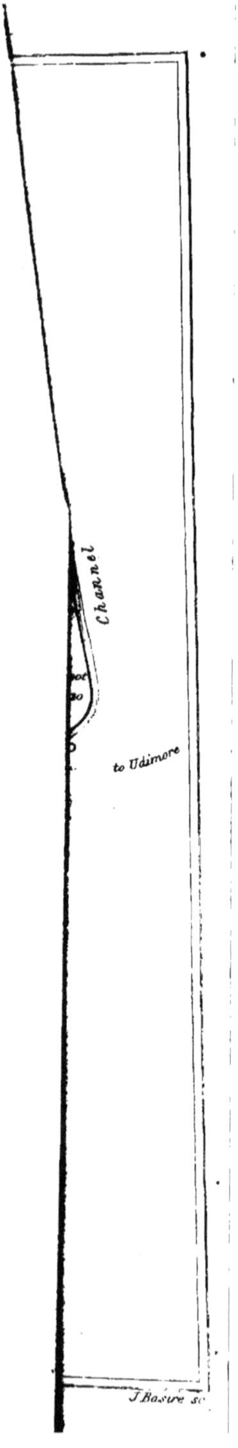
Channel
to Udimore
J Basire sc

THE HISTORY

OF

Winchelsea,

ONE OF THE

ANCIENT TOWNS

ADDED TO

The Cinque Ports.

BY

WILLIAM DURRANT COOPER, F.S.A.

LONDON:
JOHN RUSSELL SMITH, OLD COMPTON STREET, SOHO.
HASTINGS:
HENRY OSBORNE, 55, GEORGE STREET.
mdcccl.

HASTINGS:
PRINTED BY HENRY OSBORNE, 55, GEORGE STREET.

PREFACE.

The maritime importance of Winchelsea, from the days of the Conqueror to the close of the 15th Century, made it desirable to have a more extended history than is to be found in any work relating to Sussex or to the Cinque Ports: and the publications of the Sussex Archæological Society appeared to be the best mode of recording the particulars hitherto unpublished.

The following pages owe their origin to that Society. The materials, however, were too numerous to carry out my first intention; and a separate work is the result.

Many of the MSS. now printed are very interesting: the list of the owners of all the houses at the foundation of the new town, temp. Edw. I, and the accounts of the town, so early as 1388, are, I believe, peculiar to Winchelsea; and it is hoped that the entire work will be found worthy of the extensive support it has received.

My warmest thanks are due to Sir Edward Cholmeley Dering, Bart., and to the Rev. Lambert B. Larking, through whose kindness a free use was granted of the valuable collection of Dering MSS.; and to Richard Stileman, Esq., William Holloway, Esq., and the Rev. Thomas W. Richards, for the aid, which their MSS. afforded.

To E. N. Dawes, Esq., the town clerk of Winchelsea; to J. B. Freeland, Esq., secretary to the Bishop of Chichester; and to J. G. Shorter, Esq., town clerk of Hastings, my acknowledgments are tendered for the information they severally furnished from the documents in their custody: whilst much of the completeness of the work is owing to the facilities for consulting the public records, deposited in the Tower and at Carlton House Ride, most courteously rendered by Thomas Duffus Hardy, Esq., the Rev. Joseph Hunter, and Walter Nelson, Esq.

From W. H. Blaauw, Esq., George Slade Butler, Esq., the Rev. William Clarke, T. W. King, Esq., York Herald, M. A. Lower, Esq., J. Phillips, Esq., and Mr. S. Putland, jun., I have also received important assistance.

For a large addition to the illustrations I am indebted to the liberality of the Sussex Archæological Society, and of Richard Dawes, Esq., George Dawes, Esq., W. J. Denne, Esq., Mellor Hetherington, Esq., and Richard Stileman, Esq.; and the kind consideration of Mr. W. E. Baxter has enabled me to use several blocks of arms.

W. D. C.

81, Guilford St., Russell Sq., London,
15th August, 1850.

SUBSCRIBERS.

His Grace the Duke of Norfolk, E.M., Pres. Sus. Arch. Society (4 copies)
The Right Rev. the Lord Bishop of Chichester (2 copies)
Sir Henry Ellis, K.H., F.R.S., Sec. S.A., British Museum
Mr. Robert Alce, Rye
Mr. T. Arkcoll, jun., Guestling
W. W. Attree, Esq., Recorder of Hastings, Temple
John T. Auckland, Esq., Lewes
Mr. Ball, Hastings
Mr. Joseph Bannister, 4, White Rock Place, Hastings
Mr. William Edwin Baxter, Sussex Express Office, Lewes (2 copies)
Chas. Beard, Esq., Rottingdean
William Beckwith, Esq., Seacock's Heath House, Hawkhurst
John Blaker, jun., Esq., Lewes
Edgar Blaker, Esq., Lewes
W. H. Blaauw, Esq., F.S.A., Sec. Sus. Arch. Soc., Beechlands
R. W. Blencowe, Esq., the Hooke, Lewes
H. J. Bolding, Esq., 27, Tokenhouse Yard
Miss Bonnick, Hallaway Place, Hastings
Mr. E. Bowmer, Hastings
Edward Lennox, Boyd, Esq., 8, Waterloo Place, London
Mr. B. Breeds, Hastings
Sir C. M. Burrell, M.P., 5, Richmond Terrace, White Hall
Alfred Burton, Esq., St. Leonards
George Slade Butler, Esq., Rye
Rev. H. B. W. Churton, M.A., Preb. of Chichester, Icklesham
Rev. W. Clarke, M.A., Winchelsea
Mr. G. Clement, Silverhill, Hastings
The Rev. H. Cooper, B.D., Vicar of Rye
Frederick Cooper, Esq., Arundel (4 copies)
The Rev. William Henry Cooper, M.A., 44, Sussex Square, Kemp Town, Brighton
H. E. G. Cooper, Esq., Trinity College, Cambridge
Rev. Thomas Curteis, Sevenoaks
Mrs. John Daniel, Rye
Rev. Wm. Davis, Hastings
Arthur Davis, Esq., Deptford, Kent
Mr. Davies, Winchelsea
Mrs. Davies, Winchelsea
Thomas Dawes, Esq., Winchelsea (4 copies)
Richard Dawes, Esq., Camberwell (4 copies)
George Dawes, Esq., Perry Rise, Sydenham (4 copies)
Edwin Nath. Dawes, Esq., Rye, (2 copies)
E. S. Dendy, Esq., Rouge Dragon, Arundel
W. J. Denne, Esq., 6, Lower Berkeley Street
Miss Mary Julia Denne, Hythe
Miss A. M. Denne, Dover
Mr. Develin, Hastings
Thos. Dicker, Esq., Southover, Lewes
Mr. William Dobell, Hastings
Mr. Henry Dunk, High Street, Hastings
Frederick Ellman, Esq., Battle
Lt. Col. Ellwood, Clayton Priory, Hurstperpoint
Mr. James Emary, Albion Hotel, Hastings
George J. Eyre, Esq., 11, Bedford Row, London
George Fielder, Esq., Doctor's Commons
W. W. Fisher, Esq., 3, King Street, Cheapside (2 copies)
William Forster, Esq., M.A., 4, Carey Street, Lincoln's Inn
Alexander Forsyth, Esq., 47, Moorgate Street
James Bennett Freeland, Esq., Chichester
Charles Hay Frewen, Esq., M.P., Cold-Overton, Leicestershire
Mr. Walter Fuller, Winchelsea
George Edward Gatty, Esq., Crowhurst
Charles Gibbon, Esq., Richmond Herald, Yapton, Arundel
Mr. W. Ginner, Hastings
Mr. Godson, Twickenham
Mr. Goodwin, Hastings
Mr. J. Golding, Hastings
George Gray, Esq., High Street, Hastings
John Grenside, Esq., 34, Wellington Squâre, Hastings
Joseph, Gwilt, Esq., F.S.A., London

Miss Harrod, Winchelsea
Mr. W. T. Harrod, Winchelsea
Mrs. Haire, Lewes
Mr. William Harvey, Lewes
Lieut. Hennah, Winchelsea
Mellor Hetherington, Esq., Oak Lodge, Woodford (2 copies)
Charles Hickes, Esq., Rye
Mr. Hide, Hastings
H. R. Hoare, Esq., Framfield
John Hollins, Esq., A.R.A., 47, Berner's Street
Robert Hollond, Esq., M.A., M.P., Allegria, St. Leonards
Mrs. Robert Hollond, 63, Portland Place
The Rev. Dr. Holland, Precentor of Chichester
William Holloway, Esq., Rye
Mr. J. Holt, Parish Clerk, Winchelsea
Mr. George Curling Hope, Hastings
Mr. J. C. Hunter, Queen's Road, Dalston
Mrs. Hunt, Portland Place
J. H. Hurdis, Esq., Newick
Rev. A. Hussey, M.A., Rottingdean
Mr. Walter Inskipp, Hastings
Miss Jackson, 11, Pavilion Parade, Brighton
Lt. Col. Basil Jackson, Croydon
W. M. James, Esq., 34, Gloucester Place (3 copies)
Mr. Edward Jenner, Lewes
Mr. J. Jolly, Hastings
W. Polhill Kell, Esq., Lewes
Henry Lake, Esq., Lincoln's Inn
Alfred Langford, Esq., Lewes
Frederick Langford, Esq., Udimore (3 copies)
Mrs. Frederick Langford, Udimore
William Langford, Esq., 59, Friday Street, Cheapside
Nicholas Lockyer, Esq., Princess Square, Plymouth
Mark Antony Lower, Esq., M.A., Lewes
Mr. Reuben William Lower, Lewes
Charles Lushington, Esq., M.P., Palace Gardens, Bayswater
P. F. Mac Cabe, Esq., M.D., Wellington Square, Hastings
Major Mc Queen, 1, Douro Villa, Cheltenham
Mr. T. Mann, Hastings
Frederick Marrable, Esq., Rutland Gate, Hyde Park
Lt. Col. T. Marten, 1st Royal Dragoon Guards (2 copies)
Hubert Martineau, Esq., London
John Phillip Martineau, Esq., 29, Montague Place
R. Mercer, Esq., Sedlescombe
Lewis M. Meryon, Esq., St. Mary-axe
Sir S. B. P. Micklethwaite, Bart., Iridge Place
Frederick Mildred, Esq., St. Nicholas' Lane (2 copies)
Mr. E. Miller, Hailsham
Mr. Molland, 32, Budge Row,
William Monkhouse, Esq., Thurlowe Square, Brompton
Mr. Morgan, George St., Hastings
Arthur Morgan, Esq., F.R.S., New Bridge Street, Blackfriars
Cadogan Morgan, Esq., Temple
Lewis Richards Morgan, Esq., Bryn Elwy, St. Asaph
Lt. Col. George Muttlebury, C.B., K.W., London
Richard Nation, Esq., Somerset Street, Portman Square
Sir Robert Newman, Bart., Mamhead
Miss Newman, Mamhead
Mrs. Orme, Wyndham Place
Frederick Ouvry, Esq., F.S.A., 13, Tokenhouse Yard
The Rev. John Parkin, M.A., Halton Parsonage, Hastings
John Pepys, Esq., Harley Street, London
Edmund Pepys, Esq., 7, Upper Harley Street
John Phillips, Esq., High Street, Hastings
Mr. Edward Pierce, St. Leonards
Mr. J. Plane, Hastings
R. C. Pomfret, Esq., Rye
Miss Pomfret, Tenterden
Mr. William Powell, 12, Ladbroke Villas, Notting Hill, London
The Rev. William Powell, M.A., Newick
Walter Prideaux, Esq., 38, Baker Street
Robert Proctor, Esq., Holyport, Berks

The Rev. George Proctor, D.D., Rector of Hadley
Mr. Stephen Putland, London Road, St. Leonards
Rev. George D. St. Quintin, M.A., Marina, St. Leonards
W. Ramsden, Esq., Rye
Mr. Wm. Ransom, jun., Hastings
Anthony Rich, jun., Esq., B.A., 58, Cambridge Street
E. L. Richards, Esq., Bryn Elwy House, St. Asaph, Judge of the N.E. Wales County Court (3 copies)
Rev. James Richards, M.A., Hurnwick, Bishop Auckland
Rev. T. Wallis Richards, M.A., Sid. Coll. Cam., Holbeach
Mr. James Rock, jun., Hastings
Mr. Ruck, Winchelsea
Mrs. Sanders, Blackheath (4 copies)
Thomas Sanders, Esq., M.A., 37, Guilford Street
G. Scrivens, Esq., Mayor of Hastings
Mr. Seaman, Hastings
Mr. John Sharps, Winchelsea
J. G. Shorter, Esq., Town Clerk of Hastings
Miss Simmons, Icklesham
Miss Slater, Newick Park, Uckfield
W. R. Smee, Esq., Bank of England
Jeremiah Smith, Esq., Mayor of Rye (2 copies)
Thomas Smith Pix, Esq., Broomhill Lodge, Rye (2 copies)
Mr. John Smith, Hastings
Mr. Albert Smith, Rye
Francis Spilsbury, Esq., London
Mr. Stevenson, Hastings (2 copies)
F. C. Stileman, Esq., Friars, Winchelsea
Richard Stileman, Esq., Eastbourne Terrace (2 copies)
Robert C. Stileman, Esq., Eastbourne Terrace
Wm. Curteis Stileman, Esq., Eastbourne Terrace
The Misses Stileman, Friars, Winchelsea (3 copies)
William Stringer, Esq., Town Clerk of New Romney
Mr. R. Styles, Hastings
Edward Swaine, Esq., Gomersal
Mr. G. A. Thorpe, George Street, Hastings
Frederic Ticehurst, Esq., Hastings
Rev. M. A. Tierney, Arundel
W. B. D. Turnbull, Esq., Edinburgh
The Rev. Edward Turner, M.A., Maresfield
Mrs. Edmund Vallance, 2, Queen's Road East, Brighton
Miss Gertrude Vallance, 2, Queen's Road, Brighton
Rev. E. Venables, Hurstmonceux
Mr. J. Walton, London
Mr. Warrington, Strand
Albert Way, Esq., F.S.A., Wonham, Reigate
Rev. J. J. West, M.A., Winchelsea
Mr. Weston, Hastings
John Thomas Wharton, Esq., M.A., Skelton Castle
Thos. Whitfield, Esq., Hamsey, Lewes
Henry Whitmarsh, Esq., Rye
Mrs. Wilford, Lower Berkeley Street
Lt. Col. Williams, R.E., Ramsgate
John Williams, Esq., Brighton (2 copies)
Mr. J. Woods, Hastings
Mrs. Woodhams, Cleveland House, Winchelsea
Mr. C. J. Womersley, Hastings
Mr. W. L. Yates, Hastings
Wm. B. Young, Esq., Hastings

DIRECTIONS TO BINDER.

ANCIENT WINCHELSEA.

SITE.—The site of the first town of Winchelsea was a low flat island, situate at the south eastern extremity of the county of Sussex, about six miles north east of Fairlight cliff, three miles S.E. by E. of the hill on which Modern Winchelsea stands, two miles S.S.E. of the eminence which forms the town of Rye, and seven miles S.W. from Old Romney, in Kent. In the earliest times, the face of the district was very different to its present state: the town of Rye was a bare insulated rock; the hill of Higham was surrounded by water on all sides, except the south,—the waters flowed below Udimore up to Brede in one level, and to Appledore, and indeed, close to Tenterden, in the other level,—whilst in the time of the Romans, the ground, on which Old Romney is now built, had just made its head above the waters. Jeake describes Old Winchelsea as washed by the British ocean on the south and east, and by the mouth of the river Rother, (then running out there) on the north. The old town was separated, therefore, from most of the above-mentioned localities by a wide waste of waters, and the path to it on every side, save the west, was over a large estuary.

Whether the town existed at the time of the Roman Conquest, is matter of doubt. Camden does not lay it down in his maps of Roman or even of Saxon Britain: in his map of Sussex he gives it under the Roman name of Vindelis,[1] with the addition of "Old Winchelsey drowned;" but that name would be more correctly given to the isle of Portland.

[1] Butler, in his Atlas of Ancient Britain, also gives this as the site of Vindelis.

Jeake tells us,[1] that it was reported "by Johnson in his atlas, to have been a city in the time of the Romans." In Gough's edition of Camden, and in the map of Ancient Britain, published by the Society for Diffusing Useful Knowledge, the harbour is given as Portus novus. The spot on which the old town stood is accurately marked in the map given by Dugdale in his History of Embanking. The bearings indicate a place immediately on the east side of the east pier head of Rye harbour, constituting the Camber farm estate, which is in the parish of St. Thomas, Winchelsea, and must, therefore, have been the site, or adjoining the site of the original town. Norden, in his preface to the History of Cornwall, published in 1724, says, "the ruins thereof now lie under the waves three miles within the high sea." Tradition gives the same site; and report has spoken of ruins there found. A survey of the bay of Rye, however, has not brought any such to light; and the better opinion seems to be, that the ground, which was submerged at the latter part of the 13th century began partially to reappear towards the end of the 15th or the beginning of the 16th, was gradually recovered and fenced in up to the close of the 17th century, and is now a fine rich alluvial soil.[2]

Whether the town did or did not exist in the time of the Romans, it was, assuredly, built and had become an important place in Saxon days.

NAME.—From the Saxon it derives its name.[3] According to Somner, it comes from the Saxon words "Wincel," angulus, and "Ea," mare, and signifies a "waterish place, seated in a corner." Jeake, in a note, gives an old latin line of "Dovor, Sandivicus, Ry, Rum: Frig:-mare ventus." It

[1] Charters 103.

[2] Mr. Holloway has supplied us with a piece of black hard wood, or as it is here called "moor bog," taken in July 1849, from a spot dry at low water mark, and which was, doubtless, part of Old Winchelsea.

[3] The name has been variously written, Winchelsee; Winchelsey; Wynchelse, in French; 15 Rich. II, Wynchesie; in 17th Rich. II, Wynchelse; and the same in latin in 22 Hen. III, &c.

is literally "Friget mare ventus," Wind-chils-sea. "Chil, an old name," he adds, "yet in use for cold, and well might the old town deserve that name, standing in a low place open both to the winds and sea." Twine imagines it to have been written, originally, "Windchelseum," from its being exposed to the winds; for so he adds, "Olim vento frigori et ponto obnoxium, undeci nomen obvenit."[1] Mr. Holloway "agrees with all these in the general root of the name, but not in all the particulars; he would give the name and interpretation, Winchelsea, Wind-cold-Island, or more properly Cold-wind-Island."

Saxon Times.—It is not mentioned in the Saxon Chronicle, nor by name in Doomsday:[2] yet, according to Ruding, king Eadgar had a mint here (Wencles) in 959; and it was a town of sufficient importance in the time of Edward the Confessor, or St. Edward as he is called in the charter of Henry III, to be granted by him, together with the adjacent town of Rye, to the abbot and monks of Fischampe (vulgarly Féchamp) in France; to whom they were further granted and confirmed by king William and king Henry, with their liberties, free customs, pleas, plaints, and causes.

Doomsday.—The Abbot is described in Doomsday (1081-1086) to have held within the manor of Rameslie "five churches, producing 64s." These would include one in Rye, two in Old Winchelsea, St. Thomas and St. Giles, one in Brede, and the fifth St. Leonards, near Winchelsea, which was part of the

[1] Gibson's Additions to Camden, 1695.

[2] It is not strange that no mention is made in Doomsday of the towns of Winchelsea and Rye: that document was not, as is often erroneously supposed, a Record of all places and towns, it was an enumeration only of manors; and in it are mentioned the manors of Stainings and Rameslie, in Sussex, which were held by the Abbey of Fechamp. At the dissolution of the alien Priories, they held the manors of Stening, Brede, Charlton, and Wormenhurst, in Sussex, together with the patronage of their churches, and the patronage of the church of St. Leonard, near Winchelsea, and these possessions were granted to the newly founded Monastery of Syon.

town and port of Hastings, into which town the manor of Brede ran. There is also stated to have been within his possessions here, "one hundred saltpans, of eight pounds fifteen shillings," which would very readily be found in and about an island that lay in the midst of the salt waters; they were long continued, for, in 1250, cottages for salt are specifically mentioned as destroyed, and so late as 19 Henry VI, it is said that a great quantity of salt was then made on land which had been before of no value.[1] Here were "seven acres of meadow and a wood, yielding pannage for two hogs." There is great probability in the belief that Old Winchelsea was adjoining on the west to a forest called Dymsdale, and that such forest extended, at intervals, beyond Hastings. Norden tells us, that "the whole forest of Dymsdale, which lay round about this Old Winchelsea, is also eaten up of the sea." The rivulet Dimsdale flows from the valley under Bromham, through Pett level, and passing under the Military canal, enters the Brede channel half a mile below Modern Winchelsea; and in an act of 3 Rich. II there is mentioned "a certain way and marsh called Dynsdale, between the towns of Winchelsea and Hastings, which way and marsh, through neglect, were destroyed and overflowed by the sea." Near Pett, at low water, during spring tides, the remains of a wood may be seen embedded in the sand, consisting of oak, beech, and fir, the former sound and nearly black; and on the whole line of this coast, wherever ditches and dykes have been cut in the marshes, the roots and limbs of forest trees have been met with in vast numbers. The Doomsday Record goes on to say, that "in this manor a new burgh is established, where are 64 burgesses paying £8, deduct 2s." Burgh implies a town having certain rights or privileges; and the old town of Winchelsea is here plainly indicated,—it was the only new borough within the possessions of the Abbot of Fechamp, or within the hundred

[1] Pat. 19 Hen. 6, m. 19.

of Gestelinges,[1] and the number of the burgesses shows its size.

IMPORTANCE OF TOWN.—The port of Winchelsea was at the time of the Conquest, as it remained for centuries afterwards, a most convenient port for communication with France. Here, on 7th December, 1067, the Conqueror landed, and by his sudden arrival, defeated the measures agreed upon by the English for shaking off the Norman yoke;[2] and here, a hundred and twenty years afterwards, on 30th January, 1188, the king, Henry II, having taken order, as Holinshed describes it, "for his business in the parts on the further side of the sea," coming over into England again, landed on a Saturday.[3] The old town was then of far more relative importance than Rye, or than the new town afterwards became. Norden says, that it was a town of great trade and accompt, having in it when it flourished 700 house-holders, and, that the new town in its highest prosperity, was of lesser glory than the former. The property must have been valuable, since, in 1st John, (1199) James de Winchelsea gave Cs. to have such seizin of twelve acres of land as he recovered by assize of morte antecessoris, whereof he was afterwards disseized unjustly and without judgment.[4] In its neighbourhood was Bromhill or Broomhill, also called in old deeds "Alcotch," which was then populous. Camden says that it was well frequented; whilst Kilburne says it was anciently a pretty town and much resorted to: and an extract from the Dering MSS., transcribed by Sir

[1] The descriptions cannot apply to Hastings or Rye, because Doomsday expressly says that there were four burgesses in Hastings, yielding 63 shillings to the manor of Rameslie, and that Robert of Hastings held two hides and a half from the Abbot of Fechamp, who held Rameslie of the king, and Herolf half a hide: and Rye, which was not walled till the time of Richard I, was not by its situation of the same local importance.

[2] Burr. MSS. Addl. MSS. 6343.

[3] Ibid, No. 6343, fol. 140.

[4] Rot. de Oblatis, p. 14. and Madox' Exch., vol. 1., p. 485. It seems originally to have been a dispute with Simon de Catesfield about 26a. of land. Rot. Cur. Regis., vol. 2, pp. 180 and 263.

Wm. Burrell, informs us that "tradition will have it once had in it fifty inns and taverns."

ADDED TO CINQUE PORTS.—The old town of Winchelsea, together with the neighbouring town of Rye, was probably added to the Cinque Ports by William the Conqueror, as in confirming the grant of Old Winchelsea to the Abbot of Fischampe, he speaks of its liberties, free customs, &c.; and, as Henry II, Richard I, and John granted charters to the men of Winchelsea and Rye, to be free of toll, &c., in other towns, as the five ports were: to be free from shires, hundreds, &c.: and not required to plead otherwise than as the Barons of Hastings and of the Cinque Ports were.[1] Beyond all doubt, however, they were added before the time of King John, under the style of "nobiliora membra Quinque Portuum;" for, in a record, dated 2nd May, in the first year of his reign, (1200) Winchelsea and Rye are mentioned to be in aid of Hastings to do the service of their navy.[2] In the 6th year of his reign, the Quinzime of the town was accounted for to the crown.[3] In his charter of the following year, 6th June, 7th John (1205,) to the men of the two towns, he mentions and confirms to them the charters of his father, Henry II, who is elsewhere stated to have been seized of the town,[4] and of his brother Richard I; and on the 8th February, 9th John (1207-8,) there is a direct mention of Winchelsea as one of the Cinque Ports in the King's Commission,[5] directed to Vincent de Hastings, Wimund de Winchelsea, and others of the barons of the Cinque Ports, to arrest all the ships that they should find. The two "ancient towns" of Winchelsea and Rye, have, from the time of their being added to the Cinque Ports down to the present

[1] The charters of Richard (referring to that of Henry) and of John, are recited at length in the Inspeximus: see Post, 7 Edw. II.

[2] Jeake. In dors. cart. 1, R. Jo., par. 1, m. 12. Winchelsee et Rye quod debent esse in auxiliis ville de Hastings ad fac R. servicium 20 Navium, &c.

[3] Lel. Coll., 134.

[4] Madox' Firma Burgi, p. 8.

[5] Selden's Dominion of the Sea, p. 350.

day, enjoyed the same rights and privileges as the five original ports. Those rights and privileges have been so often and so well given, especially by Mr. Holloway, in his recent History of Rye, that we need not repeat them in this work.

JOHN.—In the troublous years of King John, and at the commencement of the 13th century, Old Winchelsea was in its greatest glory: it was in the enjoyment of all the privileges of the most important Cinque Ports; it had Broomhill attached to it as a member; its bay was the place of rendezvous for the fleets of England; its own commerce was large;[1] its thirty-nine squares or quarters were well calculated to give it importance and to promote its wealth; and its geographical position, directly opposite to Tréport, and not far from the direct line to Boulogne, gave it such importance, that, after Philip of France, under the auspices of the Pope, Innocent III, had, on 21st April, 1213, commanded a great army to assemble at Rouen, whence they were to march to Boulogne, where an armament of 1700 vessels was prepared to convey and guard them to England, King John, who had collected a large army at Dover, left that place on Saturday, 27th April, came from Dover to Winchelsea, and here remained to 1st of May.[2] In 1216 the Barons of England, irritated by the tyranny of king John, and menaced with the total loss of their liberties and property, offered to acknowledge Louis, the son of Philip, as Sovereign of England, on condition of his affording them protection against the king; and Philip, acceding to their request and the conditions required, sent over a large army with Louis at their head. Louis conquered almost all places opposed to him. Dover made a gallant resistance through

[1] In John's reign twelve men of Portsmouth were summoned for allowing vessels to go out of their port without paying the fifteenth; and in giving their account of the three vessels which had so gone out, the Portsmouth men return that the third vessel was the "Jacob," of Winchelsea, which had brought 61 tons of wine, of the estimated value of three marcs and a half. Cal: Rot: Orig: vol. 1, p. 94.

[2] Suss. Arch. Coll., vol. 2, p. 135.

the valour and fidelity of Hubert de Burgh: but the serious fears entertained by the king for the safety of Winchelsea and its inhabitants, may be best learnt from the following writ of the king, dated 9th June, 1216,[1] commanding the barons of Winchelsea rather to pay a ransom than allow their town to be burnt, should such be attempted by Louis.

"De componendo cum Ludovico adversario Regis ne incendio tradatur villa de Winchelseia. Rex Baronibus de Winchelseia salutem. Si in propriâ personâ suâ descenderit ad villam nostram adversarius noster Ludowicus, benè concedimus, quod priusquam incendio tradatur villa nostra, vel dampnum magnum subeatis, ei censeriam ducentarium marcarum exhibeatis." Teste me ipso, apud Divis' ix. die Junii.

Hollinshed declares that Louis took all the towns he attacked except Dover and Windsor. It is not recorded whether Winchelsea was attacked and resisted: there seems, however, much doubt whether it did follow the pusillanimous commands of the weak and wavering John.

Henry III.—In the first year of the young King Henry III (1217,) it is expressly said, that the men of Winchelsea took an active share in the naval engagement of this year between the Cinque Ports' fleet, under Sir Hubert de Burgh, and the French under Robert de Courtney; and it was to Winchelsea that the king's men of Ireland, who were on the coast of Normandy, were ordered to come in his service.[2] That Rye did not surrender, but was captured, is certain. After the fatal battle of Lincoln, it is said, "et tunc facte sunt truge inter juvenem regem et predictum Lodewycum, qui vero Lodewycum, captâ villâ de Rye in comitatu Sussexie, ibidem transfretavit."[3] "And then peace having been made between the young king and the said Louis, which same Louis having captured the town of Rye, sailed hence over the

[1] Rym. Fœd., vol. 1, p. 142. Ed. 1816.
[2] Harris Nicolas' Hist. of the Royal Navy, vol. 1, p. 176.
[3] Camden Society's Publications. Holloway's Hist. of Rye.

seas." This is the first mention we have met with of Rye being named as the place of landing or of embarkation, and not Winchelsea.

The days of Winchelsea's prosperity were now coming to a close. During the first half of the 13th century, very heavy storms are recorded to have taken place throughout the coasts of England; and in 1236, when great torrents of rain fell during the months of January, February, and part of March, and the rivers overflowed their banks, the Thames broke into the Palace at Westminster, and persons crossing Westminster Hall were forced to use a boat or go on horseback, the first inundation on record in the immediate vicinity of Winchelsea took place. In the accompt roll of the Archbishop of Canterbury, relating to the manor of Aldington, there is a payment of 41s. 4d. for the expenses of John de Walton, and the parson of Aldington, for three day's expenses at Rumenal and Winchelsea, and Appledore, together with the seneschal, to see to the saving of the marshes against the inundation of the sea.[1]

ARSENAL AND LIGHTHOUSE.—The harbour was not materially injured by this storm. And in 1240 there was here, as well as at Rye and Shoreham, an arsenal for the king's galleys:[2] and there was also a lighthouse which withstood the second inundation, since, on 30th January, 1261; there is a royal precept to pay the dues.[3] The town itself was also free from any material injury. The inhabitants, who were under the foreign abbey, became troublesome to the king and to the English government, and in the 30th Hen. III (1246,) the men of Winchelsea and Rye paid ten casks of wine to the king for a contempt and trespass.[4]

It was not against the king alone that these Cinque Ports committed trespasses and crimes: it is certain, from the

[1] Somner's Ports and Forts. [2] Nicolas' Hist. of Navy, vol. 1, p. 228.
[3] Ib., p. 237. [4] Madox' Exch., vol. 1, p. 568.

accounts of historians, that the crews of the Cinque Ports were by no means scrupulous, but very often added to their gains by piracy, and plundered the vessels of other places as they passed the coast. The complaints of such behaviour are numerous; as a specimen of which may be adduced the letter from the city of Cologne to king Henry III, from a Tower MS.[1]

To the most serene Lord Henry, by the grace of God illustrious King of England, the Judges, Bailiffs, ('scabini,' echevius) Council, and other citizens in Cologne, the most ready obedience in all things, with all devotion and reverence. We make known to your Lordship (dominationi) that we are much concerned for your adversities, but we return unmeasured thanks to your magnificence, in that our fellow-citizen merchants, with their goods, have hitherto been protected and preserved in your land by your royal authority without any grievance. Now, however, we have understood, by the shewing and serious complaint of our beloved fellow-citizen Hermann, the bearer of these letters, that he, coming with his goods into your jurisdiction, and that your citizens of Winkilse have plundered him of his goods to the value of 100 marcs, or more, by certain losses thence received. Wherefore we humbly and devoutly intreat your magnificence with earnest prayers, both for the sake of God and of justice, and by the interposition of our prayers, that you will deign to effect it, so that his goods may be restored to him, and that no dissension may arise between your citizens and ours from the aforesaid occasion, doing so much for us in this particular, that we may be able thence to commend your royal Majesty; and if no restitution shall be made to him, then we are unable to desert him in his right, but ought to assist him, so that he may be able to recover the worth from your people.

The plain hint at retaliation, probably, had more weight than the fine compliments of the rest of the letter. Many similar complaints from other cities, Bruges, Ypres, &c., are extant, and the lawless activity of the Cinque Ports seems often to have rendered the passage of the narrow seas as dangerous to commercial traffic as was the passage of the Rhine among the castles of the mediæval nobles.

[1] Tower MSS., Letter 160, Ex. inf., W. H. Blaauw, Esq.

Resumption by the Crown.—Henry took another step, which was well calculated to bring Winchelsea and Rye more directly under his subjection, when, on the 15th May, in the 31st year of his reign, (1247,) "for the better defence of this realm," says Jeake, and—"it might be to conceal from foreigners the intelligence of affairs at home, and stop them of such convenient ports of passage,"—the king took Winchelsea and Rye into his hands, and gave to the abbot and monks of Féchamp other lands in exchange. The King's charter, making the grant, which, together with a translation, is printed at length in Mr. Holloway's History of Rye, is the earliest charter relating to the town which has come down to us. It recites, that the king having felt it his duty to look with the greatest care, not only to the faithful government of his kingdom, but also to the imminent perils thereof, considering on all sides the state of his realm, and chiefly its maritime parts, he had discovered that, by means of the towns of Winchelsea and Rye, which had hitherto been held by the abbot and monks of Fischamp, to whom it was not allowed to fight against the enemies of the kingdom with material weapons, it might entail irreparable damage on him and his heirs in time of war, provided they should remain in the hands of the abbot and monks; wherefore, by the advice of his council, and by the free consent of the abbot and monks, the king resumed into his own hands the said towns, with their ports, and the advowson of their churches, and with the fourth part of the marsh of Northmareys, and the annual payment of three shillings and ninepence from thence arising, and with all their appurtenances, under the control of the king and his heirs, according to the following bounds of Winchelsea, viz., where the sea and the harbour surround the town of Winchelsea as far as to the fee of Gestlynges. Giving, and by that his charter, confirming unto the abbot and monks, as a good and sufficient exchange, the king's manors of Chilcenham, in the county of Gloucester, together with the hundred and the other appurtenances thereof; and of Scoultr, in the same county, together with the hundred of Salmanbury, and the other appurtenances thereof; and also of Naveneby, in the county of Lincoln, with its appurtenances, to be held of the king and his heirs by the abbot and monks of Fischamp for ever, as freely and quietly as theretofore they had held Winchelsea and Rye, by virtue of a deed of gift made to them by Saint Edward, of blessed memory, and, of concessions and confirmations, after the accustomed manner of William and Henry, kings of England, of the land called Stanings, with all their appendages, among which were reckoned Winchelsea and Rye: the liberties of which were set forth in the charter of King William, then given at length.

It will be seen by this charter, that the king confined himself to the resumption of the two towns of Winchelsea and Rye; and that he left in the abbot's hands the adjoining manor of Brede, which included the parish of Saint Leonard, close to Winchelsea, but within the liberty of Hastings, and a very large portion of the town of Hastings, which must then have been of comparative unimportance.[1]

The king endeavoured to conciliate the townsmen of Winchelsea by granting to the barons and bailiffs the farm of

[1] Suss. Arch. Coll., vol. 2, p. 166. The Abbot, indeed, received other immunities from Henry and his successor. In 2 Edw. I, the king directed that the men of the abbot should not be amerced. In 14 Edw. I, (1286) he had the king's consent for appropriating a piece of land in Hastings for the foundation of the Church of St. Clement there,—the date of this foundation has not been given by Moss or Horsfield,—and in 18 Edw. I, the abbot had the king's writ that Steyning church should be exempt from the jurisdiction of the Archbishop of Canterbury. See Calendar Inq: p. m., vol. 1, pp. 54-92 and 103. By the same records, pp. 92 and 204, it appears that in 14 Edw. I, Galfridus Brian, on behalf of the abbot, had an inquisition of the land in Brede, &c.; and that in 33 Edw. 1, Alan Polyngford had on his behalf an inquisition of the abbot's possessions in Rudgwick, Billingshurst, Slynfold, Stening, and Polebergh, where there were 30s. of annual rents, a messuage, and 200 acres of land belonging to the abbot.

the town, with all its liberties and appurtenances to hold during his pleasure. They duly accounted to Hen. III for the farm:[1] as they did to his successor, when, 6th February, 6th Edw. I, they were in lieu of an account to render to the king, annually, £42, half at Easter and half at Michaelmas.[2] Murage grants for the town were made in 46 Henry III, (1262) and again in the 53 Henry III, (1269.)

STORMS.—Hitherto the town had escaped without much damage from the elements; but a far more serious storm than any which had before occurred, took place on 1st October, 1250, which did a great, if not a fatal, injury to Old Winchelsea. Against foreign enemies the prowess of the men of Winchelsea was well able to protect themselves and their town; but against the formidable attacks of the elements they were without defence. Hollinshed thus records the storm:— "On the 1st day of October, the moon, upon her change, appearing exceeding red and swelled, began to show tokens of the great tempest of wind that followed, which was so huge and mighty, both by land and sea, that the like had not been lightly known and seldom or rather never heard of by men then alive. The sea forced, contrary to his natural course, flowed twice without ebbing, yielding such a roaring that the same was heard (not without great wonder) a far distance from the shore. Moreover, the same sea appeared in the dark of the night to burn, as it had been on fire, and the waves to strive and fight together, after a marvellous sort, so that the mariners could not devise how to save their ships where they lay at anchor, by no cunning or shift which they could devise. At Hertburne three tall ships perished without recovery, besides smaller vessels. At Winchelsea, besides other hurt that was done in bridges, mills, breaks, and banks, there were 300 houses and some churches drowned with the high rising of the water course."[3]

[1] Addl. MSS., 6344, p. 143. [2] Madox' Exch., vol. 1., p. 335.

[3] Hollinshed vol. 2, p. 419. In the same year there was an earthquake at St. Albans.

This second inundation by which Winchelsea suffered so greatly is elsewhere described in the following terms:—"In the month of October, in the year 1250, the moon being in her prime, the sea passed her accustomed boundaries, flowing twice without ebb, and made so horrible a noise that it was heard a great way within land, not without the astonishment of the oldest man who heard it. Besides this, at dark at night the sea seemed to be a light-fire, and to burn, insomuch that it was past the mariner's skill to save the ships; and to omit others, at a place called Huckeburn, (probably East or Hitherbourne) three noble and famous ships were swallowed up by the violent rising of the waves and were drowned; and at Winchelsea a certain haven, eastward, besides cottages for salt, fishermen's huts, bridges, and mills, above 300 houses, by the violent rising of the waves, were drowned." It is probable that at this inundation Bromhill church was lost.

Matthew of Paris, tells us, that, on the octave of the Epiphany, in the year 1252, during the day and night a terrible south-west wind prevailed,—that it drove the ships from their anchorage, raised the roofs of houses, many of which were thrown down, uprooted completely the largest trees, deprived churches of their spires, made the lead to move, and did other great damage by land, and still greater by sea: and especially at the port of Winchelsea, "which is of such use to England, and above all, to the inhabitants of London," the waves of the sea broke its banks, swelling the neighbouring rivers, knocked down the mills and the houses, and carried away a number of drowned men. And at the close of the following year the sea again broke its bounds, and left so much salt upon the land, that in the autumn of 1254, the wheat and other crops could not be gathered as usual; and even the forest trees and hedges could not put out their full foliage.

Churches, Religious House, &c.—The old town, as we

have already seen, had two churches,—one was dedicated to St. Thomas, the other to St. Giles.

Soon after the first establishment of the Franciscans, Minor or Gray Friars, in England, which, according to Stow, Dugdale, and Leland, was in 1224, a house of that order was founded at Old Winchelsea, and it survived the great storm of 1250. Richard de la Wych (St. Richard,) Bishop of Chichester, who died 1253, by his will[1] left to the Friars Minor of Winchelsea, Mark and Matthew, and 20s.; and as St. Richard does not mention the Dominicans or Black Friars, of whom he had been a brother, it is tolerably clear that they had no house in this town. The tythe of the boats of Winchelsea belonged to the Canons of the free chapel of St. Mary, of Hastings.[2] And William, son of Walwin, gave a rent of 4s. yearly, with the appurtenances in Winchelsea, to the nuns of Davinton, in Kent, which was saved from the early storms, and confirmed to them with their other possessions, by the king, 39 Hen. III, (1255.)[3] The last vicar of St. Thomas, in the old town, rendered himself famous, and did good service to his countrymen, by resisting the demands made upon him against his will, to prosecute another clerk, who had robbed him; although we are afraid that the compulsion, in more modern days, would have been carried out by a recognizance to appear and prosecute. Warner, vicar of the church of St. Thomas, of Winchelsea, had been robbed by Andrew Fincheham, clerk, who, by benefit of clergy, declined his trial, and was afterwards harboured by Warner, wherefore the barons and bailiff of Winchelsea, who had seized his houses and goods to enforce him to prosecute his clerk for the felony, were commanded by mandamus, 24th January, 1st Edw. I, to take security of Warner to answer for what he had done when called upon, but to restore to him

[1] Suss. Arch. Coll., vol. 1, p. 170.
[2] Tanner's Not. Mon., 556.
[3] Mon. Angl., vol. 1, p. 502, a. 2.

his houses and goods, for that no one, without his will, ought to be compelled to prosecute for what had been stolen from him.[1]

There was a hospital of St. Bartholomew having considerable land, as appears by the boundaries of Rye in the Resumption Charter. The Abbot and church of St. Martin, of Battle, were also possessed of land within the old town. From the abbey charters[2] it appears that Wm. de Bec released in pure alms, to this church and the almonry of the same, certain rents in Winchelsea, and land in Snelham. John, the son of Wm. Fisher, released to them the rent of a messuage here. Stephen and Roger, sons of Agnes Grig, for the health of their souls, and of the said Agnes, their mother, enfeoffed to the abbot and convent two messuages near Cornhethe, between the messuages of Roger de Oreford and John Rich, held of William de Farlegh, in his lordship of Winchelsea, one of which had been purchased by her of Samuel Adam, and one of which was afterwards let at fee farm by the abbot and convent to Ralph Ivegod, baron of Winchelsea.[3] Before 1199, William de St. Leger had granted to the abbey lands beyond Winchelsea; John, Earl of Eu, had confirmed the grant;[4] and there was a confirmation from Clarembaldus, his successor, to the abbey, of land called Maries, also beyond Winchelsea; and about 1220, Alicia, Countess of Eu, only daughter and heir of Henry, the 5th Earl, confirmed these lands and marsh, as being in Winchelsea, for the salvation of her own soul, and of the souls of her father and mother, and for the soul of her lord Ralph de Ysonden of good memory, then late Earl of Eu, who died in 1218, and for the souls of all her ancestors and successors.

[1] Ryley's Plac. Parl. app. 433. Prynne's Hist. of King John, p. 127.

[2] Battle Records, pp. 8-17-19-33.

[3] The counter part agreement bears his seal, in the centre of which is a fish.

[4] Records, pp. 40-42.

BARONS' WAR.—The Cinque Ports showed themselves extremely favorable to the cause of De Montford and the Barons. When war broke out, Henry doubted them, and on 23rd October, 1262, when he was expecting over some foreign troops to his aid, his brother, the king of the Romans, wrote to him, advising him first to ascertain whether the Cinque Ports were likely to let them land.[1] The ports refused to abide by the award made at the mise of Amiens; and notwithstanding the favor with which Winchelsea had been treated by Henry, the townsmen were in vain exhorted to lend him any aid. After the capture by Prince Edward of the Earl of Gloucester's castle of Tunbridge, in April, 1264, the King and the Prince repaired to the coast "towards the havenes with gret poer eon," coming by way of Robertsbridge and Battle, where, as elsewhere, the king's progress was marked by rapine and slaughter. The king was at Tunbridge on 30th April, reached Winchelsea on Thursday, the 8th May, and remained during the 9th and 10th. During these three days he applied in vain to the Cinque Ports for assistance, urging them to send a naval force up the Thames to attack London. The Warden and Barons of the ports sternly forbade the use of their ships, and the king, after exacting hostages for the fidelity of the Cinque Ports, or, as Matthew of Paris expresses it, having been reconciled to and taken into favor the Cinque Ports, quitted Winchelsea to collect all his forces at Lewes, the strong hold of his brother in law, the Earl de Warenne. The king arrived at Lewes on 11th May, and there, on the 14th May, the fatal battle was fought which placed Henry in the Barons' power.[2]

On 28th May, 1264, Simon de Montford committed the custody of Dover castle and of the Cinque Ports to his son Henry.

[1] Tower MS., Letters, No. 124. Ex. inf., Mr. W. H. Blaauw.

[2] Matthew Paris. Blaauw's Baron's War, p. 114. Suss. Arch. Coll., vol. 2, p. 137.

When Eleanor, Countess of the successful De Montford, in 1265, made her journey from Porchester to Dover, she came from Wilmington with her husband to Winchelsea, and here they spent Sunday, 14th June, with all their suite; and here they feasted the burghers of the town[1] and many others. The Winchelsea burghers were afterwards twice feasted by the Countess (12th and 30th July,) at Dover.

Piracies.—The success of the Barons was not unacceptable to the men of Winchelsea and of their fellow ports; they had full license for those lawless habits which made them, as marauders on the seas, the terror of foreign mariners, and the dread, even, of English vessels. For two years they enjoyed a complete immunity, and carried out to the fullest extent the practices which have left a deep stain upon their name.[2] Winchelsea, therefore, was a friendly place to which the young Simon de Montford could repair, when after his father's death, at Evesham, on 4th August, 1265, suspecting treachery on being compelled to accompany the king to London. Young Simon is recorded to have left his castle of Kenilworth on St. Clement's day, (1266) for London; whence, with the greatest secrecy, he departed and joined the citizens of the Cinque Ports at Winchelsea, who were waiting to receive him: associated himself with these rovers, and soon made himself formidable by his bold piracies at sea, and by collecting troops on the opposite coast,[3] but ultimately departed from thence and went to France.[4] The day of retribution was, however, close at hand. The young Simon had not long left the English shores and threatened an invasion, when the Prince Edward (1266,) made a terrible example of the Winchelsea

[1] Blaauw's Baron's War, p. 288, where there is a curious extract from the Roll of the expenses incurred on this journey.

[2] To this day when the boats of Winchelsea or Hastings enter some of our western ports, a hatchet is held up to them as a sign of opprobrium for their ancestors' conduct: not altogether unknown, if report speak truly, in later times.

[3] Ann. Wav. Gale, vol. 2, p. 221.

[4] Hollinshed.

marauders. Departing from Dover, says Hollinshed, "the Prince visited the sea coasts, punishing divers of the inhabitants within the precincts of the Cinque Ports, and putting them in fear, received divers to the king's, his father, peace. The inhabitants of Winchelsea only, made countenance to resist him; but Prince Edward, with valiant assaults, entered the town, in which entry much guilty blood was spilt, but yet the multitude, by the commandment of Prince Edward, was spared, and thus having won the town, he commanded that from thenceforth they should abstain from piracies, which they had before greatly used."

Pennant, speaking of this transaction, says—"Old Winchelsea had been a most powerful port; but, like the others, its vessels acted in most of their cruises, with savage barbarity. During the time that Simon de Montford, Earl of Leicester, held his iron rod over these countries, they gave full loose to their piracies, and flung over-board the crews of every ship they met, whether it was foreign or English: Leicester had share of the booty, and so winked at their enormities. In 1266, Prince Edward put a stop to their cruelties; he attacked Winchelsea, took it by storm, and put to the sword all the principal inhabitants concerned in the inhuman practices of the times: the rest he saved, and granted the inhabitants far better terms than they deserved. He at that time feared their power, and the assistance they might give to the rebellious Montford, had he been too rigorous in his measures."

The punishment was, in its results, far more severe than the prince had intended, or than the inhabitants had expected. The old town never again flourished.

EDWARD I.—When Edward ascended the throne (November 1272,) the town was gradually falling into decay; yet it was still of importance, and its port was still much frequented. In the first year of his reign, Sir Matthew Hastings was bailiff of the town; and having, as such, exacted toll from the tenants of the Archbishop of Canterbury, who were exempt, the Archbishop treated the matter in a very summary way, by sending him a peremptory letter to refrain from such exactions, and restore the pledges detained for toll within eight days, on pain of excommunication:[1] and on the 18th June, 1273, the king addressed a letter to the barons and bailiffs, by which they were directed, without delay, to expel all Jews from the place, as it was not a town which they had been accustomed to inhabit.[2] Three years later, on 2nd July, 1276, the king himself came here, no longer to chastise, but to take measures for the transfer of the town to a new, and as it was hoped, a more favorable site:[3] and in the following year,[4] according to Norden, the king had arranged his plans for the new town.

Destruction.—Year by year it became more evident that the old town would be abandoned: and at length, in 1287, the great inundation happened, which totally destroyed Old Winchelsea, and obliged almost all such of the inhabitants as escaped to quit it. In the Records of Rye, Jeake states it to have been thus recorded,[5]—"M.D. quod anno domini MCCLXXXVII, in vigilia Sanctæ Agathæ Virginis, submersa fuit villa de Winchelsea et omnes terræ inter Clivesden[6] (i.e. Cliff end) usque ad le Vochere de Hythe." Harris[7] says, "in an old manuscript, I have met with this note. Quœdam

[1] Prynne's King John, p. 129. [2] Rymer's Fœd., vol. 1, p. 503.

[3] Three writs, relating to some disturbances of the Bishop of Ely's liberties, are tested by the King at Winchelsea. Prynne's King John, p. 182.

[4] An edict was made this year to arrange the rights and usages of the ports during the fishing season at Great Yarmouth. Jeake, p. 13.

[5] Elsewhere it is said that "in a book of precedents remaining among the records of the town of Rye, p. 131, is a memorandum entered that the year Old Winchelsey was drowned, which is there said to be 1287, corn was at 2s. a quarter." Jeake's Arithmetic, p. 74.

[6] This has always been printed Climesden; for the correct reading we are indebted to Mr. John Phillips, of Hastings. The family of Clivesend were benefactors to Battle Abbey of lands at Brooke, and of 3a. of land in Guestling, lying near the wood of Cumfunte.

[7] Harris' Kent.

villa vocat: Winchelsea cum omnibus terris mariscis inter Clivesden juxta Farelythe et Hythe submersa fuit in vigiliâ Sanctæ Agathæ Virginis,—viz., quarto die Febrii, A.D., 1287. This inundation and destruction of Old Winchelsea was very sudden, as indeed I have seen it expressed in an old record to have been, per substaneam intemperiem maris."

The same inundation is recorded by Somner,[1] though he relates it as happening in 1286. "In an ancient French chronicle, (says he) sometime belonged to the church of Canterbury, and written by a monk of the place in Edward II days, which I light on in Sir John Dews his library, I read thus,—and the same year (1286,) on the 2nd of the nones of February, the sea, in the Isle of Thanet, rose or swelled so high, and in the marsh of Romenal, that it brake all the walls and drowned all the grounds: so that from the great wall of Appledore as far as Winchelsey, toward the south and the west, all the land lay under the water lost. Mr. Camden intends, I suppose, the same inundation, when he saith, 'that, in the reign of Edward I, the sea raging with the violence of winds, overflowed this tract, and made pitiful waste of people, cattel, and of houses in every place, as having quite drowned Promhill, a pretty town, well frequented; and that it also made the Rother forsake his old channel, which *here* before time emptied himself into the sea, and stopped his mouth, opening a new and nearer way for him to pass into the sea by Rye.'" *Here*, means Romney.

And Camden, giving the date of the inundation, says "what time the face of the earth, both here and also in the coast of Kent neere bordering, became much changed." The sudden stoppage of the Rother's mouth at Romney, and the junction of its waters at Appledore, with those of the estuary of Rye, must have, indeed, altered entirely the face of the country.

It is probable, that after this inundation, Old Winchelsea

[1] Ports and Forts, pp. 57-8.

became nearly or quite deserted by its inhabitants; and for many years,

> Invenies sub aquis: et adhuc ostendere nautæ
> Inclinata solent cum mœnibus oppida mersis.
>
> Ovid Met. Lib. xv. 294.

The only direct mention of Old Winchelsea, as existing in part after the great storm of 1287, which we have met with, is in Madox' Hist. of the Exch., vol. 2, p. 87, where it is said, that in 20 Ed. I, (1292) a plea being moved in Court Christian before the Bishop of Chichester concerning Sepulture in Old Winchelsey, and the said plea being in derogation of the King's right and prerogative, the King, by his writ, commands the Bishop of Chichester to put the said plea in respite, and to warn the said parties to appear before the Treasurer and Barons of the Exchequer, on the morrow of All Souls, to receive judgment therein; accordingly the parties and the bishop's official appeared at the Exchequer, but the court adjourned the proceedings therein till such time as the treasurer should send one of the barons to view the place in question: and no further account appears.

Families, &c.—The most important family in the old town was that of the Saxon family of Alard, who were settled at Winchelsea and at Treyford, in Sussex, before the Conquest, and of whom we shall have to speak at length in our account of the new town.

The family of Paulin was also of considerable importance in the old town. In the time of Henry III, Paulin of Winchelsy is a witness to a Brede charter; and in 1273 there was a lease of 1¾ acres of land from Stephen Hesel to James Fitzpaulin. The family removed to the new town. In 1290, Gilbert at Forde, of Farlegh, and Philip de Essche quitted claim to Jacob, son of Paulin of Winchelsea, half an acre "terre Flandrensis," in Icklesham.[1] Members of the family were bailiffs of Winchelsea, tem. Edward II, and Richard II.

[1] Dering MSS. Ex. inf. The Rev. Lambert B. Larking, of Ryarsh Vicarage. Henry de Winchelsy is another witness, and Reginald de Winchelsy is cited in the same Brede charter.

The old town gave birth to Robert of Winchelsey, a

prelate of great eminence and equal force of character; and who, in asserting the power of the clergy against his sovereign, has been quaintly designated "a traitor to his king, but a true subject to the pope." He was born of mean parents in Winchelsea about the middle of Henry III reign. The following sketch of his life is given by Dart.[1] Upon the death of Peckham, Archbishop of Canterbury, who was also a Sussex man, having been born at Lewes, "the monks chose Robert Winchelsey, who was consecrated on the 2d Id September, anno 1293, and was confirmed by Pope Cœlestine the Vth, on the 8th Id Septem- anno 1294; he was consecrated at Rome on the 2d Id September, by the Cardinal Sabine, and the same year coming from Rome, through Almaigne, (for there was then war between England and France,) he landed at Yarmouth on the first day of January, and went to wait upon the king, who was then in Wales, and at Aberconwey: he took his oath of allegiance, and received his temporalities from him; and returning thence on the 15th kal. April, he made his public entry into Canterbury, and was met by the convent in their coaps at the Cemitery Gate, and thence entering the church, paid his devotions, and received the prior and convent with the Kiss of Peace. And after Michaelmas, anno. 1295, he was solemnly inthroned by Henry de Estria, prior; on which day he cited Gilbert, Earl of Gloucester, who came and officiated as steward and butler, according to custom. He was educated in the grammar school of the city of Canterbury, whence, after gaining a sufficient stock of grammar learning, he went

[1] Dart's Canterbury Cathedral, pp. 139-40.

to Paris, where he commenced master of arts, according to Birchington. He went next to Merton College, in Oxford, and was D.D. in that University, and sometime Chancellor of it. His first rise in the church was to the Archdeaconry of Essex, together with a Canonry in St. Paul's. He was so much esteemed, that when he was consecrated at Rome he was offered to be made pope, and afterwards cardinal, but declined it. Soon after he was settled in this chair, Edward the First, in order to carry on his expedition against the Scots, demanded a subsidy of the clergy, which the archbishop, taking hold of the Decree of the Council of Lyons, stifly opposed; and the king, who was equally wise and valiant, resented his opposition so highly, that he seized his estate and banished him, and he continued in banishment till the king's death, and in great want, being unrelieved by the pope, for obeying whose new constitution he suffered. But yet, an ancient MS. History of this Church (of Canterbury) says, that the king seized all the estates in England, and obliged the owners to redeem them with a fifth part of the value, but the Archbishop refused such composition; but that after seizing his goods and effects for twenty-one weeks and five days, the king observing his resolution and constancy, and that there was no probability of bringing him into his measures, restored them to him on the 14th kal. August following. And three years after, viz., 1299, on the 5th Id. September, he married that Prince to Margaret, the King of France's sister, in the martyrdom of this church, and said mass, upon that occasion, at the altar, by St. Thomas Becket's shrine. Upon King Edward the Second's coming to the throne, he grew in his favour, and very rich, by arrears due from his tenants. He after this grew a generous opposer of Gaveston and the two Spencers, and other parasites of the king. He was likewise a severe punisher of vice, and as great an encourager of men of virtue and learning; and on such only he bestowed what church preferments were in his hands; and at the same time to encourage learning, bestowed much upon poor students in the universities. He bore the character of a man of singular piety, and a mirror of prelates. He was generous to his church, and gave to it vestments, together with a most rich cope, and all his books. He was exceeding charitable, for which he was generally, by the vulgar, reverenced as a saint after his death, which happened at Otteford, Id. May, 1318, according to Thorn; but more truly, according to Birchington and the obituary of this church, on the 5th Id. May, being Friday, 1313, and was buried 10 kal. June, in the upper south cross, near the altar of St. Gregory, whither the people resorted out of devotion, esteeming him a saint. And about thirteen years after his death, Thomas, Earl of Lancaster, applied to the pope for his canonization; but the pope returned, that those affairs were to be cautiously undertaken, and sought for in a different manner, with proof of miracles, and a general request of prelates: so it went off. But such was the adoration paid there notwithstanding, that it was demolished at the reformation, as giving occasion to idolatry. It must not be forgotten that this archbishop is said to have been seen in a vision at Rome, the death of King Edward. He gave ten rich benefices to the regents in divinity, and near as much to the bachelors in divinity; and to other scholars he was generous, giving to some forty shillings, and to others twenty, yearly; to the mendicants he was likewise bountiful, giving to some twenty, some ten marks. In charity to the poor he was very excellent, relieving them every Sunday to the number of four thousand; and on the four festivals of the Blessed Virgin Mary, he gave one hundred and fifty pence to as many poor persons; and on the feast of her conception, and the four days preceding it, and on the feasts of the others, and other memorable festivals, he gave one hundred pence; and to all that were ancient and infirm, he gave nourishment and subsistance; to poor persons who were too modest to beg publicly, he caused a strict enquiry to be made for such in the circuit of four miles, and then gave them annual pensions proportionable to their wants, and the number of their children. He likewise clothed large numbers of poor, at the same time that he denied himself more than two suits of apparel at one time. He was so strictly chaste that he would never speak to women but at confession. He was a constant frequenter of church service and sermons; and would not be absent for any matters of state. And, as to discipline, he was very remarkable, and would often go into the chapter-house and shut the door upon him, where he used corporal penance; insomuch that after his death, his thigh bones were laid almost bare, and the flesh livid with blows, and the bloody and watery substance visible, which some conjectured was occasioned by the hardness of the bed, but others, more justly, by his scourging. And however severe and strict he was in observing upon himself, he was to others, at table and elsewhere, affable, free, and pleasant, but hated parasites, oppressors, and sportsmen. He was as to his person lusty, but had a fair and pleasant complexion. He was moderate in his diet, and if any dainties were at his table, he never tasted them, but distributed them to women and ancient men. He was a very great devotee to the Virgin Mary, and used frequently to say the Salutation of the Angel, or the Ave, upon his fingers; and if we may credit the writers of this monastery, at his burial was a wondrous miracle, for while that was repeated over his grave, one saw the thumb of the dead corpse traverse over the fingers as usual in his life time. He visited the Convent of Worcester, and preached in the chapter-house there; and went the same day to Wyke, to visit Bishop Godfrey, who then lay sick; and the day following visited the Priory, and when he came into the great hall, it was filled with strangers, whereupon he and his retinue went away, and would not dine. Not long after, he went again into the chapter-house and deposed the sub-prior, precentor, and chamberlain; and suspended the third prior, and the pitanciary, from going out of the monastery for one year and three days. After, he was at Hayles Abbey, in Gloucestershire, with the king and many nobles, at the burial of Edmund, Earl of Cornwall. And three years after, he took from that convent the church of Doderhulle, given them by Godfrey, the bishop, for which the monks there charged him with injustice.

In the Cotton MSS. there are two Constitutions of Robert of Winchelsey: one showing in what lordships the archbishop ought to provide for the parochial duties, and in what others it was the duty of the rector: and the other in 1305, regulating the jurisdiction and obedience of rectors and vicars in celebrating the service. There is also a memorandum of his death, and of the election and enthronement of Walter Reginald, his successor. Cotton MSS., Faust. A. viii, 41 b., 116 b., 173 b.; and in the same MSS. Galba, E. iv, 67, there is a copy of the Archbishop's Statutes on his first visitation, in 1298. He bore for his arms, *Argent, between two bars, erm., a barrulet gules, in chief three cinque foils vert.* Lans. MSS., 255, p. 3.

MODERN WINCHELSEA.

Building.—When it had become evident that a restoration of the old town was impossible, and after Edward I had paid his visit, in 1277, he sent here John Kirkeby, Bishop of Ely and Treasurer of England, to view a plot to make a new town; and thereupon a site was fixed, on which a new town should be built. That site was a hill at a place in the adjoining parish of Icklesham, then called Iham, partly within the manor of Iham, which, together with the manor of Iden, then belonged to William de Grandison and Isabella his wife, but was afterwards acquired by the King, and partly on land belonging to Sir John Tregoz, to Battle Abbey, and to

others. The spot was principally an uneven sandstone rock, fit only for, and used as a rabbit warren; but there was a portion of meadow land at the north-west corner. This rock was washed by the waters on the east and north sides; on the north-west there was a communication by means of a ferry with Udimore, whence the direct road led to Battle and London; and on the south there was a road leading to Pett and Fairlight. The site is now table land, and seems to have been made level by using the surface stone for the buildings required in the new town. The whole land ultimately assigned for this town was 150 acres; and to make up the required quantity, the King, in the eighth year of his reign (1280,) directed his writ to Ralph of Sandwich, his steward, to exchange or buy of John de Langherst and John Bone, if they would sell, lands that lay near Iham, and fit for the building of the new town of Winchelsea; and it is there mentioned that the greatest part of Old Winchelsea was drowned, and the sea prevailing more and more against it, the rest was hopeless long to stand.[1] An exchange was effected, and on the 27th November, 1281, the King issued forth the following commission to Stephen de Penecester and others, to assign places at Iham (being a hill near) for the inhabitants of Old Winchelsea to plant themselves at.

Edwardus Dei gratia, Rex Angliæ, Dominus Hiberniæ, et Dux Acquitaniæ, dilectis et fidelibus suis Stephano de Pencester, Iter. Engolisma, et Henrico le Waleys, salutem. Sciatis quod assignavimus vos ad assidend. placias apud Ihamme, et eas per certam arrentationem, juxta legalem extentam per vos inde faciend. Baronibus et probis hominibus nostris de Wynch. edificand. et inhabitand. juxta discretiones vestras committend. Et ideo vobis mandamus, quod vos omnes, vel duo vestrum, quos ad hoc vacare contigerit, in propriis personis vestris apud Ihame accedatis, et placias ibidem assideatis, et eas præfatis Baronibus edificand. et inhabitand. commitatis in forma prædicta; salva tum Dominis immediatis placiarum prædictarum rationabili extenta cujuslibet acræ per vos assessæ, et ad inhabitan. commissæ, juxta discretiones vestras prædictas, sicut prædictum est. In cujus rei testimonium has literas nostras fieri fecimus patentes. Teste me ipso apud Westm. xxvii., die Novembris, anno regni nostri decimo.[2] Which letters were made patent on 15th March following. John de Cobeham was joined with them.

And to give greater confidence to those who should be willing to adopt the new town as their home, Edward, by his commission, dated at Acton Burnell, on 13th October, 1283, after reciting that he had provided a new town at Yham, "in lieu of our town of Winchelsea, which is in great part submersed by the inundations of the sea, and whose total submersion is feared," declared that he had resolved to commit the lands and tenements there to the barons of the port and town of Winchelsea, and willed that the same barons, when

[1] Jeake, p. 103. [2] Ibid.

they should have taken their abode there and begun to build, should be as free in the new town as they were in the old town and elsewhere, and should enjoy the same liberties and privileges as they did under their old charters. On 28th April, 1281, the king gave to William de Grandison and Sibilla or Isabella, his wife, his manor of Dymnok, in the manor of Dertford, Kent, in exchange for the manors of Ihamme and Idenne, with the patronage of the churches, the parks, and the knight's fees, with all the appurtenances, except land which was Henry Bertin's, in Ihamme. And on 23rd June, 1288, (the year after the fatal inundation of the old town) Edward carried out his promise to the inhabitants of Winchelsea, by granting to the barons of the royal port of Winchelsea the site and place of Ihamme, with the marsh there, except ten acres of land which the king retained to his use; and he confirmed to them all the rights and privileges which, by the charters of his ancestors and otherwise, they were accustomed to enjoy, the barons accounting annually to the treasury, as they were wont to do in the old town; he directed Salomon de Roff and others, the justices itinerant to admit of these privileges; and finally the rights of the Vicar of Icklesham were satisfied by a grant of £10 a year, in consideration of the tithes of that part of the parish, taken into Old Winchelsea: which payment was formerly made out of the revenues of the Duchy of Cornwall, but is now discharged by the Receiver General of the Land Revenue of the County of Sussex.[1]

Charters.—The whole of these Charters were afterwards exemplified by King Henry the 4th, on 10th June, 1404, in the following Charter.[2]

Henricus Dei gratia, Rex Angliæ et Franciæ, et Dominus Hiberniæ, omnibus, ad quos præsentes literæ pervenerint, salutem. Inspeximus irrotulamentum quarundam literarum patencium Domini Edwardi, quon-

[1] Horsfield's Sussex, vol. 1, p. 473. [2] Jeake, pp. 104-5.

dam Regis Angliæ primi post conquestum, in rotulis cancellariæ suæ irrotulatarum in hæc verba; Edwardus Dei gratia, Rex Angliæ, et Dominus Hiberniæ, et Dux Acquitaniæ, omnibus, ad quos præsentes literæ pervenerint, salutem. Quia pro villa nostra de Winchelsee, quæ pro majori parte per maris inundationes jam submersa est, et de cujus submercione totali cotidie veretur, quandam villam novam apud Yhame fieri providimus, et terras et tenementa ibidem baronibus villæ et portus de Wynchelsee committere, et ipsos inde feofare, edificand. et inhabitand. volumus et concedimus, pro nobis et hæredibus nostris quod cum iidem barones placias suas apud Yhame ceperunt, et eas edificare inceperunt, ipsi, cum rebus et bonis suis omnibus adeo liberi sint in eadem nova villa et alibi ubique, sicut antea fuerint in prædicta villa de Wynchelsee, et aliis locis quibuscunque; et easdem libertates et consuetudines habeant, quas habent per cartas prædecessorum nostrorum Regum Angliæ, et eisdem libertatibus et consuetudinibus gaudeant et utantur, quibus, rationabiliter usi sunt temporibus retroactis; et cartas nostras eis inde de novo fieri faciemus. In cujus rei testimonium has literas nostras fieri fecimus patentes. T. me ipso apud Acton Burnell, xiii, die Octobris, anno regni nostri undecimo. Inspeximus etiam irrotulamentum cujusdam commissionis prædicti quondam Regis in rotulis cancellariæ prædictæ irrotulatæ, in hœc verba: (setting out the commission to John de Cobeham and others, and then proceeding.)

Inspeximus insuper irrotulamenta quorundam brevium ejusdem quondam Regis in rotulis cancellariæ suæ prædictæ similiter irrotulatorum, in hœc verba: Quia propter dampnum quod di. et fi. R. Barones Portus R. de Wynchelsee, de villa sua per maris intemperiem, jam diu est, sustinuerunt, ac periculum quod eis indies imminet ibidem, Rex debit et concessit eisdem baronibus suis situm et placeam de Ihamme, cum marisco, exceptis decem acris terræ, quas in placea prædicta Rex retinet ad opus suum, quos Rex habuit ex concessione di. et fi. suorum Willielmi de Grandisono et Isabellæ uxoris ejus, ad inhabitand. et ad villam suam de Wynchelsee ibidem faciend. et tenend. de Rege et hæred. suis, sibi et hæred. suis. Ita quod ipsi Barones sunt ibidem adeo liberi, sicut prius apud Wynchelsee fuerunt, et eisdem libertatibus, quibus apud Wynchelsee, per cartas antecessorum Regis Regum Angliæ, et confirmationem Regis uti consueverunt, de cætero in omnibus gaudeant et utantur ibidem. Et ita quod de firma villæ ejusdem R. respondeatur per annum ad scaccarium Regis per manus Ballivi Regis ibidem, sicut prius de prædicta villa sua de Wynchelsee responderi consueverint. Mandatum est Vic. Sussex, quod eisdem baronibus de prædictis situ et placea, cum marisco, plenam seisinam habere fac. salvo jure cujuslibet, et ita quod alteri non præjudicetur, Rex eum in adventu suo in Angliam per se et eosdem Barones singl. jus petentibus in prædictis et clamantibus satisfaciet, nisi per dilectos et fideles Regis prius inde fuerit satisfactum. T. Edm. comite Cornubiæ cons. R. apud Westm. xxiii, die Junii, anno regni sui sexto decimo. Consimile breve dirigitur eidem vic. quod eisdem Baron. de prædictis situ et placea per metas et bundas inde factas plenam seisinam similiter habere fac. absque conditionibus prædictis. T. ut supra. Sub hujusmodi forma mandatum est Salomoni de Roff. et sociis suis Justic. itinerantibus in com. Sussex, per duo brevia R. videlicit, per unum cum condicionibus prædictis et aliud absque condicionibus quod prædictos Barones libertatibus prædictis ibidem uti permittant, nec ipsos super hiis in aliquo inquietent coram eis, seu ab aliis inquietari permittant. T. ut supra. Inspeximus similiter tenorem irrotulamenti cujusdam cartæ Willielmi de Grandisono et Sibillæ uxoris ejus, in memorandis scaccarii ejusdem quondam Regis irrotúlatæ, quem coram nobis in Cancellar. nostram venire fecimus, in hæc verba: Sciant præsentes et futuri, quod nos Willielmus de Grandisono et Sibilla uxor mea dedimus, concessimus, et hac præsenti carta nostra confirmavimus, pro nobis et hæred. nostris, magnifico principi et Domino nostro ligeo Domino Edwardo Dei gratia Rex Angliæ illustri, maneria nostra de Ihamme et Idenne, cum advocationibus ecclesiarum, parcis, et cum feodis militum, et cum omnibus alijs pertin. suis, excepta illa terra quæ fuit Henrici Bertin in Ihamme, habend. et tenend. eidem Domino nostro Regi et hæred. suis libere, quiete, absolute, et integre, imperpetuum, in escambium manerii de Dymnok, et quadraginta et sex librarum, sex solidorum, et trium denar. et unius quadr. redditus ann. in Dertford. Et nos et hæred. nostri warrantizabimus prædicto Domino nostro Regi et hæred. suis eadem maneria de Ihamme et Idenne imperpetuum in escambium prædictum. In cujus rei testimonium præsenti cartæ sigilla nostra opposuimus. Hiis testibus, venerabili patre T. Eliens. episcopo Dom. Rs. Thesaur. Petro de Cestr. præposito Beverlaci, Johanne de Cobham, Willielmo de Myddeton, Willielmo de Carleton, Baron. de Scaccario, Ph. de Wileby, Cancellar. ejusdem scaccarii, Thoma de Weylaund, Johanne de Limetot, Willielmo de Burnton, Justic. de Banco, Rad. de Sandewico, Nich. de Castello, Richardo de Standeford et aliis. Dat. apud Westm. vicesimo octavo die Aprilis anno Regni Rs. Edwardi, prædicti quinto decimo. Nos autem tenores irrotulamentorum prædictorum ad requisitionem nunc homin. dictæ villæ de Wynchelsee duximus exemplificand. per præsentes. In cujus rei testimonium has literas nostras fieri fecimus patentes. T. me ipso apud Westm. quinto decimo die Junii, anno Regni nostri quinto.—Smyth.

Jeake, after giving these charters, goes on to say that Old Winchelsea being drowned, the inhabitants, by favour of the king, and authority of his charters and grants aforesaid, brought the name of Winchelsea to their new plantation at Iham, which Jeake erroneously supposes to be that "which was before a member to Hastings, called Petit Iham, *and the rather*, because Hastings yet claims that part called St. Leonards;" but Petit Iham is in St. Leonards liberty, and the claims of Hastings did not extend into Icklesham parish; "and there built a town of about forty (the exact number was thirty-nine) squares, called quarters, after the pattern, as is believed, of the old town, with spacious streets; adorned, besides the religious houses, with three churches, called St. Giles, St. Leonard, and St. Thomas the Apostle. Fortified, besides the natural situation on a hill, with walls, part of which, and of three of the gates are yet standing,—that called Pipewell leading to Rye (viâ Udimore,) another called Newgate (on the Pett side) leading to Hastings, and the other called Strandgate, leading to the rivulet running near the foot of the hill, and so into the sea at Rye, formerly called the river Ree, which at the edifying of this new town is supposed to have run up, navigable, beyond Winchelsea into the country, and at the west side of the town, in the place called Pewes Pond, conceived to have made the harbour where ships lay at anchor, which the sea afterwards deserting, was one cause of the decay of the place." Pennant, in his Tour,[1] says he had been informed that an anchor had been found beneath the soil here.

Leland, in his Itinerary,[2] gives this account of the re-edifying of the town:—

"The oulde Toune of Winchelesey of a vi. or vii. yeres together felle to a very soore and manifest ruine, be reason of old rages of the se, and totally in the tyme of the aforesayde vi. or vii. yeres. In the space of these aforesayde yeres the people of Winchelesey made sute to

[1] Vol. 2, p. 31. [2] Fol. 58.

Kyng Edward the First for remedy and a new plot to set them a new toune on. Whereapon the Kyng sent thither John Kirkeby, Bisshop of Ely and Treasurer of England, and vewid a plot to make the new toune of Winchelesey on, the wich was at that tyme a ground wher conies partely did resorte. Syr John Tregose, a knight, was the chief owner of it, and one Maurice, and Bataille Abbay. The Kyng compoundid with them; and so was there vii. score and tenne acres limited to the new toune, whereof part is in the King Mede withoute the toune, and part in hangging of the hille. Then in the tyme of the yere aforesayde the King set to his helpe in beginning and wauling New Winchelesey: and the inhabitantes of Olde Winchelesey tooke by a litle and litle and buildid at the new toune. So that wythyn the vi. or vii. yere afore expressid the new toune was metely welle furnishid, and dayly after for a few yeres encreasid."

SITE.—Thomas of Walsingham, who is followed by Camden, calls it a Port upon a hill; and says the new town was situate upon a very high hill, very steep on that side which looks towards the sea, or where it overlooks the road where the ships lie at anchor: whence the way leading from that part of the town to the haven, goes not straight forward, lest it should by a downright descent force those that go down to fall headlong, or those ascending to creep rather on their hands than walk; but lying sideways, it winds with crooked turns often repeated, in and out to one side and the other, or as we should say "zig-zag." He adds, that on the side of this precipice the town was not enclosed by a stone wall, but by high mud or earthen entrenchments carried to the height of the human body, with intervals, and through these bulwarks was the look-out towards the ships. After giving us this description of the situation, Thomas of Walsingham goes on with an account of the accident, which happened to Edward when he was nearly thrown from his horse, of which we shall speak hereafter: but old Lambard, in his Topographical Dictionary, assumes the date of the incident to be at the building of the fortifications, and gives a very disastrous account of the accident. He tells us that whilst the townsmen were occupied building the town, "the King himself came to see the work, and as he approached, the noise of a windmill so feared his horse that he never ceased leaping and flinging till he had cast his rider. The sight whereof much grieved the beholders, howbeit they took him up without much harm." Whether the king was almost or altogether thrown from his horse is not very important for history. It is likely that Lambard copied from Walsingham, though he changed the time, and thinking the account rather dry, altered, embellished, and added to it. The visit must have been prior to the king's absence for three years in Acquitaine, and probably took place in November, 1285, when the king was at Battle, whence on the 16th of that month he issued four writs for a view of frankpledge, &c., within the liberties of the Abbot of Peterborough.[1]

The new town, thus built, was surrounded by a stone wall on all the sides, except that overlooking the ships and next the precipice, and traces of this wall may still be found. But, besides the wall, there was a stronghold or castle built by the king at the north-west corner of the town, on the ten acres reserved by him, and called by Leland "the King Mede without the town:" it immediately overlooked the parish church of St. Leonard, and commanded completely the inner harbour. Some remains of the clustered columns of the entrance gate are yet to be seen on the side of the Pipewell or Ferry Gate, leading to Udimore. Until 1828 there stood a round or watch tower, called the Roundle, of which we subjoin an engraving from a drawing made by the late Mr. Stileman; and the exact sites of both castle and watch tower are laid down in the map, which we have engraved from the original made by Mr. Stephens, in the year 1763, by order of Mr. Wardroper, and now in the possession of Mr. Thomas Dawes.

[1] Chron. Petroburgense. Camd. Soc., pp. 116-7.

PLATE 11.

T. Ross del. J. Hunter sc.

STRAND GATE.

S.W.

T. Ross del. J. Hunter. sc.

NEW GATE.

Of the three original gateways, two are standing,—the STRAND GATE, formerly leading to the harbour, but now leading by the new Military road to Rye, and the NEW GATE, leading on the south of Icklesham to Pett and Fairlight: these were three quarters of a mile apart. The present roads to Rye and across the marsh to Icklesham and Hastings were formed at a much more recent period. We give an engraving of these two gates. The original PIPEWELL or LAND GATE, now known as the FERRY GATE, led over the Ferry to the then direct road to Rye, which was by way of Udimore. This gate, which was situated one quarter of a mile north-west of the Strand Gate, has been re-built, and we shall have occasion to notice the present gate hereafter.

Besides the two churches of ST. THOMAS (the choir of which is standing) and ST. GILES within, and of ST. LEONARD without the walls, the house of the GRAY FRIARS, and the hospital of ST. BARTHOLOMEW, which had existed in the old town, were transferred to the new. There were also hospitals of ST. JOHN, and of the HOLY ROOD:[1] and there

[1] Grose mentions a tradition that Winchelsea formerly contained fourteen or fifteen chapels: upon which he hazards the conjecture that these

was afterwards added, in the reign of Edw. II, a house of the Dominicans Black Friars, or Friars Predicant. All of which we shall describe in the chapter on Ecclesiastical Foundations. Without New Gate stood the Holy Cross of Winchelsea.

There were within the walls, two greens or open spaces, one of twelve acres called the King's Green, on the road from the church of St. Thomas towards New Gate, and the other called Cook's Green, above the hanging of the hill, at the north-east side of the town, near the Strand Gate.

Water, so scarce at Rye, was amply supplied to this town from six open wells:—viz., Pipe Well, situate near the Ferry, close by the entrance of the town by the former Rye road: St. Katherine's Well, situate half way up the hill leading from Rye, and below Cook's Green, the water of which is slightly chalybeate: the Strand Well, on the hanging of the hill (above the former tan yard) destroyed a few years since by the falling in of the cliff: the Friars' Well, now enclosed, situated in a field recently called the Peartree or Wellfield, to the east of the Gray Friars; the New Well on the outside of New Gate; and the Vale Well, now called St. Leonard's Well, at the north-west of the town, under the old castle,—of whose waters the popular belief yet remains, that when once drunken the drinker never leaves Winchelsea, that is, that wherever he roams his heart is still there; each drinker realising Goldsmith's lines,

> In all my wand'rings round this world of care,
> * * * *
> I still had hopes, my strong vexations past,
> Here to return—and die at home at last.

The well-doing of the inhabitants was further secured by two market places, called Monday's Market and Little Mon-

were appendages to so many Monastic Foundations. Grose, however, must have mistaken the many vaults or crypts throughout the town for chapels. Leland and Lambard both correctly state the number of religious houses.

day's Market, and by several Windmills. One was in the liberty of St. Leonard, near the spot on which a windmill now exists. Two others were within the grounds afterwards of the Black Friars, one being near the King's Green. There was a stone mill near Pipewell, and a windmill in the parish of St. Giles, in a place then called "Le Bochery," now called the Great Millbank, which, on 1st May, 1407, Richard Londenays, of Brede, son of Robert de Londenays, then late of Winchelsea, and —— his wife, who was sister and heiress of William Oxenbridge, enfeoffed to John Gyles, of Winchelsea, miller, of whom it was purchased in 1434, by John Godfrey, and came through Matilda, widow of Simon Farncombe, the heiress of the Godfreys, in 1477, to the abbey of Battle.[1]

Among the antique seals found within the town is one bearing the impression of a lion combatant or rampant, the arms of the Londenays, with the legend SVM LEO FORTIS.

It was doubtless the private seal of one of the family, and from the style may be referred to a period not later than the middle of the fourteenth century.

The town abounds with crypts and vaults, many of which have handsome groined roofs and corbel heads well executed, affording ample store-room for the wines and other merchandise in which the merchants traded.

In the Battle Abbey Records there are mentioned in connection with the parish of Icklesham, the great ditch of Iham; the bank of the hill of Iham; the bridge of Iham; the road which leads from that bridge towards Winchelsea, that is by the Ashes Farm, entering by New Gate; and the King's high road which led from Battle towards Winchelsea.[2]

The thirty-nine quarters or squares, exclusive of the sites of the two churches, into which the new town was divided, varied in quantity. The majority were from 1½a. to 2a. and 2½a. each, but some towards the south were 3a. and 3½a.

[1] Battle Charters, pp. 96-101-114-120. [2] Addl. MSS., 6344, p. 425.

Notwithstanding the loss of fences they may yet be traced with tolerable accuracy. A glance at the map will enable us to follow them. The first quarter was at Cook's Green, at the north-east corner of the town: thence the quarters extended westward along the north side of the town: in the second quarter was the Salutation: in the third was Westbrook: in the fourth the Friars', that is, the Blackfriars' Orchard: in the fifth was the Roundle Piece. Having reached the northern point, the quarters went back again to the east, and thence again to the west, and so worked from east to west, southward, to the New Gate; in the sixth quarter were the Pendents of the hill: in the seventh was the Bear Square: in the eighth quarter was the Court House: in the ninth was Paradise (the house of Mr. Dawes): in the twelfth, on the east, was the Cliff: between the thirteenth and fourteenth quarters stood the Church of St. Thomas: in the fourteenth was the Ballad Singer's Plat: in the seventeeth, again on the east, was Tinker's Garden: in the nineteenth was Little Monday's Market and Trojan's Hall, otherwise Jews' Hall: the Church of St. Giles was between the twentieth and twenty-first quarters: next the twenty-first quarter was the Great Millbank: in the twenty-second quarter, at the extreme west, were the Furze Banks: in the twenty-third quarter, beginning again on the east but westward of the Gray Friars, was Little Monday's Market: in the twenty-eighth quarter was Monday's Market: in the twenty-ninth quarter was Packham Field: in the thirtieth quarter was Great Gallows Hill: in the thirty-fourth quarter was the Hospital of St. John: in the thirty-fifth was land near the Pewes: in the thirty-seventh quarter was the Coney Field, now part of the Gray Friars: in the thirty-eighth quarter was land, afterwards belonging to the Hospital of the Holyrood: and in the thirty-ninth and last quarter were the Hospitals of the Holyrood and of St. Bartholomew.

The parsonages of St. Thomas and St. Giles were not in

any quarter; and there were several marshes, the pendents of the hill, and land in the strand, without the quarters, but within the boundary of the town itself. The whole space occupied by the new town, and by that portion of the old parish, which is now above water, is 1120 acres.[1]

Boundary of Liberty.—From a MS. in the hand-writing of the Rev. Dr. Harris, the historian of Kent, formerly in the possession of Mr. Shadwell, and a copy of which was with the late Mr. Stileman, we find that the bounds of the Liberty of Winchelsea as they were taken and enrolled the 7th day of May, in the fourth year of the reign of Edward the Third, A.D. 1330, were as under:—"First go from the Cross, without Newgate, north, along by the Town Ditch, and so through the midst of Pewes' Marsh to a ditch of the Manor of Icklesham, leading to St. Leonard's Fleet, till you come right against a well in Pook Lane, called Vale Well,[2] and so east, up by a little lane, lying between Crooked Acre and Bell Morrice, to the King's High-street; and then north-east, through the lands of Thomas Alard to the street end, and so to the ring of Stone Mill, and so downe to Pipewell Cawsey's end, and so by the street at the right hand leading to the north and to Grind-pepper Well;[3] and then as the old Ferry-way leadeth to the Channell, and so over the Channell to a fleet called White Fleet; and as the water leadith by the Hopad Marsh into Kettle Fleet, and so taking in the whole roade of the Puddle and the Cambre along upon the Sea Coast where the Hermitage did stand, until a man can see Beachy Head, neare Bourne; and from thence through the sea to a wall called Court Wall, and so, west, to the Cross without Newgate aforesaid."

[1] Population Returns, 1841. As the sea is receding it is difficult to ascertain the exact quantity: there are only 720a. 3r. 9p., exclusive of houses and gardens, in the Tithe Commutation.

[2] Now called St. Leonard's Well.

[3] Afterwards called the Strand Well.

Dr. Harris remarks of these bounds,—"Limites Winchelseæ sunt sicut Mare et Portus circumdant villam de Winchelseæ usque ad ffœod. de Gestlinges; and that the liberty anciently extended to a cross standing on an old wall near Kettle Fleet, in North Marsh, as may be seen by depositions between Sir H. Guldeford and Thompson, about Padiham Marsh, in which also was judged to lie the North Marsh, White Fleet Marsh, and that whereon stood the Castle." The point at which a man could see Beachey Head was at Jury's Gut, to which the corporation still walk as their boundary. The corporation commissioners report[1] that "the jurisdiction extends into the parishes of Pett, Broomhill, and Icklesham. There is one house in Pett, about ten in Broomhill, and about six in Icklesham situate within it. It extends along the sea coast for six or seven miles. The western boundary is a point between the two towers numbered 31 and 32, and the eastern runs up to Rye harbour, within half a mile of that town."

The exact sites of the streets and places, together with the names of the first owners, are fully set out in a return made in the 20th Edward I, and yet remaining among the Ministers' accounts in the Carlton House Ride. The names are very curious. The Roll has the following opening:—These are the places set out, enfranchised, and on which a rent has been put, in the new town of Winchelsea, which is just now built, by the mayor and twenty-four jurats, and by Sir John de Kirkeby, Bishop of Ely, on the part of our Lord the King, commissioned to set out, enfranchise, and set a rent on the same places, who say, according to the form of their commission, that our Lord the King held of the land which belonged to Sir John Tregoz on the hill where the new town is founded, as appears by the extent made by Sir Stephen le Pencester and Gregory de Rokesle, 65½ acres, of which, one acre more or less, has been taken; in the whole, £8 5s. 1d. They say also that the

[1] Appendix II, p. 1073.

heirs of John de Langherst held on the said hill, as appears by the extent aforesaid, 35¼a. 18p. of land, of which, one acre more or less, was taken,—52s. 0¼d. They say also that John Bone held on the hill aforesaid, as appears by the extent, 24½a. 31vrgs., of which, one acre more or less, was taken, to the value of 29s. 0½d. They say also that Gilbert de Cruce held on the hill, as appears by the extent, 10¼a. 23p., value 20s. 9d. They say also that the Abbot of Battle held on the hill, as appears by the extent, 1¾a., value 2s. 4d. They say also that John Moris held on the hill, as appears by the extent, 2a., value 32d. They say also that William and Richard, sons of Tristram, held on the hill, as appears by the extent, 1a. with a house built upon it, value 5s. They say also that John Moris held on the hill, as appears by the extent, ¾a., value 12d. They say also that the heirs of Bartholomew Wymund and his partner, held on the hill, as appears by the extent, 1½a., value 2s. 6d. They say also that John, son of Reginald Alard, held in a certain place which is called the Trecherie, as appears by the extent, 1a., value 3s. They say also that the heirs of John Bacan held on the hill, as appears by the extent, 1¾a. 16p. of land, value 3s. 1d. Also that the same heirs held a certain mill with the site, which contains 8p., which mill and site the said heirs held in their own hands, and is not necessary for our Lord the King or the town. They say also that John Moris and his partner, held on the hill, as appears by the extent, 2a., value 40d. They say also that the heirs of John Bacan and his partner, held under the pendents of the hill, as appears by the extent, 2a., value 20d. Total value £14 11s. 5¾d. Sum total of the aforesaid acres, 149¾a. 8vrgs.: of which total of the said lands are taken away 12a., which are retained for the use of our Lord the King, by the said Bishop of Ely. Also that there are taken out of the said total for the cemetaries of St. Thomas and St. Giles, 5a., of which the right of patronage remains in the hands of our

Lord the King. Total subtracted from the land aforesaid, 17a.; and that there remained for the building of the town, out of the said total, $132\frac{1}{2}$ acres and a quarter of an acre, and 8 virgates. And the said mayor and jurats say that of these $132\frac{1}{2}$ acres and a quarter of an acre, and 8 perches of land, 87 and a half acres, and half a quarter of an acre, and seven and a quarter perches are set out for buildings; and that there remain in waste, some for the markets, some in streets, and some in the pendents, which cannot be built upon, 45a., the 8th part of an acre, and $5\frac{3}{4}$ perches. Which waste, 87 and half acres, and a half a quarter of an acre, and $7\frac{1}{4}$ perches of land, are charged in the sum of is £14 11s. $5\frac{3}{4}$d.

They then go on to give the names of every owner, the quantity of his holding, and the free rent he was to pay, in divisions of eight streets or ways, and 39 quarters.

FIRST STREET OR HIGHWAY.

In the First Quarter.

Simon le Machon
Stephen Blaunchpain
Robert called Burnel
Walter Bosce
Thomas of Pevensey
Robert le Meleward
Alan de Ferne
Walter Salerne
Henry Dagard
Roger Wyliam
Adam Schewere
Roger Averil
The Heirs of Adam le Meleward
Thomas le Meleward
Stephen Ryngemere
Robert Colyn
Nicholas Codelawe
Peter Geneinde
Gervase Mot
Reginald Robert
Stephen of Canterbury
Walter Johan
Peter of Portesmouth
Reginald Alard, junior

Total in this quarter, 1a. 8 parts 12v.: rent, 4s. $0\frac{1}{4}$d.

In the Second Quarter.

John Madour
Clement Doning
John Sneke
Thomas Werterer
Nicholas Richard
William Pret
The Heirs of Alan Buchard
Richard of Dover
Clement Langters
John Folke
Andrew Passelewe
William Blanc payn
Gervase Coleman Paul
Lawrence Ferbras
Gervase Frost
John Galp
Petronilla, relict of Cok Scolard
Richard Witloc
Walter le Botre
Geoffry Roberd
Sampson Seli de Pucto
Godard Petit
Andrew of the Monastery
Nicholas Fimelyte
Nicholas de Apeltre
Philip Matip
Gervase Hambuc
Richard Hambuc
Beatrix Hambuc

Total in this quarter, $1\frac{1}{4}$a. $16\frac{1}{4}$v.: rent, 4s. $11\frac{1}{4}$.

In the Third Quarter.

John, son of John Roger
Justin Alard
William Beaufrount
John Large
Stephen of Bidindene
John of Scotenye
Andrew of Folkestane
William Batayle
John Austin
John Liteman
Stephen Russel
William Hamer
Maurice Cocus (Cook)
Petronilla Queynte
Henry Clement
Richard of Pevensey

Total in this quarter, 1¾a. half a quarter 8½v.: rent, 4s. 8¾d.

In the Fourth Quarter.

Richard Cely
Goda pore Voghel
John Treygen
Symon of Scotenye
Jacob, son of Thomas Barber
John, son of Thomas Barber
Colin Alard
Thomas Alard
Gervase Alard, junior
Walter de Rackele

Total in this quarter, 1½a. 35¾v.: rent, 5s. 8¾d.

In the Fifth Quarter.

Henry le Palmer
Joseph of Hasting
John Orpedeman
Walter Sand
Ralph Harding
Lucas Beneyt
Andrew Hardi
John Hardi
William de Orewelle
Thomas, son of Th. Weterledere
Simon Hughet
Margory, relict of Peter Austyn
William Halfhering
William atte Velde
Nicholas Bosce
William Mot large
John de Farlegh
Poteman Bod
John Bod
William Romeming

Total in this quarter, 1½a. 3½v.: rent, 3s. 10d.

SECOND HIGHWAY.

In the Sixth Quarter.

Gervase le Coupre
Gervase Skele
Robert ate Carte
John Crask
Peter Torold
John Jacob
Parvus Galfridus
Thomas Large
Jacob de Lidehame

Total in this quarter, ½a. half a quarter 10¾v.: rent, 2s. 3½d.

In the Seventh Quarter.

The Heirs of Stephen Dinder
John de Herewyco (Harwich)
Richard Finor
Roger Toneman
William Wade
John Dawe
John Batayle
John, son of John Bochard
John Ine
William Mancap
William Mazote
Robert Stalle
The relict of Gabriel Gudloc
John Romeming
Philip le Seltere
Sampson atte Crouche
Standanore
Peter Faber
Elyas Lambin
Juliana Nightyngale
The Heirs of Richard de Hethe
Alice Busch

Total in this quarter, 2a. 8¾v.: rent, 6s. 10d.

In the Eighth Quarter.

Henry Yve
Petronilla Clobbere
Alice, relict of Rob Gerveys
Nicholas Alard
Gervase Alard, junior
Nicholas Alard
Reginald Alard, senior
Gervase Alard, senior
Thomas Alard
William Seman
William Mot de Hasting
Adam Pistor

Total in this quarter, 2¼a. 18¾v.: rent, 7s. 10½d.

In the Ninth Quarter.

John of Ihame, clerk
Robert le Barebour
Ralph Cocus
Adam, called Cok of Wynchester
Pote called Chepman
Henry le Bakere, son of Benedict
Roger Scappe
Thomas Colram
The Heirs of Richard Batayle
Henry Jacob
Vincent Herberd
John Pistor Witegrom
Walter of Dertemouth
John Pistor Wytegrom
William Pistel
Godfrey the clerk
Stephen Germeyn

Total in this quarter, 2a. 13¾v.: rent, 6s. 10¼d.

In the Tenth Quarter.

John Takesnaw
Stephen of Wynchester
Stephen Wyncard
Adam Pope
Stephen Holt
Ralph Bertelot
Laurence Arniz
Richard Stevening
Stephen Wincher
Eustace Holt
Hugh Wymund
The Heirs of John Adrian
Ralph de Gillingham
Christiana Weldisse
William Quiliere
William of Maghefeld
William le Palmere sen
Maurice Ingelard
Matilda, relict of John Carite
Adam Stain
Hamo Campion
William Hannile
Bartholomew Bone
Adam Faber
Symon Burne
William Bakere
John Ingelard
The Heirs of Gervase Turepin
Adam Cheke

Total in this quarter, 2⅝a. 19¾v.: rent, 9s. 6d.

In the Eleventh Quarter.

Batecok le Passur
Thomas Alard
Roger Mortumer
Gervase Hughet
John Ledelone
John Nowynd
Adam Weterledere
Gabriel Tristram
Hamod Blakeman
Matilda Stevening
Milicent Piggesteil
Wymarch Piggesteyl
Alan Goman
Henry Savveney
Reynard le Palmer
Motting Clobbere
Richard le Coggre
Broumeng Cristyn

Total in this quarter, 1a. 25½v.: rent, 3s. 8d.

THIRD HIGHWAY.

In the Twelfth Quarter.

William Burgeys
John, the clerk
John Yevegod
John Gascoign
Robert Codelaw del ord
John Nase
John Yve, son of Henry Yve
Richard le Vetre
Charles Faber

Total in this quarter, 1¾a. and half a quarter of a virgate: rent, 4s. 3½d.

In the Thirteenth Quarter.

Henry of the Church
Richard Inthelepe
John Colekyn le Paum
Richard Trace
William Thursteyn
Walter Scolloc
William Gerveys
Alan Brounetesone
Richard Scot del ord
Herbert, called Brouning, clerk
Petronilla Ingelberd
Lawrence the clerk
John Tailleur
Petronilla, relict of John Purveaunce
Johanna de Stoke
Petronilla de Hertepole
Richard Pace
The Heirs of Stephen Cornman
John, son of John Pace
John Streyl
John, son of Ralph Pace
John Seman
Walter Songre
Lawrence Haskard
William Skorefeyn
Magnus William

Total in this quarter, 2½a. and half a quarter of a virgate: rent, 7s. 6d.

In the Fourteenth Quarter.

Robert, son of Ralph Cocus (Cook)
Elecote Adam
John Palmer, son of John Palmer
Elyas Hamer
John Pollard
Johanna Petronilla, daughter of Geoffry Russel
Robert Taunay
Henry Bacun
Robert le Gric
John of Maghefelde
William de Brokeye
Stephen Colram
Nicholas Carpenter
Alan Maynard
John Manekyn
William le Alblaster
Geoffry Ponderous
John le Dore, senior
Benedict Penyfader
John, son of Gervase Alard
The Heirs of Colewif of Ihame

Total in this quarter, 2a. 12v.: rent, 6s. 10¾d.

In the Fifteenth Quarter.

Stephen Moris
Richard le Ropere
Roger de Eldinge
Roger Godard
Richard Adam
William Belde
John Chipian
Henry Heved
Vincent Goldine
Geoffry de Tened
Robert Germeyn, senior, son of Richard Germeyn
John Cralbere
Stephen de Cruce
William Hoghelyn
Benedict le Botere
Ralph Favel
William de Burne
Richard Blobbere
Adam Kenting
Robert Broker, near the mill, heir of John Bazan
William Suift
Richard Neam
Roger Cotesone
John Lamb
William Neel

Total in this quarter, 2½a. half, and half ¼ of a virgate: rent, 7s. 6¼d.

In the Sixteenth Quarter.

Geoffry Banek
John Brouning
Bonne Botercoke
John Ancel
John of Dover
John Hannile
William Bredeware
John of Ihame, clerk
William Pace
John Gerveys of Pevensey
William Godinogh
Gervase Scopeheved
William Scopeheved
Walter Spytewymbel
John Remys
Richard Albard
Hugh Page
Richard Rucke
Gervase Aldwyne
Stephen Wyting
Henry Felipe
Robert Isonde
Adam Stonhard
On the side of this quarter Gervase Alard, junior, held one acre

Total in this quarter, 3¼a. 14¼v.: rent, 11s. 1d.

FOURTH HIGHWAY.

In the Seventeenth Quarter.

John Dada
John Ripecherl
Nicholas Whif
Walter Stoket
John Bateman
Adam Lokyere
Lawrence Yon
Sir Roger de Leukenore
Sir William de Echingeham
Simon de Echingeham
Nicholas Pistor, forester
Henry Seman
Rose Picard
John Bakere, son of Benedict
Robert Aubin
Henry Dorivall
Laurence Burgeys
John Boghiere
Matilda Beneyt
Robert Lef
Roger Mite Wlle
Rengerùs Wylekin

Total in this quarter, 2¼a. half a quarter 5¼v.: rent, 8s. 1d.

In the Eighteenth Quarter.

Henry Heaved
Robert Londeneys
Geoffry Trippe
Godefry Langters
Ad. Aleman, bochre
Isabella Machon
John, son of William Alard
William of Canterbury
Richard Wibelot
William of Sandherst, bochre
Simon ate Helme
Robert le Hane
Adam Eufeme
Juliana, relict of Alan Godefrey
John Panifader
Gerald, called Batecok ate Welle
Henry, son of John Aurifaber (Goldsmith)
Salerne, relict of William Maynard
Gervase Pechun
Matilda Bakestre
William Trottesmale
Richard Cocing
Henry Cornman
Henry Port
John Vetre
Robert Reyne
Robert le Botere
Alexr of the Church
Ralph Yring
Geoffry Dali
The Heirs of Nicholas Quic
John Martin
Henry Moning
Robert Jolivet
John Large
John, his son
Reginald Carpentre
William de la Carette

Total in this quarter, 3⅝a. 9¾v.: rent, 10s. 8¾d.

In the Nineteenth Quarter.

Henry de Strode
William de Apeltre sutor
Hamo Sutor of Rye
Henry de Monigeham
John, his brother
John of Sandwych
Gervase le Cordwaner
William le Barebour
Richard Scot Cotiler
William Aurifaber
Stephen Aurifaber
Henry Bron
Walter Scappe
Reginald Alard, junior
Paul de Horne
Thomas Godefrey
John Andrew
John le Dore
Richard Godefray

Total in this quarter, 3½a. 7¾v.: rent, 12s. 9¼d.

In the Twentieth Quarter.

William Pate
Walter of Scotenie
Andrew Goddard
Matthew Godard
William Toly
Henry, son of John Alard
John Pontre
Henry Bakere
John Wallere
Simon Salerne, Roger and John his brothers
Adam of Bidindene
Robert, son of Roger of Bidindene
John Squathard
William Aurifaber, brother of Stephen
The Heirs of Mathew le Machon
Godard Cocus
John Alard
Robert Paulyn
Jacob Paulyn
John Godefrey

Total in this quarter, 3⅝a. 17v.: rent, 11s. 1d.

In the Twenty-first Quarter.

Agnes Panifadre
The Rector of St. Giles
Roger Paumer
Sampson Heaved
William of Ihame
John Sperke

Robert Salerne
Margaret, daughter of Stephen Roberd
Roger Soutre, piscator
Robert Yevegod

William Kenting
Henry Goldine
Sander de Brokeye, long.
Peter Goldine
Robert of Canterbury

Total in this quarter, 1a. half a quarter 7¼v.: rent, 6s.

In the Twenty-second Quarter.

Bartholomew Roberd
William de Pulham
Walter Scappe
John Alard and Justin, brothers, jointly
John Buchard, ingulf
Thomas Pannoc
Cok Badding

Hamo de Marisco
Muriele Scrith
John Roteline
Alexander Pistor of Westune
William Grubbe
John Noreys, pistor

Brouningus Paumer
Richard Quiliere
Gervase Popelote
Jordan, the clerk
Stephen Speche
William Passelewe
John Jone sone

Total in this quarter, 3a. 23v.: rent, 10s. 6d.

On the side of the above Quarter.

John de Rackele
Walter de Marisco

William and Richard, sons of Tristram le Frere, with a house

Total of this land, ½a. 10v.: rent, 22¼d.

FIFTH HIGHWAY.

In the Twenty-third Quarter.

Richard Digon, trompour
John Scheylard, pistor
Peter Maynard
John Alard, son of John Alard
Hamo Cotiler

Henry de la Haye
Geoffry Draneke
William Frost
John of Brede
Peter Blosme
Robert Russel

Roger Mathon, bochre
John Beneyt
Adam Vader
Adam Erl
Beneyt Bochre
William Dod

Total in this quarter, 1a. ¼v.: rent, 6s. 9¼d.

In the Twenty-fourth Quarter.

John le Palmer of Upredinge
William Heved
Robert Germeyn, junior
Stephen de Brokeye
Petronilla de Brokeye, his mother
Richard Germeyn, son of Richard

Richard Germeyn, his father
Robert Crips, pistor
Stephen Wichon
Bartholomew Campion
Henry ate Merse
Thomas Malherbe
John Valer
Walter de Marisco

William de Marisco
Givido Cissor
Robert Spec, called Jolif
Johanna Dore
Henry Lovecok
William Citeneste
Walter ate Walle
John Deth

Total in this quarter, 1¼a. 5¼v.: rent, 7s. 5¼d.

In the Twenty-fifth Quarter.

Richard de Bilesham
William Deryng
Sampson Cok moris
Nicholas Albard, son of Richard Albard
John, son of William Burgeys
Ralph le Bufre
John Picard
John le Iwherst
Petronilla of Iwherst
John, son of Robert Paulyn
Hamo Roberd
Richard Bonenfant, clerk
William Griffin
Robert Gotobedde
Lawrence Cupre
Alexander de Brokeye, curt.
Thomas Roger, pistor
Henry Jordan
Golding Pistor

Total in this quarter, 2a. 8½v.: rent, 6s. 10d.

In the Twenty-sixth Quarter.

John, son of Godefrey Buchard
Adam Palmer
Dionisius, son of Henry Paumre
Mathew Songre
Thomas Cissor
Benedict Carite
John Grik
Robert, son of Stephen Aurifaber
Robert Scalle
William of Canterbury, sutor
Henry Stronge
Richard le Cannere

Total in this quarter, 1½a. 19v.: rent, 5s. 4¾d.

SIXTH HIGHWAY.

In the Twenty-seventh Quarter.

Gervase Alard, senior
Philip, son of Lawrence, clerk
Robert, son of Robert le Hane
Richard Bene
Alan Dagard
Walter Coting
Stephen Fachel
Nicholas Dodlef
Thomas Dodlef, his brother
John Forester, pistor
Henry Jacob
The Mayor of Winchelsey for the time being

Total in this quarter, 2a. half a quarter 15½v.: rent, 9s. 10¾d.

In the Twenty-Eighth Quarter.

Thomas le Mathon
Robert, son of John Valer
Alice Cogger
Mabile Cogger
Juliana Gotebedde
Dionisius Whitloc
John Calot
Alan Grindelof
Adam Randulf
Mabille Lynleggestre
Reginald Cokalayn
Goda Charles
Alexander, called Lovecok Redegrom
Richard Aleyn
Walter Longe
John le Vischre
William de Salcote
Gilbert Ledzetre
Roger Bulloc
John ate Merse
John Specre
Henry of Leycestre
Robert Chauri
Richard Deth
Robert Bertelot
John of Arundel
William, his brother
Peter of Arundel
Robert Codelawe
William de Pulham
Robert Withon
William of Romene, pistor
Henry Bochre
Henry Atenende
Jacob, son of Thomas Godefrey
Lucy, called Douce Martin
Theobald Pistor
Alice, daughter of Hamo of Colchester
John of Lindherst
Mabille Pollard
John of Portesmuth
William Cupar de Apeltre

Total in this quarter, 3¾a. half a quarter 2v.: rent, 12s. 2¾d.

In the Twenty-ninth Quarter.

Robert le Hore
Robert Prest
Simon Linct
Walter le Frye
Cronnok, relict of Wileman
Ancel Candelarus
Spakeman Cocus
Alexander Hugheman
Andrew Rape
John Faber
Ranulf de Oclynge
Robert of Glynde

Stephen, son of William Pate
Dionise, relict of Simon de Hydeme
Philip of Bernehorne
William of Odimere
Thomas Bone
Alan Kenting
John Crutel
Coraldus Taverner
Thomas Suift
John Hever

Robert of Promhell
Simon Aurifaber
John, son of John de Carecta
Bartholomew, his brother
Henry ate Carte
Walter Prinkel
Henry Vischre
Gilbert Coggre
Ralph Modt
John Thomas
Thomas de Green

Total in this quarter, 2a. half a quarter 10¼v. : rent, 9s. 1¾d.

In the Thirtieth Quarter.

Lawrence Cuppere
John of Ho
Thomas Teppe, sutor
John, son of Reginald Alard
Henry Honne
Peter, son of William Kenting
Vincent, son of Robert Gyteveste

Agnes Panifader
John Alard
Henry Jacob
Robert le Lodeleghe, pistor
John Hewe
John Pollard
Petronilla Brokeye
Walter, her son

Nicholas Beilwerghte
Alexander Rope
Ralph Porter
Roger Pote
John Trem
John Schenchere
William, son of Sampson called Guillot

Total in this quarter, 2a. half a quarter 5¾v. : rent, 8s. 4¾d.

In the Thirty-first Quarter.

Reginald Alard, senior
Robert Stoket
Bate Pellipar

Alan Yonge, peliparius
John Andever, peliparius

Philip Cardinel, peliparius
Juliana, relict of John Michel

Total in this quarter, 1a. ¾v. : rent, 3s. 4½d.

SEVENTH HIGHWAY.

In the Thirty-second Quarter.

John, son of Walter Scappe

William Burgeys
John, son of Ralph Pate

Nicholas Alard
Thomas Godefrey

Total in this quarter, 1½a. 26v. : rent, 4s. 11¾d.

In the Thirty-third Quarter.

Godefrey Bochard
John le Cupre
John le Bakere, schipwerghte
William Scot
Robert Wlward
Robert, son of Adam of Wynchester
Gervase Andrew
Stephen Osebarn

Thomas White, pistor
Adam Erl
Roger Fikeys
Angus Dinder
John de Beilwerghte
John Barete
Agnes Pilchere
Pagan Coggre
Coleman Petit, sutor

Thomas, called Boun Mounyer
Robert Balloc
Gervase Scot
Thomas de Meydestane
Gervase Coneman
John Terri
William Denote
Walter Schyve

Total in this quarter, 1a. half a quarter 5¾v. : rent, 5s. 5d.

In the Thirty-fourth Quarter.

Adam Faber
Theobald Walterman
William of Chelintone
John, son of Benedict le Bochre
John Kemese
The house of St. John
Petronilla, relict of Maurice Jacob
Petronilla, his daughter
Richard of Pulham
Joce Tigelere
John Eve

Total in this quarter, 1a. half a quarter 5v.: rent, 5s. 0¾d.

In the Thirty-fifth Quarter.

John and Bartholomew, sons of John de Carcet
Adam Stonhard
Henry le Carect
Walter le Granger, called Mite Stene
Isabella, daughter of Morekyn Jacob

Total in this quarter, 1a. half a quarter 13v.: rent, 3s. 6d.

EIGHTH HIGHWAY.

In the Thirty-sixth Quarter.

Gervase Alard, senior
Vincent Herberd
Stephen of Bidindene
and John of Ihame, clerk
Thomas Colram

Total in this quarter, 1a. 14½v.: rent, 3s. 2d.

In the Thirty-seventh Quarter.

Vincent Herberd
Stephen Germeyn
Johanna, daughter of Maynard Cornhethe
Robert Ricard
William Russel
William de Esche
The Heirs of Ralph Chot
Dionisius Mareys
William le Lung
Sampson Heved
John, son of Martin of the Church
Thomas Boltan
Ranulph Skele
Stace, his mother
Matilda Beauchef
William Page
Stephen Roper
Thomas le Mas
Lawrence, the clerk
Jacob, son of Thomas of Meydestane
John Seman
William Seman

Total in this quarter, 3¼a.: rent, 8s. 8¾d.

In the Thirty-eighth Quarter.

Tho. ate Curt, bochre
Dyn Chaper
William de Morile, bochre
William de Potesterne, carpentre
John Mathon
William de Schettele
William of Brede
Thomas Haldan
William Lamb
Gilbert de Cruce
Richard Guillot of Kyngestone
John Godefrey
Alexander de Brokeye, curt.
Henry Yve
John, son of Reginald Alard
Jacob Paulyn

Total in this quarter, 3¼a. and 19¼v.: rent, 9s. 11¼d.

In the Thirty-ninth Quarter.

Robert, the clerk
The house of St. Bartholomew
The house of the Holy Cross

Total in this quarter, 3½a.: rent 10s. 6d.

These are the places enfranchised for building, and the rents fixed, under the Pendents of the Hill on the north side, in the land next the salt water, (salt marshes) and dangerous at all flowings of the tide.

Stephen Aurifaber
Nicholas Alard
Henry Jacob
Stephen Cloram
John of Maghefelde
Justin Alard
John Seman
Alexander de Brokeye, curt.
Jacob Paulyn
Jacob Paulyn of Upredinge
John Takesnau
John le Visch
William Seman
Henry, son of John Aurifaber
John of Scotenie
Henry Bakere
Adam of Bidindene
Stephen Withon
Simon of Scotenye
Vincent Herberd
John Grik
Reginald Alard, junior
John Alard
Gervase Alard, junior
Thomas Godefrey
John Andrew
William Neel
Stephen Moris
Peter Goldine
William Pate
Henry Bacun
Richard Baytaile
William Batayle
Mahende Horn
Jacob, son of Thomas Barbatus
Walter de Rackele
John Lamb
Robert de Carett
Thomas Alard
Godard Cocus
John Godefrey
John Thomas
Stephen de Brokeye
Paul de Horne
William de Salcote
Richard of Pevensey
Reginald Cokaleyn
John, son of John, pistor
Robert ate Merse
The Heirs of John Batan
Geoffry Banok
Adam Stonhard
William de Brokeye
Reginald Alard, senior
Walter Scappe
John Pace, son of John Pace
John Batayle
Copyn of Lydehame
Robert Hane
John Yve
John, son of Henry Yve
Henry Yve
Stephen Germeyn
Thomas Bone, and Bartholomew his son
Stephen of Bidindene
John Bochard, son of Godefrey
Henry ate Carte
William of Poleham
William Mancap
John Folke
Richard Pate
John Pate, his brother
Henry Broun
John of Ihame, clerk
William Bingeys
Thomas Colram
Gervase Alard, senior
Robert Scalle
John, son of Gerveys Alard

Rent, 13s. 0¾d. Total of the land under the Pendents 3½a. 20¾v.

Total of all the rents, £14 11s. 5¾d.

Total of the land aforesaid, 87½a. half a quarter of an acre, 7¾v.

And the said mayor and jurats say that in the 16th year of the reign of King Edward, about the Feast of St. James the Apostle, (25th July, 1288,) Sir J. de Kyrkeby, then Bishop of Ely, gave seizen to the commonalty of Winchelsea of all the lands and tenements in these Rolls, in the presence of the Sheriff of Sussex and other nobles, as well as knights, and many others of the said county, on the part of our lord the King, repromitting (guaranteeing) the said commonalty absolute and quiet possession, free from payment of the said rents from the feast above named for seven years succeeding; by reason of which repromission, from the building and rental of the town to the present time, nothing has been paid; upon which repromission the will of the king is in all things to be performed. And for greater (certainty) the mayor and jurats, with the assent of the whole commonalty aforesaid, have caused to be affixed to this present Roll, the seal of the said commonalty. Given at Winchelsea, the Saturday next before the Feast of St. Michael the Archangel, in the 20th year of our lord King Edward, 1292.

HISTORY.

EDWARD I.—The relative importance of Winchelsea to the neighbouring ports, at the time of its reconstruction, is evident from the large compliment it had to furnish to the king towards the Cinque Ports' navy. Hastings and its members had twenty-one ships, each equipped and manned with twenty men and a master, for fifteen days, at their own cost; and temp. Edw. I, these twenty-one ships were thus distributed:[1] Winchelsea furnished ten; Rye five; Hastings three; Seaford and Pevensey one; Bulverhithe, and Petit Higham, next Winchelsea, one; and Hidney, Grange, and Beakesbourne in Kent, one. The new town soon realised the best hopes of its founders. The port was in a very flourishing condition: trade and merchandise flowed into its waters, and gave to the inhabitants an apparent security for a lengthened prosperity. The king had his hunting seat close by, at Newenden, and one of his chief friends, and we believe relative, William de Echingham, had a large mansion, with parks and estates, in the adjoining town, (as it then was) of Udimore,[2] to which

[1] 31 Edw. I, there is an Inspeximus stating which are the five ports and their services. It is there said, that Hastings is a head port, of which the members are Winchelsea, Rye, the Leucate of Pevensey, and Bolewereheth, in the county of Sussex, and Beakesborne and Greneth, in the county of Kent: which port, with its aforesaid members, ought to find, on the king's summons, twenty-one ships, and in each ship there ought tó be twenty-one men, armed, equipped, &c. Dering MSS.

[2] The manor house at Udimore stood near the church: a more modern structure, called Court Lodge, marks the site. Between the house and the church, was the Little Park; further on, in the parish of Brede, was the Great Park: and these names, together with those of the Ladies' Well

the king not unfrequently resorted, and thence he came to the new and thriving town of Winchelsea. When Edmund, the king's brother, was about to sail for Gascony, the king, on 3rd Sept., 1294, directed the ships of the five ports to attend him. A general writ was directed to the warden of the Cinque Ports: and there was a separate writ to the barons and bailiffs of the two most important of the ports, Winchelsea and Sandwich.[1] An account of the Cinque Ports' ships furnished for this expedition is preserved among the MSS. in Carlton House Ride, in a petition for payment of the wages to the seamen[2] for going and returning, between the 7th March and the 3rd May: viz. sixpence a day for each master, sixpence for each constable, and threepence for every seaman. No less than fifty ships were furnished; of which Winchelsea supplied thirteen, Sandwich twelve, Rye seven, Dover seven, Romney five, Hythe three, and Hastings three. The names of the Winchelsea vessels, and of their masters and constables, were

NAME OF VESSEL.	MASTER.	CONSTABLE.
La Cog St. Edward	John Pate	John Alard
La Cog St. Mary	Adam Stonhard	Edmund Andrew
La Plente	William Kyngesone	Robert atte Carte
La Lunge Cog	Reginald Payn	Robert Badding
La Nicholas	John Muleward	
La Holop of St. Giles	Henry Baker	Henry Baker, son of Benedict
Staw Den	Benedict Alard	Henry Alard
De la Bochere	Benedict Seman	Richard Spayn
De la Faucon	Gervas Touman	Roger Touman
De Holop of St. Thomas	Elias Lambyn	William of Iham
La Margaret	Robert Germeyn	Matthew Batell
Ship de Langeton	Hendman Aubyn	Robert Paulyn
Ship of the Bishop of Durham	John Magefeld	William Heved

Wood, the Great Lord's Wood, and the Little Lord's Wood, are still retained. In 22nd Edw. I, Wm. de Echingham obtained a survey of his manors, including Udimore; and in 23rd Edw. I, a grant of free warren for his park as well in Brede as in Udimore. An excellent history of the Echynhams of Echyngham has (1849) been published by Mr. Spencer Hall.

[1] Rym. Fœd. vol. 1, p. 809.

[2] The petition is in 24 Edw. I. In the same MSS. there is another roll of the payments.

As the king's foreign affairs became more urgent, the walls of Winchelsea were strengthened,[1] and the king repaired himself to Udimore, to be near this most important port. From Odymer, on 2nd November, 1295, he addressed a letter,[2] "Vicecomtatibus Angliæ de prorogando parliamento," giving as a reason for proroguing parliament, the necessity of assembling and preparing a fleet for the defence of the kingdom. On the 5th of the same month, he there tested his writs to the archbishops and several bishops, directing them to remove all beneficed persons, who were foreigners, and within thirteen miles of the sea, further up into the country.[3] From Odymer, is also dated a commission for the custody and defence of the sea coast in Kent and Sussex.[4] The king subsequently left Udimore, but returned in a few days. On the 17th November, 1295, he was at Bury St. Edmunds, and on the 18th at Westminster, but on Sunday, the 20th, the feast of St. Edmund, he was at Winchelsea; on 21st he was at Winchelsea and Odymer; on 22nd at Winchelsea and Robertsbridge,[5] and returned thence to Westminster. The immediate danger had then passed: it was, however, soon to return. On 31st January, 1297, the king found it necessary to issue his writs to his officers in all the chief port towns of England, and among others to Winchelsea, not to suffer any person to pass out of England without his special license;[6] and, in the month of August following, he repaired to Winchelsea, preparatory to his embarkation for Flanders. On Friday, August 9th, the king was at Brede; on the 10th, 11th, and 12th, at Odymer;

[1] Muragium Pat. 23 Edw. I. m. 7. In the same year Osbert de Spaldington accounted for his expenses going with three squires, six horses, and several ships, from Lene to Berwick, attacking the king's enemies and bringing the ships to Winchelsea, a service of seventy days; and also for his expenses whilst sent with Lady Eleanor, the king's daughter, from Winchelsea beyond the seas. Carlton House Ride MSS.

[2] Rym. Fœd. vol. 1, p. 832. Suss. Arch. vol. 2, p. 141.

[3] Prynne's Hist. of King John, p. 630. [4] Suss. Arch. vol. 2, p. 141.

[5] Ib. and Rym. Fœd. [6] Prynne's Hist. of King John, p. 729.

on 13th, at Odymer and Winchelsea; on 14th, 15th, and 16th, at Odymer; on 17th, 18th, and 19th, at Odymer and Winchelsea; and on 20th, 21st, and 22nd, at Odymer.[1] A letter in French, addressed "Adolpho Regi Romanorum de festinando ad succursum comitis Flandricæ," is tested, August 13, at Winchelsea.[2] The king's writ, prohibiting the Archbishop of Canterbury from excommunicating any of his ministers, is tested at Winchelsea,[3] 19th August; and there are two other writs tested there on 21st August: on the following day he embarked, having been first attended here by the deputies of the nobles, with a remonstrance of the grievances of his kingdom, and a petition for their redress, to which he, for the present, returned an evasive answer, and desired the matter might be put off till his return. He landed in Flanders 27th August. Thomas of Walsingham says,[4] that the king having gone over into Flanders to assist the Earl against the King of France, took up his residence for some days in the neighbourhood of Winchelsea, which was the port he had appointed to sail from, watching for the coming in of those of his subjects of the kingdom, who were to join his army.

It was during this visit that the king met with what was likely to have been a serious accident, which Thomas of Walsingham[5] thus describes, under the title of the miracle of the King's salvation:—Whilst the king was dwelling near Winchelsea, he proposed to go one day to the port to take a view of his fleet, and having entered the town, when he had just ridden over against the bulwarks, and was about to survey the fleet at the lowest station, it happened, that he approached a certain windmill, of which there were several in the town; and his horse being frightened with the noise of the mill and

[1] Suss. Arch. Coll., vol. 2, p. 142. Rym. Fœd. vol. 1, pp. 873-5, &c.

[2] Suss. Arch. Coll., vol. 2, p. 162. Rym. Fœd. vol. 1, p. 873.

[3] Rym. Fœd. vol. 1, 875.

[4] T. Wals. p. 71, l. 10. Addl. MSS., 6343, fol. 160 and 397.

[5] T. Wals., p. 71, l. 20.

with the quickly revolving sails, refused to proceed; and as the horse was vigorously urged on by the king by whip and spur, he lept over the bulwarks: upon which, out of the multitude of horse and foot who followed the king, or had assembled to have a look at him, no one thought but that the king had perished, or had, at least, been stunned by the leap. But divine providence so disposing, the horse fell upon his feet, even from such a height, into a road, which, from recent rains, was softened with mud, into which the horse was able to slip for twelve feet, and yet did not fall; and being turned round with another bridle, by the king, he ascended directly to the gate, through which he entered unhurt, and the people, who were waiting for him, were filled with wonder and delight at his miraculous escape.

On 20th October in the same year (1297,) the king directed the barons and commonalty of Winchelsea to proclaim the armistice between the King of France and himself;[1] and on 15th December, to proclaim the enlargement of the armistice. On 4th February, 1298,[2] however, he directed them to meet him with their ships at Exclusos in Flanders: and at the close of the same year, he required their service against the Scots, desiring them to assemble at Skymburnese (Kircudbright,) near Carlisle.[3] In the year 1300, the mayor and bailiffs were directed by the king's writ[4] not to suffer the exportation of any silver from their port. On 7th November, 1302,[5] the king again summoned their ships to Newcastle, but he was enabled to dispense with their service; and, on 2nd December, directed them to proclaim the truce between himself and the Scottish king. On 22nd March, 1303, a proclamation of the extension of the truce between France and England was ordered to be made here. On 12th July, peace itself was directed to be likewise proclaimed here: and, on 9th April,

[1] Rym. Fœd., vol. 1, pp. 880-882. [2] Ib. 886. [3] Ib. 901.
[4] Ryley, p. 482. [5] Rym. Fœd., vol. 1, pp. 945-947-950-958-962.

1304, the king went one step further, and gave instructions for ships to be taken hence to aid the King of the French.

The names of the ships last furnished by the ports for the war in Scotland have been preserved in a certificate,[1] returned 34 Edw. I, (1306) by William de Woodforde, clerk, and William de Benefeld, locum-tenentes of the lord warden, in pursuance of a writ from Chancery, of the services due from the Cinque Ports. The Winchelsea return was made by Henry Paulyn, mayor, Thomas Alard, bailiff, and Nicholas Alard, Gervase Alard, junior, Vincent Herberd, Henry Alard, Henry Jacob, Matthew de Horne, William Seman, Stephen Cobran, Bartholomew Bone, and Thomas Roger, jurats: they say that Winchelsea[2] ought to furnish five ships properly armed and equipped: viz.

NAME OF VESSEL.	MASTER.	CONSTABLES.
The Cog Edward	Adam Shipman	Adam Bidendenter and Peter Paulyn
Ship La Katerine	Henry Weldisshe	Matthew Kingessone and William Heved
Cog St. Thomas	Robert atte Carte	William Brokex and Walter de Rackele
Cog Spirit	Bartholomew Robert	Robert de Wynton and Simon Curteys de Pevense
Cog St. Giles	Simon Boylequer	Peter Kentyng and Robert Brotex

Whilst the ships were thus often employed for the public service, the merchants of the town found ample opportunities for prosecuting their own mercantile transactions, and some of the records which have reached us are curious, as—On 18th June, 1294, John Alard, Hugh son of Baldwin, and Walter Pyl, merchants of Brabant, had the king's license to pass with three ships to Herewych.[3] On the 10th June, 1299, there is a safe conduct, dated from Dover,[4] given to "Benet Seman, mestre de la Blithe de Winchelse, Bauf le Boef et Willm de Ihamme, mestres de la neef Dame le Cour de

[1] MSS. in Chapter House, Westminster, Press z, No. 11.

[2] For this fleet Dover furnished nine ships, Rye two, and Hastings one.

[3] Rym. Fœd., vol. 1, p. 802. [4] Rot. pat. 27 Edw. I.

Winchelse, et pur Beneit Carytee, mestre de la Barge de Winchelse, et Robert Paulyn pur Alexandre Badding, mastre de la nef La Lyttel Nanspie de Winchelse." Among the receipts and expenditure of the King's garderobe,[1] in 29th Edw. I, there is the following entry, "Simoni de Waynflet, magistro de la ffaucon de Wynchelse, de prestito super radiis suis et sociorum suorum nautarum ejusdem navis. vi. marcas."

In 31st Edw. I, (1303) Gervase Alard, of this town, was made admiral of the Cinque Ports' navy;[2] and, in the 34th Edw. 1, he was again admiral of their navy and admiral of the western ports,[3] and required to proceed with them to Skymburnesse to act against the Scotch.

EMBANKMENTS.—The new town seems, at the close of the first quarter of a century, to have been almost of as much note as the former town; yet, even thus early, the old enemy the sea, gave fresh causes for alarm, and the embankments required constant care and attention. In 29th Edw. I, (1300) there was an inquisition of the walls and ditches of Spadlond marsh, as repaired by the different tenants, against the inroad of the sea.[4] And Dugdale[5] tells us, in his History of Embanking, only three years afterwards, that

> In 31 Edward I, (1303) the king being informed that the banks and ditches which had been made in the marsh of Winchelse, for the defence of his lands there, and preservation of the adjacent parts, were then so broken by the overflowing of the sea, that the said lands were in danger of being drowned and lost; and, that his tenants of those lands, by reason of a certain ancient composition made betwixt them and the tenants of the other lands in that marsh, which was, that the said king's lands should be defended by such reparations by the other land owners there, refused to contribute to the repair of those banks and ditches; and being also informed that the tenants of the other lands were not able to undergo those repairs, by reason of the great expense, which would be requisite thereto: taking care, therefore, of his own indemnity and the

[1] Carlton Ride MSS., E.B. 2052. Ex. inf. Mr. W. H. Blaauw.
[2] Pat. 31 Edw. I, m. 39. [3] Spelman's Glos. p. 16.
[4] Cal. Inq. p. m., vol. 1, p. 166. [5] Dugd. c. 19.

preservation of those marshes, he directed his precept to Thomas Alard, guardian of his lands of that marsh, commanding him that he should, for the present occasion, cause an equal contribution to be made out of those lands, according to a just and proportionable tax with the said other land-holders, lest for want thereof, a greater loss might afterwards happen, for which he, the said Thomas, was to receive allowance out of the Exchequer. But after this, the very next ensuing year (32 Edward I,) upon an inquisition taken by Robert de Septem Vannis, Will. de Hastings, and Rob. Paulyn, whom the king had assigned to take view of the banks and ditches in this county, and to cause them to be repaired, (which was returned into Chancery) it was found, that the said marsh of Winchelsea could not be defended and preserved by the old wall, situated towards the east, and that if it ought to be defended, it would be necessary to have a new bank there, of the length of 350 perches; and that the said new bank could not be made by those who, according to the ancient composition before mentioned, had wont to repair the old bank, forasmuch as they who were in the soil liable to the repairs of the said bank were not able, in regard of the diminution of their lands, to bear the whole charge thereof themselves. He, therefore, directed another precept unto the said Thomas Alard, requiring him to take care that such contribution should be made thereto out of his own lands and the lands of others, as is above expressed. And hereupon the said king issued out a commission to the said Robert, William, and Robert, to see that the contribution which the said king's bailiff was to make therein, should be well and also faithfully assessed.

Estates.—Among the particulars of property held by persons connected with the town, in this reign, we find that in 18 Edw. I, William Maufe and Johanna, relict of Thomas de Hipegne, prayed to farm the returns of the town, that they might receive £10, which they were accustomed to receive, and which was badly paid to them, whereupon it was ordered, that unless they were paid, they should distrain the bailiffs;[1] and in the same year, Robert Paulyn, of this town, whose house had been destroyed by the sea, sought to be allowed to farm the manor of Iden.[2]

Edward II.—The young King, disregarding the oath he had sworn to his father, to carry on with vigour the war

[1] Rot. Parl. vol. 1, 56 a. [2] Ib. 55 b.

against the Scots, and to bear his father's bones against them, withdrew his army ingloriously from Scotland. At the commencement of his reign, however, he called for the services of the Cinque Ports against his own, and his father's enemies.

In 1309 [1] the king directed his writs to Winchelsey, Rye, and other large ports, to prevent any earl, baron, knight, or notable person, from going beyond seas during his war with the Scots. On 2nd August, 1310,[2] he summoned their ships to Dublin and Drogheda, for service against the same enemy. In a fragment of the Carlton House Ride MSS.[3] we have a record of the names of the vessels, from Winchelsea, employed in pursuance of this order, and of their captains, with the sums paid for wages: "Wynchelse, Gervasio Toneman, magistro navis que vocatur, Cog Edward, ii., Constabulariis at lvii. sociis suis nautis predicte navis pro radiis suis per xv. dies; xi*l.* xvi*s.* iii*d.*; viz., magistro capiente per diem, vi*d.*; et cuilibet constabulariorum per diem, vi*d.*; et cuilibet nautarum per diem, iii*d.*; summa xi*l.* xvi*s.* iii*d.* Reginaldo Payn, magistro navis que vocatur Sante Marie cog," &c., in the same words.

On 26th June, 1313,[4] John de Insula and Robert de Halliwell, were directed to arrest and take thirty of the best ships that could be found between Plymouth and Shoreham, with the best men, and all that should be in the port of Winchelsey, for the king's service. On 1st April, 1314, the king[5] summoned the ships of Winchelsey and the other ports, to be at Skymburnesse on the nativity of St. John the Baptist, ready to proceed against Robert de Brus and his confederates. The ships of most of the ports disobeyed the order, and an inquisition was thereupon taken with the view of amercing them; but in their return, the men of Winchelsea

[1] Rym. Fœd. vol. 2, pt. 1, p. 95. [2] Ib. 114. [3] Ex. inf., Mr. W. H. Blaauw.
[4] Rym. Fœd. vol. 2, pt. 1, p. 223. [5] Ib. 246.

adroitly excused themselves, by declaring [1] that they had sent two ships (less, however, than their proper number) which were unable to get up, owing to contrary winds and stress of weather.

The customary wrecking propensities of the Sussex men, early showed themselves at Winchelsey, Rye, and Romney. In 8th Edw. II, (1314-5) they were not only concerned in plundering the wreck of a vessel called the Blessed Mary of Fonte Arabia, laden with goods of very great value, and going to Gascony, and wrecked off the bank of Aungemaris (Dungeness,) but the king was petitioned to prosecute an enquiry,[2] the taking of which they had impeded.

And their true character was shown in 1321, by one of their full armed ships, with a ship of Greenwich, plundering a ship of Albrith de Breme, a German merchant, driving the master and nine men out of the ship, pursuing them on land, and killing one of them, Wulrich de Breme.[3]

CHARTERS CONFIRMED.—On the 26th July, 7 Edw. II, (1313) the king granted the following Charter to the men of the new town, reciting and confirming the Charters which Henry II, Richard, and John had granted to the two towns of Winchelsea and Rye.

PRO HOMINIBUS DE RIA ET WYNCHELSE.[4] Rex Archiepiscopis, &c., salutem. Inspeximus cartam quam Dominus Ricardus quondam Rex Angliæ progenitor noster fecit hominibus de Ria et de Wynchelse in hæc verba. Ricardus, Dei gratiâ, Rex Angliæ, Dux Normanniæ, Aquitaniæ, Comes Andegaviæ, Archiepiscopis, Episcopis, Abbatibus, Comitibus, Baronibus, Justiciariis, Vicecomitibus præpositis, Baillivis, Castellanis, et omnibus fidelibus suis totius terræ suæ, Salutem. Sciatis nos concessisse et præsenti carta nostra confirmasse, quod homines de Ria et de Wynchenesell', sint liberi et quieti per totam terram nostram citra mare et ultra ab omni theolonio, et lestagio, et tallagio, et passagio, et chaiagio, et rivagio, et sponsagio, et omni Wrec, et de Rocato, et de omnibus consuetudinibus per totam terram nostram quocumque venerint. Concedimus etiam eis quod habeant inventiones in mari et terra, et quod sint quieti de omnibus rebus suis et de toto mercato suo sicut nostri liberi homines. Præcipimuse tiam

[1] MSS. in Chapter-house, West., 8 Edward II, Kent bag, No. 12.
[2] Rot. Parl. vol. 1, 329 b. [3] Ib., 397 a. [4] Charter Roll, 7 Edw. 2, No. 47.

quod nullus eos vel res eorum disturbet super decem librarum forisfacturam et quod sint quieti de syris et de hondredis et si quis versus illos placitare voluerit non respondeant neque placitent aliter quam Barones de Hastingiis et de quinque portibus placitant et in tempore Henrici patris nostri placitare solebant. Pro hiis etiam libertatibus invenient ad plenarium servitium nostrum duas naves ad perficiendum numerum viginti navium de Hastingiis. Hæc autem omnia suprascripta concedimus et præsenti carta nostra confirmavimus hominibus de Ria et hominibus de Wynchenesell', sicut pater noster eis concessit et carta sua confirmavit. Hiis testibus, Johanne de Pratell', Rogero de Pratell', Dapifero nostro Ricardo de Caumvill', et pluribus aliis. Data per manum Magistri Rogeri-Mali catuli clerici nostri apud Messanam xxvii., die Martii regni nostri anno secundo.

Inspeximus etiam cartam quam Dominus Johannes quondam Rex Angliæ progenitor noster fecit prœdictis hominibus in hæc verba. Johannes, Dei gratia, Rex Angliæ, Dominus Hiberniæ, Dux Normanniæ, Aquitaniæ, et Comes Andegaviæ, Archiepiscopis, Episcopis, Abbatibus, Comitibus, Baronibus, Justiciariis, Vicecomitibus præpositis, Ballivis, Castellanis, et omnibus fidelibus totius terræ suæ, Salutem. Sciatis nos concessisse et præsenti carta nostra confirmasse, quod homines de Ria et Wynchelese sint liberi et quieti per totam terram nostram citra mare et ultra, ab omni thelonio, et lestagio, et tallagio, et passagio, et cayagio, et rivagio, et sponsagio, et omni Wrec, et de Rocato, et de omnibus consuetudinibus per totam terram nostram quocumque venerint. Concedimus etiam eis quod habeant inventiones in mari et terra, et quod sint quieti de omnibus rebus suis et de toto mercato suo sicut nostri liberi homines. Præcipimus etiam quod nullus eos vel res eorum disturbet super decem librarum forisfacturam. Et quod sint quieti de syris et hundredis, et si quis versus illos placitare voluerit non respondeant neque placitent aliter quam Barones de Hastinges et de quinque portibus placitant et in tempore Henrici Regis patris nostri placitare solebant. Pro hiis etiam libertatibus invenient ad plenarium servitium nostrum duas naves ad perficiendum numerum viginti navium de Hastinges. Hæc etiam omnia suprascripta concedimus et præsenti carta nostra confirmavimus hominibus de Rya et hominibus de Wyncheles', sicut pater noster eis concessit et carta sua confirmavit et sicut carta Regis Ricardi fratris nostri quam inde habent rationabiliter testatur. Testibus, R. Comite Cestr,' Comite David, Comite W. Sarum, R. Constabulario Cestr', Willielmo de Breosa, Willielmo Briwere, Sayero' de Quency, Roberto filio Walteri, Willielmo de Alben'. Data per manum Hugonis de Well', Archidiaconi Well', apud Stok' sexto die Junii anno regni nostri septimo. Nos autem concessiones et confirmationes prædictas ratas habentes et gratas eas pro nobis et hæredibus nostris quantum in nobis est præfatis hominibus de Rya et Wyncheles', hæredibus et successoribus suis, concedimus et confirmavimus sicut cartæ prædictæ rationabiliter testantur. Hiis testibus, Venerabilibus patribus, W. Wygorniæ, J. Bathoniæ et Wellen', et W. Exon', Episcopis, Gilberto de Clare Comite Gloucestriæ et Hertford', Johanne de Britannia Comite Richemond, Adomaro de Valencia Comite Pembroke, Hugone le Despenser, Roberto filio Pagani, Edmundo de Malo lacu Senescallo Hospicii nostri et aliis. Data per manum nostram apud Westmonasterium xxvi die Julii. Per ipsum Regem et consilium.

WALLS.—When the Mayor and Barons had obtained this confirmation of their charters, they, in 15th Edw. II, (1321-2) by the King's command,[1] repaired the walls, and enclosed the town with a ditch round the place; but, in so doing, they took in a large part of the tenements of the Abbot of Fischampe in Iham, upon which, in the same year, the abbot prayed for an indemnity by exchange or otherwise.[2] It was at this time, therefore, that the greater part of the liberty of St. Leonards came within the walls of the town. A portion of the Castle Fields still pays a free rent to the manor of Brede.

GOVERNOR, &c.—SIR THOMAS COLEPEPPER, who was governor of Winchelsea at that period of the king's reign, as well as governor of Leeds castle, took part with Thomas Earl of Lancaster,[3] the grandson of Henry III, and leader of the Barons. Philpots, in his History of Kent, says, with little probability, that he defended Winchelsea to aid the rebellious barons, for the principal scene of the contest was in Yorkshire. Sir Thomas, however, suffered with his great leader, (according to Weever) without having the

[1] Muragium pro. Winchelse et Sandwich, Rot. pat. part 1, m. 19.
[2] Rot. Parl. vol. 1, 393 b. [3] Hollinshed, p. 331.

honor of being, like the earl, beheaded, but he was "hanged, drawn, and quartered."

Towards the close of the reign of this wayward monarch, the ships of the ports were again required for service.[1]

On 13th April, 1323, writs[2] were directed by the king to the mayor, barons, and bailiffs of Winchelsea, and to the other ports, to have the 57 ships they were obliged to furnish, and 27 other ships, well equipped and furnished, at Dalkey, near Dublin, and to proceed thence against the Scots, the king's enemies and rebels. And, on 10th May, 1324, the ships[3] of Winchelsea were directed to be prepared for service, and to be at Portsmouth ready for the king's expedition into Aquitaine. The last service required of them, was after Phillipa of Hainault had landed at Orwell. On 24th Sept., 1326, the king sent his writ[4] to Winchelsea amongst many other places, dated from Marsfield, requiring the mayor and bailiffs diligently to search their port for, and arrest or report all suspected persons, particularly foreigners.

Property.—Few notices of the property, held in the town during this reign, have reached us. In 1 Edward II, there was an inquisition ad quod dampnum (No. 114) for Robert de Langhurste, for lands in this town. Among the Dering MSS. is a charter, 32nd Edw. II, wherein Joan Thogar, daughter and heir of Simon Thogar, grants to her uncle, William Bertam, of Iham, lands, &c., in Dengemarsh; and amongst the witnesses we have Gervas Alard, junior, mayor of Winchelsea, and Robert Paulin, bailiff of Iham. We find also,[5] in the same year, a release from Godfrey, the son of Alan Godfrey, of Winchelsea, to his brother Theobald, of property in the neighbourhood; and, that in 14th Edw. II, lands and

[1] In 15 Edward II, the sum of £27 4s. was allowed to Margaret, widow and executrix of William de Greye, for a voyage from Dublin to Winchelsea, during the war with Scotland. Rot. Parl. vol. 1, 389 b.

[2] Rym. Fœd. vol. 2, pt. 1, p. 516. [3] Ib. p. 552. [4] Ib. p. 642.

[5] Cal. Rot. orig. vol. 1, p. 308.

tenements in the town of Winchelsea and marsh of Iham escheated to the crown, by the death and bastardy of John, illegitimate son of John de Rakle.[1]

In this reign, Robert Battail, of Winchelsea, was admiral of the Cinque Ports fleet;[2] and in the 18th year of this reign (1324,) Stephen Alard was captain and admiral of the Cinque Ports' navy and of the King's fleet, in the western seas.[3]

It was during this reign that the religious house of the Blackfriars or Friars' Preachers, was founded by the king.

Edward III.—The townsmen did not at first take very kindly to these new comers of the Friars; and among other places where the religious and townsmen quarrelled and came to blows, in 1327,[4] Winchelsea is mentioned. And on 3rd April, 1327, the mayor and bailiffs were not to allow any friar predicant, friar minor, carmelite, or any other religious man to go out of the kingdom without license.[5]

The new King very soon required the naval aid of the ports. On 5th April, 1327, he commanded Winchelsea and the other ports, to meet him at Skyburnesse, that the presence of a naval force might expedite his negociation for peace with Robert de Brus.[6] The negociation did not proceed so prosperously as the king expected, and, on 29th April, he required the aid of other towns to resist the invasion of England. The men of Winchelsea remained true to the naval duties they owed to their sovereign, and to their own peculiar notions of dealing with the ships of other nations: we find, that on 30th April, 1327, Edward was obliged to assure the Burgomasters of Bruges, that if they would state their claims, he would give them redress for the injuries inflicted on them by the capture of one of their ships, after the truce had been agreed on, by certain "malefactores de villis de Sandwico et Winchelse."[7]

[1] Rot. Parl. vol. 1, 168 a. [2] Ib. vol. 2, p. 413. [3] Pat. pt. 1, m. 22.
[4] Hist. and Antiq. Univ. Ox., vol. 1, p. 63. [5] Rym. Fœd. vol. 2, p. 701.
[6] Ib., p. 703. [7] Ib., p. 705.

In Dec., 1330, the mayor and bailiffs were required to search the port and take care that John Mautravers and others did not escape the kingdom.[1] On 20th Sept., 1335, the king directed his writs to them and others, that no exchange of florins or other money to be carried out of the kingdom, should take place, except according to the exchange which had been committed to William de la Pole.[2]

An account of the ships furnished this year, (9 Edw. III,) by the Cinque Ports, is extant among the MSS. in the Carlton House Ride. The number of ships furnished was thirty, of which Winchelsea[3] supplied these nine:

NAME OF VESSEL.	TONS.	MASTER.	CONSTABLE.
La Blith	160	Gervase Whything	John Adrian
La Laurence	140	John Roger	Richard Large
La Cog John	140	John Alard	Benedict Cely
La Jonete	130	Richard Swaine	Walter Salerne
La James	120	Stephen Lambyn	Henry de Bedinden
La James Coleyn	100	Gilbert Careman	Roger Kyldar
La Andrew	100	Walter Glaunde	William Potacas
La Margaret	100	John Henry	Philip de Oxene
La Lightfote	100	John Downey	Thomas Codelowe

Making a total of 1090 tons: the wages, at 6d. a day for each master, 6d. for each constable, and 3d. for each man, amounted to £145 9s. 3d.

In the following year, 6th Nov., 1336, the ships of this town, with all the western fleet, were required to rendezvous at Portsmouth.[4] And in the same year the mayor and bailiffs were directed not to permit the exportation of wool or woollen goods of any art, device, or colour, until the full duty had been paid.[5]

[1] Rym. Fœd. vol. 2. p. 801. [2] Ib. 922.

[3] Rye furnished the four following:—

NAME.	TONS.	MASTER.	CONSTABLE.
La Michael	240	John Pennethorne	Robert Goldwyn
La Edmund	170	Ralph Hombroys	Helyas atte Halle
La Nicholas	120	John Yefegod	Richard Gaylard
La Palmere	60	William Floure	Stephen Alard

Making a total of 590 tons; and the wages of the seamen 84s. 9d.

[4] Rym. Fœd. vol. 2, p. 951. [5] Ib., p. 944.

THE ATTACKS of the French along the southern coasts were carried on with great vigour during this reign. Speaking of the year, 1337, Joseph Barnes[1] says,—"About this time there came a fleet of Frenchmen, consisting of twenty great ships, fifteen smaller ones, and thirty-two gallies, riding before the Sandwich haven, and they durst not take land because they saw the county Militia ready up to receive them. Thence, therefore, they tacked about to Rye, where they did much mischief; but while they were there a squadron of English came up with them, whereupon the Frenchmen hoisted sail and fled before them, the English all the while making after them with a full sail till they came to Boulogne, where they set fire to part of the town, and hanged twelve captains of the fleet, whom, among others, they had taken." The extent of the mischief done at Winchelsea and Rye in this attack, is evidenced in two inquisitions still preserved among the Carlton Ride MSS. The first was taken at the close of the 20th Edw. III, (1347) before William de Bellcrd, John de Bredon, and others, and shows that in ninety-four houses in Winchelsea, there was not then, and had not been, for several years before, any thing on which a distress could be levied for the King's rents, no one having been able to inhabit them; and that fifty-two tenements and one mill at Rye, which had been burnt by the French, and which paid yearly 38s. 4½d., were not re-built, except a few, which, from the feast of All Saints then last, had begun to be inhabited. The same return was made to a like inquisition in the 30th Edw. III, (1356.)

NAVY, &c.—In 13 Edw. III, (1339) the ships of the Cinque Ports and of the Thames, under the Earl of Huntingdon, were directed to rendezvous here, and all persons having charters of pardon were required to repair hither in the service of the navy.[2]

In the same year, when eighteen Flemish vessels had taken

[1] Hist. Edw. III, p. 137. [2] Rot. Parl., vol. 2, 108 a.

several English vessels, laden with wool and other merchandise, the king directed the mayor, bailiffs, and collectors of many ports, and among them of Winchelsea, to take great care that the Flemish ships were prevented from escaping, if they should come into any of these ports.[1] And, on 6th Oct., 1340, the mayor was directed to proclaim the truce, which had just been concluded between the King and Philip of Valois.[2]

The attacks of the French still continued, and on 12th Feb., 1341, many towns, including Winchelsea, were required to send the names of two ships that could be used for a channel fleet to protect the coast.[3]

In the same year, Winchelsea is named as one of the ports from which wool might be exported,[4] on payment of a customs duty of 50s. a bag.[5]

In April, 1342, when the maritime affairs of the country were in great danger, several of the chief ports, including Winchelsea, were required to send two of the best and most discreet naval men of the port to Westminster to consult and advise with the king.[6] And, on 20th June, in the same year, the mayor and bailiffs of this town were required to furnish their quota of ships to assemble at Portsmouth, and transport William de Bohun, Earl of Northampton, and his fleet into Brittany.[7] Two years afterwards, on 6th February, 1344, the king again commanded the mayor and bailiffs to send two of the most sufficient men and of the best naval knowledge to London to meet other naval men and consult on the state of the navy.[8] A few days afterwards, 9th February, the mayor and bailiffs of this town, amongst others, were commanded not to let any earl, baron, knight, or esquire, or any other armed person, or religious person, or pilgrim, depart the kingdom

[1] Rym. Fœd., vol. 2, p. 1078. [2] Ib. p. 1137. [3] Ib. p. 1150. [4] Ib. p. 1158.

[5] In this year, John, Duke of Brittany and Earl of Richmond, died seized of the lastage in Winchelsea. Cal. Inq. p. m., vol. 2, p. 100.

[6] Rym. Fœd., vol. 2, p. 1193. [7] Ib. p. 1201.

[8] Ib., vol. 3, p. 4. Rye, Hastings, and Seaford, sent only one man each.

without the king's special license. And, on the 12th of the same month, they were commanded to search all persons going out of the port, and see that they did not take out of the kingdom any coin, or silver plate, or gold or silver vessels.[1] The townspeople did not very carefully carry out the royal commands for preventing persons from departing the realm without license; and on 25th March, when eight ships of the Cinque Ports were summoned for preparation, a special writ was sent to the mayor and bailiffs, again enjoining the former order, which, as the king had been informed, had not been attended to: many men, as well military as travellers, having been allowed to go out from Winchelsea and others of the ports.[2] On the 10th July, 1346, immediately before Edward's expedition to France, the mayor and bailiffs of this town,[3] as well as of London, Dover, and Sandwich, which were then the chief ports for embarkation, were enjoined to keep such strict watch in their respective ports that no one might by any means pass therefrom to foreign ports, for eight days, except those who were going with Hugh de Hastings, who had been appointed, on 20th June, Captain General of the king's forces in Flanders, in the king's service to that country. This order was to prevent spies from carrying the king's secrets to his enemies.

The victory of Crecy for a time gave the ascendency to Edward. His army, however, were very short of supplies; and on 6th September, 1346, the king desired proclamation to be made at Winchelsea and many other towns, that, whoever would take victuals, bows, arrows, or bow strings to Calais, for the supply of the army, should be protected from loss or molestation, and should be free to sell their commodities for such price as might be agreed upon between the buyer and seller.[4] In the month of February, 1347, two of their best informed naval men were again summoned to advise the king

[1] Rym. Fœd., vol. 3, p. 5. [2] Ib. p. 10. [3] Ib. p. 85. [4] Ib. p. 90.

on the state of the navy, which was again in danger; and, on the same day, the 15th, the mayor and bailiffs were required to arrest such ships as they could find, and detain them in port ready for the public service.[1]

The Seige of Calais was at this time occupying all the attention and exercising all the energies of Edward. A list of the fleet employed by him at the seige is still extant,[2] and shows how valuable a naval town Winchelsea then was. The King's ships were 25, carrying 419 mariners, being somewhat less than 17 men to a ship; and the number of the whole fleet was 700 ships, manned with 14,151 mariners, which, upon the general average, was little more than 20 men to a ship. Among the south fleet, were—

Winchelsea	ships	21	Rye	ships	9
	mariners	596		mariners	156
Hastings	ships	5	Seaford	ships	5
	mariners	96		mariners	80

Winchelsea supplied the largest number of ships and men to this fleet of all the forty-nine southern ports, except London; Feversham, which supplied 22 ships, but only 504 mariners; Dartmouth; Plymouth; Fowey; Bristol; and Southampton: the last supplied the same number of ships, 21, but only 576 mariners.

Ship Building.—At this period Winchelsea was a good place for building ships. The king had not many ships of his own; but we find, among the Carlton House Ride MSS., some interesting particulars of the making and re-making of royal vessels, and of the wages of the workmen. They are in an account rendered 7th Dec., 1352, by Richard Large of Winchelsea, master of the King's Cog Thomas, from 25th August, 1347, (21st Edw. III) when he was appointed to the mastership, to 22nd August, 1349: he accounts for the receipt of £390, and for the expenditure of £377 2s. 5d. in some slight repairs of the Thomas, and for the making of two skumers, one named

[1] Rym. Fœd., vol. 3, p. 106-7. [2] Arch., vol. 6, p. 213.

the John and the other the Jonette, out of a galley or cog called the John, under the survey of William Elewayre, clerk. The whole work seems to have extended over a period of 175 days. The shipwrights were employed on an average 120 days: the best were paid sixpence a day each, (the same rate as a master of one of the Cinque Ports' ships,) others received fivepence a day, others fourpence, and the common workmen threepence a day. The sawyers were employed 28 days, at fivepence a day each: the castlewrights 50 days, at sixpence a day each: watchers were employed for 175 days, at threepence a day each: and men were employed to dig a way out of the float for three days, at threepence a day each.

Gallants of Fowey, &c.—The bravery of the men of Winchelsea was accompanied with somewhat of unnecessary insolence, which was well repressed by the men of Fowey. Carew[1] says, that the ships of Fowey sailing by Rye and Winchelsey about this time, would vale no bonnet, being required, whereupon the Rye and Winchelsey men and they fought, when the Fowey men had the victory, and thereupon bore their arms next with the arms of Rye and Winchelsey, and thence rose the name of "The Gallaunts of Fowey."

On 28th Oct., 1347, the mayor and bailiffs were commanded not to permit any knights or armed men to go out of their port without the king's special license.[2] The surrender of Calais did not immediately terminate Edward's difficulties in France; and as he needed support and supplies there, he, on 1st Oct., 1348, required the mayor and bailiffs of Winchelsea to unlade any vessels in the port that might be laden with wool or other merchandise, and send them to meet the other ships at Sandwich.[3]

After the pestilence of 1349, the country having been much depopulated, and the public treasury being very much

[1] Survey of Cornwall, B. 2, fol. 134-135. Addl. MSS., 6344, p. 153.
[2] Rym. Fœd., vol. 3, p. 141. [3] Ib. p. 174.

exhausted, the king directed the mayor and bailiffs not to permit any one except a merchant, notary, or king's messenger, to leave the port.[1] On 23rd July, 1350, they were again commanded to prevent any earl, &c., from going out of the port.[2] The town appears in all the writs directed to the principal towns in the kingdom, during this reign, whether to prevent the exportation of corn, iron, or food, to any place except Calais; or any horses, falcons, woollen thread, or linen; or to stop military persons, or persons carrying the secrets of the king, or travellers departing the realm; or to regulate the price of wine; or to observe the truces; or to further any other public object.

Naval Engagement off Winchelsea.—On the 29th August, 1350, was fought, off Winchelsea, the celebrated engagement with the Spaniards; the English fleet being commanded by the King in person, assisted by Edward the Black Prince. Froissart,[3] in his Chronicle, gives a full and graphic account of this fight. "When the Spaniards," he says, "had completed their cargoes and laden their vessels with linen cloths, and whatever they imagined would be profitable in their own country, they embarked on board their fleet at Sluys (in Flanders.) They knew they should meet the English, but were indifferent about it, for they had marvellously provided themselves with all sorts of warlike ammunition; such as bolts for cross-bowes, cannon, and bars of forged iron to throw on the enemy, in hopes, with the assistance of great stones, to sink him. When they weighed anchor, the wind was favourable for them; there were forty large vessels, of such a size and so beautiful, it was a fine sight to see them under sail. Near the top of their masts were small castles, full of flints and stones, and a soldier to guard them; and there also was the flag-staff, from whence fluttered their streamers in the wind, that it was pleasant to look at them.

[1] Rym. Fœd., vol. 3, p. 191. [2] Ib. p. 199.

[3] Johnes' Ed., vol. 1, p. 197.

If the English had a great desire to meet them, it seemed as if the Spaniards were still more eager for it, as will hereafter appear. The Spaniards were full ten thousand men, including all sorts of soldiers they had enlisted when in Flanders; this made them feel sufficient courage not to fear the combat with the King of England, and whatever force he might have at sea. Intending to engage the English fleet, they advanced with a favourable wind until they came opposite to Calais. The King of England being at sea, had very distinctly explained to all his knights the order of battle he would have them follow: he had appointed the Lord Robert de Namur to the command of a ship called Le Salle du Roi, on board of which was all his household. The King posted himself in the fore part of his own ship: he was dressed in a black velvet jacket, and wore on his head a small hat of beaver, which became him much. He was that day, as I was told by those who were present, as joyous as he ever was in his life, and ordered his minstrils to play before him a German dance, 'Sir John Chandos,' which delighted him greatly. From time to time he looked up to the castle on his mast, where he had placed a watch to inform him when the Spaniards were in sight. Whilst the king was thus amusing himself with his knights, who were happy in seeing him so gay, the watch, who had observed a fleet, cried out, 'Ho! I spy a ship, and it appears to me to be a Spaniard.' The minstrils were silenced, and he was asked if there were more than one: soon after he replied, 'Yes: I see two, three, four, and so many that, God help me, I cannot count them!' The king and his knights then knew they must be the Spaniards. The trumpets were ordered to sound, and the ships to form a line of battle for the combat, as they were aware that since the enemy came in such force, it could not be avoided. It was, however, rather late, about the hour of vespers. The king ordered wine to be brought, which he and his knights drank; when each fixed their helmets on their heads. The Spaniards now drew near; they might easily have refused the battle, if they had chosen it, for they were well freighted, in large ships, and had the wind in their favour. They could have avoided speaking with the English if they had willed, but their pride and presumption made them act otherwise. They disdained to sail by, but bore instantly down on them, and commenced the battle.

"When the King of England saw from his ship their order of battle, he ordered the person who managed his vessel, saying, 'Lay me along side the Spaniard, who is bearing down on us; for I will have a tilt with him.' The master dared not disobey the king's order, but laid his ship ready for the Spaniard, who was coming full sail. The king's ship was large and stiff, otherwise she would have been sunk, for that of the enemy was a great one, and the shock of their meeting was more like the crash of a torrent or tempest; the rebound caused the castle in the king's ship to encounter that of the Spaniard, so that the mast of the latter was broken, and all in the castle fell with it into the sea, when they were drowned. The English vessel, however, suffered, and let in water, which the knights cleared, and stopped the leak, without telling the king any thing of the matter. Upon examining the vessel he had engaged lying before him, he said, 'Grapple my ship with that, for I will have possession of her.' His knights replied, 'Let her go her way: you shall have better than her.' That vessel sailed on, and another large ship bore down, and grappled with chains and hooks to that of the king. The fight now began in earnest, and the archers and cross-bowes, on each side, were eager to shoot and defend themselves. The battle was not in one place, but in ten or twelve at a time. Whenever either party found themselves equal to the enemy, or superior, they instantly grappled, when grand deeds of arms were performed. The English had not any advantage; and the Spanish ships were much larger and higher than their opponents, which gave them a great superiority in shooting, and casting stones and iron bars on board their enemy, which annoyed them exceedingly. The knights on board the king's ship were in danger of sinking, for the leak admitted water: this made them more eager to conquer the vessel they were grappled to: many gallant deeds were done; and at last they gained the ship, and flung all they found in it overboard, having quitted their own ship. They continued the combat against the Spaniards, who fought valiantly, and whose cross-bowmen shot such bolts of iron as greatly distressed the English.

"This sea fight between the English and Spaniards, was well and hardy fought; but, as night was coming on, the English exerted themselves to do their duty well, and discomfit their enemies. The Spaniards, who are used to the sea, and were in large ships, acquitted themselves to the utmost of their power. The young Prince of Wales and his division were engaged apart: his ship was grappled by a great Spaniard, when he and his knights suffered much; for she had so many holes, that the water came in very abundantly, and they could not by any means stop the leaks, which gave the crew fears of her sinking; they, therefore, did all they could to conquer the enemy's ship, but in vain, for she was very large, and excellently well defended. During this danger of the prince, the Duke of Lancaster came near, and as he approached, saw he had the worst of the engagement, and that his crew had too much on their hands, for they were bailing out water: he, therefore, fell on the other side of the Spanish vessel, with which he grappled, shouting, 'Derby to the rescue.' The engagement was now very warm, but did not last long, for the ship was taken, and all the crew thrown overboard, not one being saved. The prince, with his men, instantly embarked on board the Spaniard; and scarcely had they done so when his own vessel sunk, which convinced them of the imminent danger they had been in.

"The engagement was in other parts well contested by the

English knights, who exerted themselves, and need there was of it, for they found those who feared them not. Late in the evening, the Salle du Roi, commanded by Lord Robert de Namur, was grappled by a large Spaniard, and the fight was very severe. The Spaniards were determined to gain this ship; and the more effectually to succeed in carrying her off, they set all their sails, took advantage of the wind, and in spite of what Lord Robert and his crew could do, towed her out of the battle: for the Spaniard was of a more considerable size than the Lord Robert's ship, and therefore she more easily conquered. As they were thus towed, they passed near the king's ship, to whom they cried out, 'Rescue the Salle du Roi,' but were not heard; for it was dark; and, if they were heard, they were not rescued. The Spaniards would have carried away with ease the prize, if it had not been for a gallant act of one Hanequin, a servant to Lord Robert, who, with his drawn sword on his wrist, leaped on board the enemy, ran to the mast, and cut the large cable which held the main-sail, by which it became unmanageable; and, with great agility, he cut other four principal ropes, so that the sails fell on the deck, and the course of the ship was stopped. Lord Robert seeing this, advanced with his men, and, boarding the Spaniard sword in hand, attacked the crew so vigorously, that all were slain or thrown overboard, and the vessel won.

"I cannot speak of every particular circumstance of this engagement. It lasted a considerable time; and the Spaniards gave the King of England and his fleet enough to do. However, at last, victory declared for the English. The Spaniards lost fourteen ships: the others saved themselves by flight. When it was completely over, and the king saw he had none to fight with, he ordered his trumpets to sound a retreat, and made for England. They anchored at Rye and Winchelsea, a little after nightfall, when the King, the Prince of Wales, the Duke of Lancaster, the Earl of Richmond, and other barons, disembarked, took horses in the town, and rode to the mansion[1] where the Queen was, scarcely two English leagues distant. The queen was mightily rejoiced on seeing her lord and children: she had suffered that day great affliction from her doubts of success; for her attendants had seen from the hills of the coast the whole of the battle, as the weather was fine and clear, and had told the queen, who was very anxious to learn the number of the enemy, that the Spaniards had forty large ships: she was, therefore, much comforted by their safe return. The king, with those knights, who had attended him, passed the night in revelry with the ladies, conversing of arms and amours. On the morrow, the greater part of the barons who had been in this engagement, came to him: he greatly thanked them all for the services they had done him before he dismissed them, when they took their leave, and returned every man to his home."[2]

[1] In another translation, it is called a religious house; but the term is, "le Manoir:" it was, most probably, William do Echyngham's house.

[2] Barnes' account of this sea fight gives some additional particulars. It is quoted at length by Mr. Henry Noel Humphreys, in his Record of the Black Prince, (1849;) he gives an illuminated picture of this sea fight. "The king being soon furnished with a fleet of fifty good ships and pinnaces, and taking along with him his eldest son, Edward, Prince of Wales, then in the 20th year of his age, together with the Earls of Lancaster, Northampton, Warwick, Salisbury, Arundel, Huntingdon, Gloucester, and other lords and knights, with their several retinues, and a good number of stout archers, went on board at Sandwich, with design to meet the Spanish fleet at its return with wares from Flanders, and, at last, on a Monday, the iv. of the kalends of Sept., being the 29th of August, and the feast of the Decollation of St. John the Baptist, he met with them upon the coasts of Winchelsea and about Rye, near the hour of matins." He adds, "This victory the King of England thought too dearly bought, with the loss of many brave knights, especially Sir John Goldsborough, a young knight of great valour, of comely shape and noble deportment, who was much lamented by the king and his son the Prince of Wales, to whom he was always very dear, upon the account of his extraordinary qualities, and almost equal age and conformity of will and inclination. His loss King Edward endeavoured to repair by advancing no less than fourscore young gentlemen, who performed best in the fight, to the honor of knighthood."

At this battle Richard Fitz Alan, Earl of Arundel, who had led the second battalion of the English army in France, greatly distinguished himself.[1]

Some doubts have existed as to the date of the battle; but, by a writ, tested 2nd November, 1350, granting a pardon to Thomas de Banastre for the murder of Ralph de Blackburn, committed before the 29th August, in consequence of Banastre's good services in this battle, the king fixes the 29th as the day[2] of the victory. One of his writs is dated from Winchelsea on the 28th August, and another on the 3rd of September.

Attacks of the French.—When war again broke out between France and England, the town of Winchelsea was seriously injured. In 1359, (on the ides of March, 15th, according to Thomas of Walsingham, but on St. Matthew's day, 21st Sept., according to Henry of Knighton) whilst King Edward was in France, the French, from the coasts of Normandy, to the number of 3,000, with a considerable fleet of ships, came ashore at Winchelsea, and entering the town, set fire to, and partly burnt it, and killed all that withstood them without regard to age, sex, degree, or order. Meeting with no opposition to signify, they carried off with them the matrons, and all the handsome young women they could lay their hands on, and abundance of plunder; and whilst they were there, committed the most abominable acts: for when they landed the townspeople were at mass in the church; thither the Frenchmen immediately directed themselves, and after butchering many of the congregation and despoiling the church, they met with one woman of more beauty than the rest of her neighbours, and had come there together with them to her devotions: her the brutes seized upon, and, in that very place, most grossly assaulted, one after another, till

[1] Dallaway's West. Sussex, vol. 2, p. 126.

[2] Rym. Fœd., vol. 3, p. 207.

the woman died.[1] Henry of Knighton says, that there were nine illustrious women ravished; that the French killed forty townsmen; and that 400, who came to the succour of the town, were drowned in the harbour, out of which the French took thirteen ships well freighted with wine and victuals. According to Leland,[2] they stayed in the town a day and a night, and then returned to their ships, but were obliged to leave two behind, being fast in land.[3] The slaughter seems to have been heaviest at the west of the town and near the Pewes. The slain were buried in St. Giles' church yard, which was thereupon enlarged, and the lane near is called to this day, Dead Man's Lane.

The king was very indignant at this attack, and immediately turned his army towards Paris. Whilst he was occupied under its walls, and a short time before the 15th March, 1360, the anniversary of the last attack, the French landed at Winchelsea with a large number of armed men and horses, besieged and took the town, inhumanly killed, as the king's writs say, all the men found in the town; and were riding all about the country, there killing, burning, and destroying all about them; when, on the 15th March, the king directed an array of the several southern and midland counties to repel these invaders.[3] Lambard says, that the French came under the command of the Admiral of France,

[1] Thomas of Walsingham, p. 174.

[2] Notable Things, translated into English by John Leylande.

[3] In Devon's Issue Rolls of the Exchequer, p. 173, is the following entry connected with these French attacks, Michaelmas, 34 Edw. III, (1360.) To John de Thorpe, (a clerk of the King's Exchange in the tower) lately sent beyond the sea to my lord the king upon secret business, in money paid to him in discharge of the ten marks, which the lord the king commanded to be paid to him: for the twenty marks, which the king granted to him in recompense of the damage and loss which he sustained at the town of Winchelsea during the time the French enemy hostilely entered into the said town, and burnt the same. By writ, &c., £6 13s. 4d.

[3] Rym. Fœd., vol. 3, p. 477.

that they landed at night, took the town, slew the townsmen, fired their houses, spoiled their goods, and returned laden to their navy. They were speedily obliged to retreat from the southern coasts, as an English fleet, under Sir John Paveley, swept the seas between the two countries, and forced the French to keep within the Norman ports.

The French, in their turn, received full retribution: in vengeance of the arrival of the Normans, there assembled in 1360, under the king's auspices at Winchelsea, the navy of the Cinque Ports and the north navy, to the number of 80 ships. This fleet went with 1,000 armed men, and 1,500 archers, to the Isle of Sans, within fifteen days after Easter, and won the town of Luce, and burnt it. "But this jorney, says Leland, was lettid to procede by commandement of Edward, that was, by the French counsail meanes, in treatice of trewes."

On 18th March, in this year, 1360, the king landed at Rye in the evening, and immediately started on horseback for London, where he arrived at nine o'clock the next morning; and on 24th March his writ was sent (amongst others) to John Cronhastyng, master of the ship called La Seinte Marie Cog de Winchelsea, requiring him forthwith to unlade the said ship in the port of Southampton, notwithstanding the said ship was freighted for another place, and to fit her out to go at the wages of the king with the other ships of the armed fleet, which were getting together with all expedition to withstand the French, who had invaded the kingdom.[2]

The attack on the Isle of Sans was not the only return which the French received from the English for their misdeeds; for, in the year 1361, the Isle of Caux, in Normandy, was taken by the English navy "in the revengeing of the Frenchmen displeasure doone to Winchelsey."[3]

[1] Notable Things, by J. Leylande. [2] Rym. Fœd., vol. 3, p. 479.
[3] Leland's Collect., p. 479.

ROADSTEAD.—The Roadstead off this town was, at this time, as much a place for dispatching the fleet and embarking troops as Portsmouth or Spithead, at the present day. In the summer of 1370, a very large force was sent to France, under Robert de Knolles. Winchelsea was the place whence this force sailed; and in Mr. Devon's Issue Roll of Thomas de Brantingham, the Lord High Treasurer,[1] 44 Edw. III, we have full particulars of what took place. On the 3rd July, William Fox, a courier, was sent to Winchelsea with letters of Privy Seal, directed to the mayor and bailiffs of the same town, to certify to the king, and also by himself to certify concerning the ships that were in this port. Letters were also sent by messengers and couriers to divers admirals in all parts of the country, to detain ships for the expedition, and hasten and take them to Winchelsea and Rye, for the passage of Knolles and his retinue; and there are several entries of wages paid to the seamen to hasten them. John Lord de Neville, admiral of the fleet, and others were required to find as many armed men and archers as were necessary to secure the safe passage of the ships.[2] The royal commands were obeyed with alacrity. On 18th July, William Lord de Latymer, steward of the king's household, was sent to Winchelsea and Rye to superintend the passage of Knolles and his retinue, and embarking the men at arms and archers, receiving £25 for his expenses. On the same day, John de Thorp was sent with £4,000 to Winchelsea towards payment of the wages of the ships, &c. From the 22nd to 26th July, Lord Latymer had constant communications sent to him at Rye, where he had taken up his abode, and whence he, in company with Lord Neville, Henry de Scrope, and others sent to assist him, went by barge to the Camber, to inspect the ships: no less than 8,464 horses, besides foot men and archers, were embarked

[1] See pp. 180-181-205-206-212-213-269. [2] Rym. Fœd., vol. 3, p. 896.

before the last day of July; and a sum of 5,000 marks was sent from London on four horses to pay the expenses.[1]

Towards the close of his reign, Edward again visited the town; and hence he dated, on 6th Oct., 1372, his writs adjourning the parliament that had been summoned to meet fifteen days after Michaelmas, to the 3rd November following.[2]

EMBANKING.—The exertions which had been made during the two preceding reigns to protect the town from the further encroachments of the sea, to reclaim the land,

> And, sedulous to stop the coming tide,
> Lift the tall rampire's artificial pride,

Were continued under Edward III. In the 5th year of his reign, (1331) he granted[3] to Stephen Padiham, of Winchelsea, 28a. of land, in Laddemarsh, part of Higham, which had been submerged by the sea, yet still existed, rendering a yearly rent of 28s. if he should be able, by ditches and banks, to defend these acres from the sea.

In 6 Edw. III, (1332) Thomas de Faversham, Richard de Grofherst, and Robert de Bataille were appointed commissioners for Northmarsh, near Rye, and Spadeland Marsh, between Winchelsea and Danise Wall.[4] In 10 Edw. III, (1336) it having been found by inquisition that the king held 128a. in Roothmershe, near Rye, which belonged to his manor of Ihamme, and that the king's bondmen there held 30a. of land called Spadeland; and that the king's lands there could not be preserved, except contribution were made towards the expenses of their safeguard; the king commanded the commissioners to assess his lands according to their quantity, as they did others, and he commanded Stephen Padiham, his bailiff of Ihamme, to contribute his proportion out of the profits of that manor; and in 16 Edward III, (1342) he

[1] There are particular entries of the cost of the planks, &c.

[2] Parl. Hist. Eng., vol. 1, p. 113.

[3] Cal. Rot., orig., p. 50. [4] Dugd. Embank., c. 19.

directed his precept to John Glynde, then bailiff of the manor, reciting his commands to Padiham, and giving him strict charge not to omit the contribution.

But (says Dugdale) notwithstanding this great care, which it appears the king had, the work was not perfected of three years after: for, in 19 Edw. III, (1345) I find the like precept directed to the same Stephan, who was again his bayliff of the said mannour in that year. What was done in the marsh of Spadelonde before mentioned, in pursuance of the said king's precept, I cannot say: but this is certain, that within few years after through the force of great tempests, the sea banks between Winchelse and Dauneswalle, and betwixt Pykammyll and Trecherie, were so broken and decayed, that, as well the king's lands as the lands of divers other persons in that marsh, were overflowed at every tide, to the danger of their utter ruine, and the apparent depauperation of the town of Winchelse and the parts adjoyning.[1] "The king, therfore, for the speedy repair thereof, did, in the 25th of his reign, (1351,) assign John de Ore, Stephan de Horsham, Robert Arnald, and Stephan de Pageham, his commissioners, to view them and to take order therein," and they were to repair all the walls and ditches.[2]

In 1370 we find that the first bridge to supersede the ferry had been built. In this year

The king being informed that the burghers of Wynchelse had, for the advantage of the town and benefit for the whole countrey, built a certain bridge at Pypewel, over a water, called the Chanel of Wynchelse, upon the said king's soyl, on both sides of the water, for the passage of people and all carriages; which was not done with little chardge: and, that by the violence of the tides and flouds of fresh water passing to the sea,

[1] By two inquisitions, taken 21st Edw. III, and 30th Edw. III, for the purpose of the bailiff's discharges, and to be found among the MSS. at the Carlton House Ride, it appears that the sea had recently submerged eighteen tenements at Rye, which had formerly paid 4s. rents; two acres of land near Rye; and two tenements in Higham, belonging to the heirs of Pette: that Adam atte Clive had land uncultivated that used to pay a rent of 2s. 10¾d.; that Stephen Padiham had expended £11 16s. 8d. in repairing the walls, &c., between Winchelsea and Daneswall: and, that in 1356, in spite of all exertions, 128 acres of land in Spadeland, which had formerly paid a rent of £42 16s. 2d., had been submerged.

[2] Rot. Pat., 25 Edw. III, part 1, m. 23.

the said bridge and banks, on each side of the said water, betwixt the said town of Wynchelse and the towns of Odymere and Rye, were so broken down and ruined, and all the highwayes about the said town of Wynchelse so overflowed, that scarce any one could come in or out thereof; he granted commission to the Abbot of Bataille, Thomas de Reyns, (Lieut. to the Constable of Dovor Castle) William Batesford, Roger de Ashborneham, and others, to view the said bridge and banks, and to take order for the repairing of them.[1]

Among the seals found at Winchelsea, is one of the family

of Glinde. It is the seal of JOHN, son of Robert Glinde, and was discovered some years since in a garden, then the property of Mr. Thomas Lamb, mayor of Rye, and bears the inscription, ✠ S: IOH: IS: FILII: ROB'TI: GLINDE: Sigillum Johannis filii Roberti Glinde. The scroll seems to be a merchant's mark, from which it is premised that he had no arms.[2]

PROPERTY, NAMES, &c.—In consideration of their peculiar burdens, the Freemen of the Cinque Ports claimed, and were allowed exemption from the subsidies imposed upon other subjects of the king. Among the MSS. in the Carlton House Ride, are several rolls to the time of Henry VI, of freemen non-resident in their respective ports, but resident in several parishes in Kent and Sussex, who were exempted from contribution: and there is one roll, Non. Inq. of 15th Edw. III, (1341) which contains the names of the resident freemen who were thus exempted; and we are enabled to mark the changes, which half a century had produced in the new town. The Roll of Winchelsea is very incorrectly printed in the Nonæ Inquis., p. 403, and the names of several freemen who afterwards claimed exemption are omitted.[3] We,

[1] Dugd. Imb., p. 91. In 8th Henry VIII, the Burgesses paid 20s. for a confirmation of the charter of Edw. III, for building the bridge at Pipewell. Rot. orig. Carl. Ride MSS., m. 54.

[2] The seal is engraved in the Arch., for 1794, vol. 7, p. 430, pl. 19.

[3] In the same roll the names of 49 freemen in Hastings, 30 in Rye, and 28 in Pevensey, are given.

therefore, print from the original roll, with the additions among the Subsidy Rolls in the MSS. at Carlton House Ride:

Stephen de Padyham
John Wallere
Joab de Bidendenn
Robert Bataille
William Brokex
John Brokex
John Cole
Matilda Arnold
William Manell
William Coupre
John Longe
William Longe
Bartholomew Longe
Robt. and Stephen, sons of Stephen Alard
Thomas Geffrai
William Wellard
John de Brede
John de Folke
William Yonge
Robert Lende
Thomas Lende
John de Pette
Richard Coupre
Roger Coupre
Stephen Tregen
William Tribuler
Johanna de Pette
Margaret Palmer
William de Brede
Richard Frere
Robt Malerbe
Robt Alard de Ihamme
Margaret Germayn
John Glynde
Beatrice atte Gate
John Jacob
John atte Carte
John Yonge
Alan Alard
John Paulyn de Stich-erton
Roger Salerne
Dionisia Tannere
Thomas Lynter
Richard Swayn
Johanna Hywe
John Patrik
Stephen Lambyn
Richard Large
Philip de Oxnoo
John Curteys
John Wyndere
Richard Kenne
Ralph Enogle
Roger Flechre
Roger Waterman
Richard Webbe
Willm. Godynton
Paul Hore
Geoffry Hereward
Nicholas Ofemute
Richard Suerpe
John Suerpe
John Ryngemere
Roger Spycer
Walter Blandy
John Heved
Richard Moys
John Rypecherl
John and Thomas de Clavering
John Cely
Reginald Alard
Henry Vynht
John Seman
John Vynht
Thomas de Maydestan
Charles Colyn
Simon Ambreis
Peter Fihs

The additional roll, certified by the mayor and bailiff on 4th April, is very much defaced, but it contains the following nineteen names:—

Reginald Alard
Henry —
The Heirs of Robert Bataille
James Paulyn
Walter Paulyn
Margaret —
Gilbert Kareman
John Paulyn
John —
Matilda Arnold
Isabella de Bidendene
The Heirs of John de Bidendene
The Heirs of John Yonge
Charles Co (upre)
William Manew
John Fynh
Thomas G (odfrey)
Robert Alard of Ihamme
Philip de Ox (ene)

Among the Battle Abbey Records and the Dering MSS., we have some additional names. In January, 1341, we find a feoffment from James, son and heir of Gervase Alard, to Richard Mory and Joan his wife, of seventeen virgates of land, in St. Thomas, abutting on the north to the messuage of

Henry, son of Richard Alard. And we find Henry Alard, Walter Clerk, John Andrew, and others, witnesses to the feoffment from Stephen and Roger, sons of Agnes Grig, of Winchelsea, for the health of their own souls and of their mother, of two messuages near Cornhethe.[1] In 1345 we have a release from Peter Fich, of Winchelsea, to the Abbot and Convent of Battle, of two wax tapers, wont to be rendered by the sacrist of the monastery on the day of the Purification of our Lady.[2] In the same year, we find John de Brede, of Winchelsea,[3] in an inquisition taken at Winchelsea in 1349 before John Longe, bailiff,[4] the jurors were Robert Portesmouth, Geoffry Gateward, Philip Barbour, John Hodere, John Bronketre, John Dranke, Samson Sneppe, John Hardyng, Thomas Nede, Henry Folde, William Colhepe, and John Edouse; and in 1355, the name of Finch instead of Herbert first appears as immediately connected with this town, in a bond in the penalty of £40 given by Vincent Finch, who was bailiff in the following year, to Robert Arnold, Robert Londencys, Robert Badding, and William de Batesford, of Winchelsea.[5]

Richard II. Attacks of the French.—During the last year of the last reign, great fears were entertained of some renewed attacks by the French. On the 8th May, 1376, the mayor and burgesses of Rye were directed to array and put all the able-bodied men in arms, and to fortify their town, that they might be able to resist their enemies, should any presume to attack them by sea or by land: and they were required to make proclamation that no one, of whatsoever state or condition, should withdraw himself from the town, or remove his property, under a penalty of the loss of all his possessions. These directions to the faint-hearted men of Rye, and these preparations, were not made without a necessity; for in the

[1] See ante, p. 16. [2] Thorpe's Battle Abbey Records. [3] Dering MSS.
[4] Tower Records, Inq., 23 Edw. III, p. 2, (1 nrs.) No. 173.
[5] Dering MSS.

following year, (1377) a few days only after the new king had ascended the throne, the French invaded Rye, and the inhabitants of that town ".turned their backes." Let us see how bravely the men of Winchelsea behaved.

Stow thus describes the attack.[1] "Upon the feast day of St. Peter and Paul the Apostles, (29th June) in the morning, the Frenchmen, with five vessells great and small, invaded the towne of Rye, and with small labour tooke the towne: albeit the towne dwellers, upon confidence of strength, had taken order that none should remove their goods from the towne, that at the least wise, for love of their goods, they might with more courage abide the conflicts; yet, notwithstanding, they turne their backs in the time of battell, whereupon it came to passe, that by their want of heart and courage, the towne was taken with all their goods. The Abbot of Battayle, (Hamo of Offington) hearing of so lamentable a report, put all his men in armour to defend the villages nigh adjoyning, and one of the enemies going forth for forage, being taken by one of the Abbot's men, declared that the Frenchmen purposed to keepe the said towne for ten dayes, whereupon the Abbot removed with his power to the towne of Winchelsey, which towne (as the prisoner reported) the French purposed to assault; but when they saw the Abbot and his men armed in that towne, dispayring of further entrance into that countrie, they beginne to set fire on the towne of Rye, and within five houres brought it wholly unto ashes, with the church that then was there of a wonderfull beauty, conveying away foure of the richest of that towne, prisoners, and slaying sixty-six, left not above eyght in the towne. Forty-two hogsheads of wine they carried from thence to their ships, with the rest of their booty, and left the towne desolate."

After the French had burnt Rye they set sail for the Isle of Wight, and according to Stow, they devastated its towns,

[1] Chron., pp. 278-9.

slaughtered the inhabitants, and bound them by an oath not to resist them for the space of a year, whensoever they should please to land there.[1] This done, they again, in the same year, visited the Sussex coast, and "came to the town of Winchelsey, where, understanding the Abbot of Battell was come to defend it, they sent him word to redeeme the towne: unto whom the Abbot answered, he needed not to redeeme the thing that was not lost, but willed them to desist from molesting the towne upon paine of that which might follow. The French, exasperated with this answeer, requested him that if hee would not have peace, hee would send forth to fight man to man, or more in number if hee would, to trye the matter in view of armes; but neyther would the Abbot admitte the one request or the other, saying hee was a religious man, and therefore not to admitte such petitions, and that hee came not hither to fight, but to defend and preserve the peace of the country. These things being heard, the Frenchmen supposing the Abbot and his people wanted courage, they assaulted the towne with such instruments of warre, as cast forth stones far off, not ceasing from noone till evening; but by the laudable prowes of the Abbot and such as were with him, the French prevailed nothing, but left it as they found it. In the meane time, whilst they were busie thus at Winchelsey, they sent part of their company unto Hastings, where, finding the towne almost empty, they burnt it."

Speaking of this attack and defence of Winchelsea by the Abbot, old Fuller says, in his quaint language:[2] "I behold this Abbot the saver, not onely of Sussex, but England. For as dogs, who have once gotten an haunt to worry sheep, do not leave it off till they meet with their reward: so, had not these French felt the *smart* as well as the *sweet* of the English plunder, our land (and this county especially) had never been free from their incursions."

[1] Chron., p. 279. [2] Fuller's Worthies, ed. 1662, p. 106. See also T. Wals.

In this year, 1378, Stow tells us,[1] that the men of Winchelsea and Rye, in retaliation, gathered a great number of people together, and sailed for the coast of Normandy, "desirous to requite the losses which before they had received; and so, in the night, arriving in a town called Peter's-Haven, entred the same, slaying so many as they met, and those whom they thinke able to pay ransome, they carry to their ships; they spoyled the houses, with the churches, where they found many rich spoyles, which sometime had been by the Frenchmen fet (fetched) from Rye, and especially the bells, and such like, which they shipped, set the rest on fire, and then they land at Wilet, not farre from thence, where they practised the like cheuance, and so, with their rich spoile, turned home."

Two years afterwards, on 15th March, 1380, the unfortunate town was again attacked by the French and burnt, and the valiant Abbot put to flight. Holinshed[2] states, that among other incursions which the French made this summer on the coasts, we find that they burnt the town of Winchelsea, and put the Abbot of Battle to flight with his people, coming to succour the town, and took one of his monks that there was in armour with the Abbot. "Some write, also, that they burnt Rie, Hastings, and Portsmouth." Stow[3] gives the account that "John Vian, knight, with the French King's gallies, tooke the towne of Winchelsea, put the Abbot of Battell to flight, and tooke one of the monkes that came thither armed. Hee also burnt the townes of Appledor and Rye, Hastings and Portesmouth, about the feast of St. Laurence." Leland also says that they burnt Appledore and Rye. And Thomas of Walsingham[4] adds, that the capture of Winchelsea was among the most disastrous injuries which the French inflicted during the summer of that year upon this country.

The damage done to the town was very severe. It is cer-

[1] Chronicle, p. 281, following Thomas of Walsingham, p. 210.
[2] Holinshed, p. 427. [3] Stow, p. 282. [4] T. Wals., p. 241.

tain that the walls were seriously injured, and that the Land or Pipewell Gate was destroyed: and there is good reason to suppose that the nave of the church of St. Thomas was burnt to the ground.

The king lost no time in endeavouring to ascertain and repair the loss; he immediately issued his writ[1] to the Abbot of Battle, Edward Dallyngrugge, and William Batesford, reciting that the town was not sufficiently secured, and was liable to the hostile attacks of the enemy, and directing them to survey the town, and enquire how it could best be secured, and at whose expense it ought to be done. The parliament took up the cause as a national question; and the Commons (1384,) petitioned the king that some remedy might be applied for the defence of the fortresses of Rye and Winchelsea, which had been so often injured and almost destroyed by the burnings and invasions of the enemy; "because if those towns were taken, which God forbid, the whole country would be destroyed."[2] This petition was referred to the Council; and the king, carrying out the wishes of the Commons, not only applied himself to a reparation of the walls, but directed that certain persons, who had tenements there, which were injured, should forthwith re-build and inhabit them, or give them up to others, who should be willing to inhabit them. The energy and vigour of the inhabitants did much to restore the devoted town: they so far succeeded as to stop for a time these attacks. But the town, although it was well resorted to by traders, never afterwards recovered its original importance.[3]

[1] Rot. Pat., 4 Richard II, pt. 1, a tergo, m. 40.

[2] Rot. Parl. vol. 3, p. 201, a.

[3] Holinshed (p. 440) gives an account of another sea exploit. "About the same time, (1382,) certeine English ships of Rie and other places, went to sea, and meeting pirats, fought with them and overcame them, taking seven ships, with three hundred men in them. One of those ships had beene taken from the Englishmen afore time, and was called the 'Falcon,' belonging to the Lord Will. Latimer; they were all richelie laden with wine, wax, and other good merchandize."

Rye gradually rose in wealth and commerce, and we find that Winchelsea as gradually became of less national interest.

Grose, quoting Leland, ascribes the attack of 1380 to the Spaniards, and not to the French; and says that they (the Spaniards) entered by night at Fairlight, about midway between Winchelsea and Hastings. All other authorities, however, agree in stating the French to have been the aggressors. They are recorded to have entered the town before sun-rise; and tradition has it that the New Gate was, by treachery, thrown open to them.

The orders sent to the town in this reign, included one in 1382, in which the hosts of this town, and of Rye, London, Yarmouth, and Scarborough were forbidden to forestal fish or other victuals;[1] and another in which the mayor and bailiffs were required to proclaim and enforce an order against the exportation of provisions.[2]

EMBANKING.—In 3rd Richard II, (1379 or 1380,) "upon complaint being made to the king by the commonalty of Wynchelse, shewing that there was a common way called Cop-greys, then lately leading from the said town unto Battaile; as also a certain marsh called Dynsdale, lying betwixt the towns of Wynchelse and Hastings, which way and marsh, through the neglect of some persons who of right ought to repair and maintain them, were destroyed and overflowed by the sea," the said King, by the assent of parliament, "assigned the Abbot of Battaile, Robert de Bealknappe, and William de Battesford to enquire through whose default these damages had happened, and who had used and ought to repair them, and to compel them thereto," according to the laws and customs of Romney marsh.[3]

Where this town or common way, called Cop-greys, was, we are unable to determine; but it must have been in the direction from the Newgate towards Icklesham or Pett.

[1] Rot. Parl., vol. 3, p. 142 b. [2] Ib. p. 396 b.

[3] Dugd. Imbank., p. 91; Holloway's Romney Marsh, p. 121; and Rot. Pat., 3 Rich. II, pt. 1, a tergo, m. 40.

PROPERTY, NAMES, &c.—Very few traces of the change of property, or of new names, in this reign, have come down to us. We learn only from the Battle Abbey Records, that, in 1379, ROBERT PORTER of Winchelsea, enfeoffed certain lands at Westham; and, that in 1389, Robert Scot and Petronilla his wife, enfeoffed to John Benglesthorpe and Godiva his wife, a messuage in Winchelsea, to which feoffment William Skele then mayor, the then bailiff, John Geffrey, and others were witnesses.

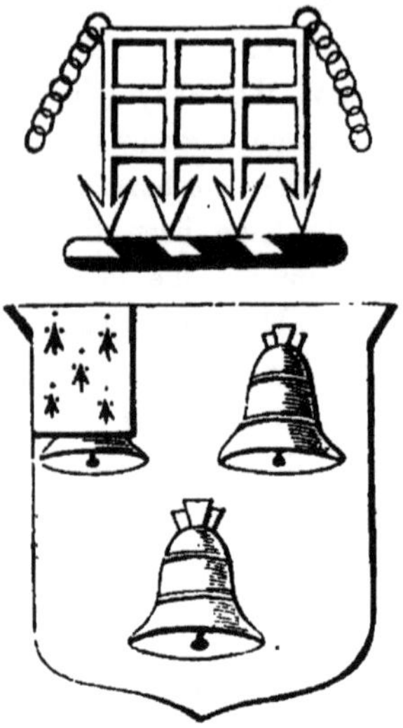

HENRY IV.—On 9th June, 1400, (1 Hen. IV,) the king's writs requiring proclamation to be made, that no one should carry out of the port any ship or armed vessel of war to go against or hurt the French, or any of their allies, except the Scots, contrary to the then present truce, were directed amongst others, to the mayor and bailiffs of Winchelsey.[1] In the early part of the following year, many arrests of vessels were made in the Camber; and proclamation was made that no strangers should be abroad in the town after a certain hour of the evening.[2] About 1404, says Holinshed,[3] great loss happened in Kent, by breaking in of the waters that overflowed the sea banks, as well in the Archbishop of Canterbury's grounds as other men's, whereby much cattle was drowned. The townsmen, as we have seen, on 10th June, 1404, obtained

[1] Rym. Fœd., vol. 3, pt. 3, p. 185.
[2] Corporation Accounts of the Town. See post, from Dering MSS.
[3] Holinshed, p. 526.

PLATE 111.

A. Hull Jr. del. J. Hunter sc.

STRAND GATE.

N.E.

M. J. Denne. del. J. Hunter, sc.

PIPEWELL GATE.

a confirmation of their charters, and set themselves to work in good earnest to repair the injuries their town had received.

PIPEWELL GATE, &c.—The repairs of the town walls, which had been commenced during the last reign, were carried on and completed in 1404. Tradition says that the windows in the north aisle of the church were repaired; and it is beyond doubt that the Pipewell Gate was now rebuilt. The gateway has, on the side without the town, next Udimore, a shield having the arms,—*a squirrel sejeant*—and above, in old English letters,

John Helde was mayor in 1404-5, and this sufficiently fixes the date of the gate. It was originally of more elaborate workmanship than the others; and there are now to be traced on the western side, the remains of shafts, from which clustered columns rose.

PROPERTY AND NAMES.—The additional names to be met with during this reign are not many. Among the Battle Abbey Records we have a feoffment on 26th Jan., 1405, from Bartholomew Marle and Alicia his wife, to Walter Seman, of the same place, and Juliana his wife, of land in the parish of St. Thomas, which was the gift and feoffment of Robert Scharp of Hastings, witnessed by John Gascone, Thomas Thondyrr, and others. And on 25th April, 1410, we have a feoffment from John Tamworth of Winchelsea, of land in the borough of Monjoye. Among the Inquisitiones post mortem,[1] is one,

[1] Cal. Inq., p. m., vol. 3, p. 328.

11th Henry IV, in which it appears that Agnes, widow of John Orlaston, died seized of a messuage and divers lands and rents in Winchelsea. And, on 20th Sept., 1412, Alan Kynton of Winchelsea, had a demise of the land here, which belonged to the Abbot and Convent of St. Martin, at Battle.

HENRY V.—The tenements which had not been rebuilt since the French attacks, and the changes which the land around was undergoing from the gradual retirement of the sea, rendered it desirable to contract the space included within the walls. Accordingly, we find in 3 Hen. V, (1415) an inquisition ad quod dampnum[1] on the proposal of the mayor and commonalty, to have a murage grant, because the site of the town, as it had theretofore existed, was too large for the then necessary habitation of the town; and this was followed by a patent for fortifying the town on the proposed plan.[2]

Several notices of the shipping of the town and of the use of the port occur in this reign.

In 3rd Henry V, (1415) the sum of £12 1s. 6d. was due from the King to Thomas Walsh, master of the ship called Gabriell de Wynchelse, for the wages of himself and his mariners, sailing with the said ship with the King, in his voyage beyond the sea, viz., for six weeks, after August 1st then last past; and he had a grant, Oct. 12th, for the payment of that sum out of the King's Customs in the port of London.[3] In 1415, the king preparing for the invasion of France, directed his ships to rendezvous at London, Sandwich, Winchelsea, and Southampton.[4] On 13th Oct., 1417, safe conduct was granted to John Bernard and three of his servants, in a ship or balinger, with twenty-five or thirty armed mari-

[1] Inq., ad quod dampnum, 3 Hen. V, No. 16.

[2] Rot. Pat. 3 Hen. V, pt. 2, No. 28.

[3] Rym. Fœd., ed. 1740, vol. 4, pt. 2, p. 148.

[4] Burr. MSS. Addl. Humphrey, uncle of Henry V, Lord Warden of the Cinque Ports, issued the summons from the king to the ports, to furnish ships to rendezvous at Winchelsea at the feast of St. George, to go to France with an army.

ners from Southampton, Winchelsea, Sandwich, or Dover.[1] From Winchelsea, 6th Id. i.e. 8th June, 1420, Henry Chichele, Archbishop of Canterbury, set sail on his passage to the king in France.[2]

In 7th Henry V, (1420) at a meeting of the Commissioners of the King of England and Philip, Duke of Burgundy and Earl of Flanders, at Calais, to treat concerning the prorogation or renovation of the truces between the kingdom of England and Flanders, and concerning the reformation and reparation of what had been done contrary thereto by either party, among some things of that sort particularly specified, is a complaint of the arrest and detention of a ship laden with wood, belonging to Winchelsea.[3]

PROPERTY, NAMES, &c.—The Battle Abbey Records have two additional feoffments during this reign: one from Thomas Reynolds of Winchelsea and Joan his wife, to John Coket, of the same place, and Alicia his wife, of a messuage in the parish of St. Thomas, situate towards the lands of the heirs of John Burghalsherte; and, in the other, John French of Winchelsea is mentioned as conveying lands in Willingdon.

HENRY VI.—The town still continued to be a convenient place for embarkation to the Continent. Its merchants were yet of importance; but with this reign, the prosperity departed.

In the 3rd Henry VI, (1425) four ships of Brittany, laden with wine, salt, &c., were taken by Lord Talbot and carried into Winchelsea, where an inquisition was held upon them.[4] In the Issue Roll of the Exchequer,[5] in Easter term, 5th Henry VI, we find a sum of £5 paid to John Talbot, the King's serjeant at arms, appointed in the first year of his reign, to detain and seize divers ships in the ports of London, Sandwich, Deal, and Winchelsea, to embark Thomas Duke of Exeter, John the Earl Marshal, Robert Lord Willoughby,

[1] Rotuli Normanniæ, vol. 1, p. 179.
[2] Addl. MSS., 6344, p. 801.
[3] Rym. Fœd., vol. 4, pt. 3, p. 152.
[4] MSS. Carlt. Ride.
[5] Devon's Issue Roll Exch., p. 400.

and other knights, esquires, and archers of the King's retinue in the aforesaid ports, proceeding to Calais, and for other services. In 9th Henry VI, (1430) Richard Sueleham[1] of Winchelsea, and others, merchants of England, complained to James King of Scots, that, about the feast of St. Andrew, 1428, one Simon Logane, and three other Scots, plundered them of two ships, commonly called the Gabriel of Hundeflete, and George of Wynchelsea, together with other goods, things, and merchandizes, to the value of £1,500: whereupon the king, on 5th January, granted his letters patent, giving liberty to all persons in authority in any of the ports of England and Flanders to arrest and detain those offenders, and any other merchants and mariners of his kingdom and their ships and goods, at the request of any of the said complainants, till such time as they should be fully satisfied of the said £1,500; which letters were confirmed by those of the King of England, on 26th January. On 2nd December, 1430, there is a writ of Privy Seal, for carrying from the town of Winchelsea to Dieppe, a sum to pay the ships, archers, and mariners;[2] and in Easter term, 11 Henry VI., Roger Minster, teller of the Exchequer, was paid for being sent to Winchelsea, and thence to Dieppe and Rouen, with £2,500 for John Duke of Bedford, to pay the wages of the men at arms.[3] On 28th Nov., 1431, an order was made for stopping the ships at Winchelsea.[4]

PILGRIMAGES.—During this reign the pilgrimages to the shrine of St. James of Compostella, became frequent, and the merchants of Winchelsea largely availed themselves of this source of profit. On 26th Feb., 1434, Robert Porter, master of a barge,[5] called Le Trinite de Wynchelse, had the king's license to carry therein sixty of the king's subjects, who were

[1] Rym. Fœd., vol. 4, pt. 4, p. 171.

[2] Proceedings and Ordinances of the Privy Council, vol. 4, p. 73.

[3] Devon's Issue Roll of Exch., p. 422.

[4] Proceedings of Privy Council, vol. 4, p. 103.

[5] Rym. Fœd., vol. 5, pt. 1, p. 4.

going on a pilgrimage to St. James', provided that they made oath to the keepers of the passage, when they were taken on board, that they would carry no gold or silver above their reasonable expenses with them; and that they would not reveal the secrets of the kingdom to any one abroad. And, on 8th May, in the same year, the same Robert Porter, master of a barge, called Le Kateryn of Winchelse, had the king's license[1] to carry therein forty of the king's subjects, &c., as before. Licenses were granted in this year for no less than 2433 pilgrims.

In Sir Henry Ellis' Original Letters, second series,[2] there is a singular letter, showing that ships were every year fitted out from different ports in England with cargoes of pilgrims. From other countries these pilgrimages were continued even in the last century.

In the earliest English sea song, preserved in a MS. of the time of Hen. VI, in the library of Trinity College, Cambridge, and printed by the Percy Society in Mr. Halliwell's Early Naval Ballads, p. 1, the discomforts of these pilgrims to the shrine of St. James are pointed out: and from the opening verses it is clear that Winchelsea held a prominent place among the ports for these articles of exportation.

> Men may leve all gamys,
> That saylen to Seynt Jamys:
> For many a man hit gramys;
> When they begyn to sayle.
> For when they take the see,
> At Sandwyche, or at Wynchelsee,
> At Brystow, or where that it bee,
> Theyr herts begyn to fayle.

These pilgrimages from Winchelsea occupied the attention of the principal merchants for several years. The last entry of a license which we have found, is 22nd Feb., 1456, (34 Hen. VI;) it was granted to Simon Farnecombe, owner of the ship

[1] Rym. Fœd., vol. 5, pt. 1, p. 6. [2] Vol. 1, p. 110.

called Le Helene of Wynchelse, to carry therein fourscore pilgrims to St. James'.[1] In this same year, ships for the same destination went from Portsmouth, Weymouth, Plymouth, and other places, and there is extant a MS. Itinerary[2] of William Wey, Canon of Eton, who was one of the pilgrims in this year.

PORT.—Up to this time the Port was large enough to have constantly a Custumer and Deputy Custumer.[3]

In 14 Hen. VI, (1435) William Morfote, a mariner of Winchelsea, who was at sea at his own expense with an array of one hundred persons "for to withstand," as he called privateering, "and depresse the kyng's enmys, and his rebells, and of this worthy realme," complained that he was prevented from victualling at many places, and dare not come to land, in consequence of his having broken prison at Dover Castle, and he prayed for letters patent granting him a pardon: upon which parliament recommended the king to inflict an easy fine upon him for his prison breaking, and after payment thereof to grant him the desired pardon.[4] This Morfote married Alice, the widow of John French of Winchelsea, who died possessed of lands in Pevensey, which afterwards became the property of Battle Abbey.[5] On 29th May, 1421, there was a letter of attorney from Morfote and his wife to deliver seizin of the lands in Pevensey; one of the witnesses to which letter is Alex. Beuelay of Winchelsea. Wm. Morfote was member for the town in 1428 and 1429. And, on 21st May, 1433, William Skele of Winchelsea, was party to a release and concession in respect of the Pevensey land to this William Morfote, who, on 2nd July, 1446, enfeoffed to John Godfrey of Winchelsea, John Tamworth of Hastings, and Thomas Grevt of Winchelsea, all his lands and tenements within the liberties of Winchelsea and Pevensey.

[1] Rym. Fœd., vol. 5, pt. 2, p. 65. [2] Penes the Camden Society.
[3] Rot. Parl., 10 Henry VI, (1432) vol. 4, p. 417 b.
[4] Rot. Parl., vol. 4, p. 488 a. [5] Batt. Abb. Rec.

In 17th Hen. VI, (1439) we find a payment of £61 10s. 2d. for the conveyance of lead, tin, saltpetre, quarell-heads, lances, bowstrings, sheaves of arrows, &c., from London to this town,[1] to be shipped for the service of our army in France. On 8th July, 21 Hen. VI, (1442) an ordinance[2] was made for the better defence of the realm, by which it was directed that eight ships with forecastles, armed with 150 men each, were to be at sea from February to November, and every large ship was to be attended by a barge with eighty men, and a balinger with forty men. Each man to receive 2s. a month wages; and the masters and quarter-masters 3s. 4d. each more than the men. They were first ordered to assemble at Camber, but afterwards were directed to meet off the Isle of Wight. Winchelsea furnished a barge. In addition to this, two barges were directed to be stationed at Winchelsea, one of Morefore's called the Marie, and "that other Pratte barge" called Trinity.[3] In 1443, a letter was sent to Winchelsea to enquire who were takers of the Hollander's or Zealander's goods.[4] And on 8th July, in the same year, Godard Pulham, the bailiff of the town, was directed to be spoken with for a balinger to victual the bastile at Dieppe.

In the next year, five ships of the ports were required to attend the queen from France.[5]

Last Attack of the French.—It was during the severe struggle of England to keep possession of the places she held in France, and a few years before the conquest of Bayonne, which completed our expulsion, that the French made their last attack upon the two ancient towns. Jeake tells us, that "Both Winchelsea and Rye were burnt in the time of Henry VI, about the 26th or 27th year of his reign, (1448 or 1449,)

[1] Devon's Issue Rolls of the Exch., p. 437.
[2] Proceedings and Ordinances of Privy Council, vol. 5.
[3] Rot. Parl., vol. 5, p. 59 b.
[4] Proceedings and Ordinances of Privy Council, vol. 5, p. 308.
[5] Boys' Sandwich, p. 673.

in which I suppose the old charters and records of the town of Rye perished; because none older than his 27th year, save only some fragments, are to be seen." The attack, probably, took place in the summer of 1449, when the array of the county was called to the aid of the inhabitants; for, on the 30th July, 1449, (27th Hen. VI) there is a muster roll,[1] taken before Thomas Yerde, Richard Dalyngrygge, John Devenish, Thomas Thondre, and Robert Thorpe, commissioners, of 55 men at arms, and 508 archers, in the retinue of the Duke of Somerset, who were then at Winchelsea, well armed and arrayed, under the command of William Ipetot.

On 17th Feb., 1450, the king's letter was sent, amongst seven places, to the bailiffs, burgesses, and commonalty of Winchelsea, not to permit any gatherings or assemblages, except such as were by the king's proclamations justified.[2] In March, 1452, Calais being in much danger, a large fleet was placed under Lord Clifford, who was directed to bring them to the Downs or the Camber, without delay.[3]

In 33 Hen. VI, (1455) great apprehension was felt for the safety of the kingdom from the designs of foreigners, and the Commons[4] petitioned the king, praying that the Italian merchants, strangers who used to ride about buying woollen cloths, wool, wolfelles, and tyne, in several parts of the realm, whereby they learned the secrets of the kingdom, might be restrained from so buying; and that they should not be permitted to buy at the ports, unless driven by stress of weather into the ports of Fowey, Falmouth, Plymouth, Dartmouth, or Winchelsea. More active measures for the safety of the country were taken two years afterwards, when an array was directed to be made in London and in all the southern counties and towns. The patent[5] for the array at Winchelsea, was

[1] MSS. in Carlton Ride. The name of every man is recorded.
[2] Proceedings and Ordinances of Privy Council, vol. 5, p. 91.
[3] Ib. p. 121. [4] Rot. Parl., vol. 5, p. 335 a.
[5] Rot. Pat., 36 Henry VI, part 1, a tergo, m. 13.

issued on the 30th Sept., 1457, and the inhabitants were ordered to be mustered and arrayed, not only to guard and defend the town itself, but the other parts of Sussex.

SEA SHORE.—Hastings and other ports asserted their right to the Sea Shore between high and low water marks, against the claim of the Lord Warden, upon which an inquisition was taken at Winchelsea[1] on 9th May, 21 Hen. VI, (1443) before Reginald Cobham, Knt., locum tenens for Humphrey Duke of Gloucester, Constable of Dover Castle, and Lord Warden of the Cinque Ports; in which the claims were returned.[2] And we have two commissions for embanking, issued during this reign. One in the 34th year, (1456) for embanking both sides of the common watercourse between Sedlescombe and Winchelsea; and the other in the 37th year, relating to the lands between a place called Fodyr and this town.

PROPERTY, NAMES, &c.—The Battle Abbey Records give us feoffments from Godyng Bongylstherst of this town, on 5th April, 1425, to Henry Medehurst and William Tabbe, of a messuage in St. Thomas, adjoining on the east the messuage of Simon Flesher, formerly John Kokets; and on 5th April, 1428, from Medehurst and Tabbe, to John Godfrey and Joan his wife, which same John Godfrey, on 20th June, 1443, obtained a grant from Alicia Lyndrigge of Winchelsea, of a cottage adjoining his lands on the west: and as we have seen, was, in 1446, one of the feoffees from Wm. Morfote. In the same records, we find also a feoffment, on 22nd Oct., 1434, from John Hyll, clerk, and John Downe, to William Werthe and Isabella his wife, of a house and land adjoining on the south the rectory of St. Thomas. The Dering MSS. have, in 1430, among the abutments of land in the same parish, the heirs of William Batelesford, land formerly Richard Burgham's, the four Capellans of the Chantry of St. Nicholas, and the heirs of Robert Arnold: and a confirmation from Richard

[1] Dering MSS. [2] Dugd., p. 101.

Lundeneys to Nicholas de Bury and Dionesia his wife, of a tenement in the town.

EDWARD IV TO HENRY VIII.—From the commencement of the Wars of the Roses, Winchelsea affords very few materials for history. The sea was year by year retiring; the ships were unladen at the Camber or at Rye; and the town gradually fell to decay. Winchelsea, however, contributed its quota to the fleet called out on 26th May, 1475, to do their service. And in 21st Edward IV, (1481) the allowance of the town, towards three parts of one-fifteenth and a tenth,[1] amounted to £20 12s. 9¾d.

In 5th Edw. IV, (1465) we have the last of the commissions for embanking.[2] It related to the lands in Yham, in the parish of St. Leonards, and from Yham to the lands called Cregge, and the lands of John Fynche. Among the additional charters in the British Museum, No. 959, et seq., are several relating to the embanking of Huyteflet or Whyteflet marsh.

The marauding propensities of the townsmen remained uninjured by the gradual decay of their town.

On 31st Jan., 1483-4, (1 Rich. III) a commission[3] was issued to John Fysshe, mayor of Winchelsea, John Baseley, Richard Davey, and Robert Wood, on the petition of Luder Brames (master of a Hamburgh ship or "creyer") and of certain Hans merchants, to make inquest concerning and restitution of the said ship which had, on 20th Jan., 1 Rich. III, been seized and brought to the town of Winchelsea by certain servants of John Lord Clynton. And in the same year, there was a warrant[4] to Andrew Brown of Calais, to seize certain herrings furtively conveyed out of the ship Laureres of Calais, and sold by certain mariners of the said ship, in the river of Winchelsea.

[1] Dering MSS. [2] Dugd., p. 101.
[3] Rot. Pat., 1 Rich. III, mem. 19 d., No. 3 d.
[4] Harl. MSS., No. 433, p. 164 b.

In the 3rd Hen. VII, (1487) the town allowance[1] for half one-fifteenth and one-tenth, amounted only to £12 2s. 7d.

In 1491, (6th Hen. VII) the service of the ports' navy was required to transport horses to France; and in the same year the king fixed the allowance to be paid for the Cinque Ports' navy at £500: out of this sum Winchelsea had £80 allotted for furnishing ten sail of ships.[2] And even in 1496 the town had not wholly fallen in importance. It is one of the chief trading and sea ports, the mayors and bailiffs of which were to enter into an obligation[3] for the due observance of the treaty of friendship and intercourse concluded between Henry and Philip Archduke of Austria.

Very soon after this, the merchants must have left the place. In the return made to the writ of knighthood in 15th Hen. VII, (1498) it is stated that there were no persons, who had above £40 in goods:[4] and Rye[5] was the seat of the trade when Henry the VIII, in 1538 or 1539, built the castle of Camber. The dissolution of the religious houses completed the ruin of the town.

The only general document of any interest connected with the town at this period, is a list of the persons in Winchelsea, who contributed to the Benevolence, 36th Henry 8th,[6] (1544.) The list is preserved among the Carlton Ride MSS. It was a voluntary benevolence; such of the townsmen as wished

[1] Dering MSS.

[2] Rye supplied half the number of ships, and had £40. Boys' Sandwich, pp. 679-778.

[3] Rym. Fœd., vol. 5, pt. 3, p. 86. [4] Dering MSS.

[5] In 1513 the Cinque Ports furnished 57 ships and 1197 men, with provisions; and on account of that charge they refused to contribute to the general subsidy. Boys' Sandwich, p. 682. In 1533 very few ships were required, and care was to be taken that they did not come from ports infected by the plague. The ports furnished their full number in 1541 and 1562. Ib. pp. 684-5-9.

[6] It was, temp. Hen. VIII, that the costume of the Cinque Ports' mariners was laid down: "every person that goeth in the navy of the ports is to have a coat of white cotton with a red cross, and the arms of the ports underneath." Boys' Sandwich, p. 775.

to stand well with the crown made contribution: the names of the contributors were

	£	s.	d.		£	s.	d.
John Watts, mayor -	3	0	0	Richard Clerke - -		26	8
Richard Ferrat - -	3	0	0	John Prawle - -		26	8
George Lewesse - -	3	0	0	Thomas Collens - -		20	0
Thomas Hinkstead -	5	0	0	John Sharpe - -		20	0
John Lewesse - -		40	0	Dr. Chepman - -		16	0
Henry Smyth - -	6	13	4	Sir Thomas Edwardes -		8	0
John Smyth - -		20	0	Sir Thomas Nyx -		5	0
Robert Lucas - -		30	0	John Bell - - -		8	0
William Hoode -		40	0	Thomas Holloke -	3	16	8
Robert Holden - -		40	0	Goderd Heyman -	4	0	0
Richard Sergeant -		40	0	Nicholas Clerke - -		26	8
Edward Sargeant -		40	0	Thomas Babb - -		20	0
Thomas Hoke - -		26	8				

ELIZABETH.—The town had been entirely abandoned as a place of trade by the merchants, when Elizabeth ascended the throne, though it was still the residence of some persons of local importance. There smouldered, however, the embers of the ancient fire, and the inhabitants left no stone unturned to rekindle the flame: but all in vain. In 1570, they addressed themselves to the Council,[1] and they graphically set forth the then condition of the town, and propose a mode of relief, in a statement of the causes "why the town of Winchelsey is worthy to be advanced and raised up out of the present poor and most lamentable state it is in."

The statement sets out that in the memory of man it had been a town of great prosperity, of excellent traffic, and of most worthy service, in many ways to the realm. That its situation was most excellent, on a high rocky hill within half a mile of the main seas; that it was divided into squares, and the streets were large and broad, all straight as the same were laid with a line, and so cast that at the end of every street the town was to be seen through, and having yet remaining a great many costly vaults, arched and set forth with pillars of Caen stone, as meant to have houses over them fit for famous merchants; that there was in the narrow seas no place so fit to have a good haven made, as it was midway in a fair bay between Rye and Hastings, with rocks within half a mile, to make piers and jetties; that there were three fathoms at low water, without any sand, flat

[1] Domestic Documents in State Paper Office, 1570, No. 567.

bar, or other danger near; and that, with less than a hundred rods of cutting, through good firm marsh ground, the sea might be brought into a great fleet two fathoms deep, and so into the old channel where the tide ebbed and flowed: that such a haven would be of use to the fishermen of Hastings and Rye, and a safeguard for the navy and all voyagers on the narrow seas: and that such a place for defence was more necessary since the loss of Calais.

The appeal was made in vain. The only solace the inhabitants received, was a visit made to their town by the Queen,[1] in August, 1573; when Her Majesty "beholding the goodly situation, ancient buildings, grave bench of a mayor and twelve jurates in their scarlet gowns, and city-like deportment of the people (there being then several gentry,) as well as the projection of the place, she gave it, as she thought deservedly, the name of LITTLE LONDON." Members of the county families of Ashburnham, of Fane, of Stapley, of Weekes, of White, and of PECKE were residents; but, nevertheless, the good folks must have mustered all their forces for this display, to make this favorable impression on their sovereign; for Lambard, who published his Topographical Dictionary only two years afterwards, 1575, declares[2] that there were not then "above sixty households standing, and those, for the most part, poorly peopled: all which happened by reason of the sea having forsaken the town."

[1] This description is taken from Jeake. Mr. Nichols, in his Account of this Progress, (vol. 1, p. 334) makes no mention of the Queen's visit to Winchelsea. After leaving Mr. Guilford's, at Hempstead, the only entry is, "thence to Rye, where the Queen remained three days."

[2] Lambard, p. 429.

This favorable impression of the grave bench was turned to a good account, for, on 28th November, 29th Elizabeth, (1586) the queen granted the following estates to the mayor, jurats, and commonalty of Winchelsea, to hold as of her manor of East Greenwich, in free and common soccage, paying certain small free rents to the Receiver General for Sussex, half-yearly at Michaelmas and Lady-day, with powers of distress, &c.[1]

Property, the former owners of which are not named.	*Name of tenant at time of the grant.*
Messuage and premises in the Strand - -	Henry Pecke
Common passage, called Winchelsey Ferry -	Thomas Swallowe
Seven acres of land in the parish of St. Leonard next Winchelsea - - - - - -	Mayor and Jurats
Three acres of hanging wood in St. Leonard -	Mayor and Jurats
One acre, called Pettit Higham, in St. Leonard	Mayor and Jurats
Twelve acres arable, near Catsfield -	Ashburnham Pecke
And all those seven messuages or tenements formerly William Pope's, and given for life by one of the Queen's ancestors (they appertained to the office of Bailiff) - - - -	
Property, formerly part of the Dissolved Monastery or House of Black Friars, or Friars' Preachers.	
The King's green in Winchelsea, containing twelve acres - - - - - - -	
Four acres in Winchelsea - - - -	Mayor and Jurats
One acre in St. Leonard - - - -	Thomas Swallowe
A mill - - - - - - - -	The Mayor and Jurats
A windmill in Winchelsea, near the King's green	Ashburnham Pecke
A messuage and two gardens in the twenty-fourth quarter - - - - - - -	Ashburnham Pecke
Two acres near St. Giles' church - - -	John Pixle
Land in Winchelsea, in first quarter - -	Jacob Wace
House and apple orchard in ninth quarter -	Robert Gouldsmythe
Two messuages and two gardens in fourteenth quarter - - - - - - - -	Christopher Mockett and Richard Breadman

[1] Grant now among Corporation Records. The names of the tenants seem to indicate the principal inhabitants at the time, and include many good families.

Two acres in seventeenth quarter	Christopher Mockett
A garden in third quarter, and half an acre of land in fourth quarter	John Love
One rood in eighth quarter	Goddard White
A messuage, two gardens, and one acre in twenty-ninth quarter	Henry Wood
Orchard in twenty-seventh quarter	Thomas Neighbor
Messuage and garden in tenth quarter	Adam Moyle

Property, formerly parcel of the House of Friars Minors.

Half an acre near Monday's Market	John Asheburnham
Tenement, orchard, and garden in fourteenth quarter	Joseph Denison
Messuage, garden, orchard, and one acre in nineteenth quarter	Richard Whiblye
Two messuages, and two gardens in thirteenth quarter	John Asheburnham
Messuage, garden, and orchard in eighteenth quarter	George Rockley

Property lately part of the dissolved Hospital of St. John.

A messuage and ten acres of arable land, called the Hospital of St. John	Phillip Durrante

Property, lately parcel of the dissolved Priory of St. Bartholomew.

A toft and two acres of land in Winchelsea	Francis Bolton

Property, lately part of the dissolved Chantry, called Farncombe's Chantry.

A messuage and one rod in the Strand	Goddard White
A messuage and one acre in the Strand, called the Brewhouse	Robert Pearce
Half an acre of land, and two acres in St. Leonard, juxta Winchelsea	
A house, called the Storehouse, in the Strand	Thomas Fane
A messuage, and garden in the Strand	Thomas Egleston
Two messuages, and two gardens in the Strand	Thomas Vyncente
Two acres of land, and one acre of fresh marsh in the Strand	Thomas Swallow
A messuage, and two gardens in the Strand	Agnes Beesen

Property given for the perpetual sustentation of Two Lights and Six Lamps in the Church of St. Thomas the Apostle.

A messuage and garden in ninth quarter -	Thomas Swallowe
A messuage and garden in tenth quarter -	John Welles
A messuage and garden in tenth quarter -	Richard Parker
A messuage and garden in eighteenth quarter -	Hugo Wigg
A messuage and garden in seventh quarter -	John Love
A messuage and garden in seventh quarter -	Anthony Stapley, Knt.
A messuage and garden in seventh quarter -	Henry Pecke
A messuage and garden in fifteenth quarter -	Richard Parker
A messuage and garden in seventh quarter -	Matthew Harrenden
A messuage and garden in thirteenth quarter -	Thomas Tokeye
A messuage and garden in nineteenth quarter -	Richard Whiblye
A messuage and garden in eighth quarter -	Edmond Weekes
A messuage and garden in twenty-eighth quarter	Andrew Love
A messuage and garden in ninth quarter -	Robert Gouldsmythe
A messuage and garden in thirteenth quarter -	Nicholas Bottynge
Another messuage and garden in thirteenth quarter - - - - - - -	Goddard White
A garden in seventh quarter - - -	Richard Waterman
A garden in second quarter - - -	John Parle
Another garden in twentieth quarter - -	Thomas Swallow
A garden in twenty-ninth quarter - -	John Pearle
A garden in eighth quarter - - - - -	John Love
A garden - - - - - - -	Anthony Stapley
Another garden in eighth quarter - -	Philip Denne
A garden in twenty-first quarter - -	Thomas Egleston
An orchard in twenty-fourth quarter - -	Thomas Woodland
A garden at the Strand - - - - -	John Allen
A garden in ninth quarter - - -	John Durrante
A garden at the Strand - - - - -	Goddard White
Two acres of land in St. Leonard, juxta Winchelsea - - - - - - - -	John Pearle
A barn in tenth quarter - - - - -	Thomas Fane
A barn or stable in tenth quarter - -	John Whitfeilde
Another barn or stable in thirteenth quarter -	Dorothy Middleton, widow

Property given for the perpetual sustentation of a Lamp in the Parish Church of Icklesham.

A messuage and seven acres of arable land in Icklesham - - - - - - -	

W. J. Denne, del.ᵗ J. Basire, Lith.

THE FRIARS.

FROM THE WEST

Ten years afterwards, (1596) when five ships and a pinnance were offered by the Cinque Ports to the Queen, Winchelsea could not offer any part.

MODERN STATE.—Since the days of Elizabeth the sea has receded nearly another mile, and it is now a mile and a quarter from the town: which, however, has remained almost stationary. In 1705, only four freeholders, viz., James Briggs, Thomas Barnham, Benjamin Jackson, and Thomas Cooper voted at the great county contest: the principal inhabitants in 1710 may be found in the Chamberlain's rental of that year, referred to in our account of the Corporation: in 1719 Dr. Harris describes the town as without trade, under his own house there were two disused crypts; and in Sliford's Collections it is said, that in 1730 the streets were over-run with grass, though well paved. The exact state of the town in 1763 is accurately given in Capt. Stephen's map, which we have engraved, and to which we have added the St. Leonard's boundary, the principal highways, and the numbers of the quarters, wherever they can be clearly ascertained. We have also marked the spots, where crypts exist on land now without buildings: under many houses, particularly the New Inn, there are also crypts. They abound in the northern quarters of the town: here, therefore, the merchants resided, whilst the tradesmen occupied the centre of the town, near Monday's Market. In 1763, the chief proprietors were Capt. Pigram, who held the *Grey Friars'* estate, of which, and of the house, we shall speak presently; Mr. Nesbit, who owned *Bear Square*, (now called Barrack square, from its having been used for barracks during the last war) and the greater part of the next quarter, westward, (No. 8,) on which, next the town hall, stood a large mansion, reported to have once been the house of the Finches, and which was afterwards the residence of the Rev. Drake Hollingbery, and was pulled down about 1830; Mrs. Harcourt, who owned St. Leonard's Church field, White Horse field, Ferry marsh, Roundle field, and Friars' orchard;

the EARL OF EGREMONT, who owned Holyrood field, the Castle field, and Chesnut field; and Mr. Richard Wardroper, who owned Cook's green and the mansion-house in the ninth quarter, called *Paradise*, which is still standing, and is the residence of Thomas Dawes, Esq.

Mariteau House, in the twentieth quarter, was not then built, it was erected soon afterwards by Mr. Mariteau on the land called Truncheons. During the prevalence of that scourge, the small pox, it was converted into a hospital, for patients attacked with that frightful disease. The house was, in 1783, purchased by and became the residence of RICHARD DENNE, Esq., a member of the Kentish family, who bear for their arms,—*Quarterly:* first, *three leopard's heads, affrontee, couped at the neck, or.* second and third, *ar. three bars erm. in chief, as many fleurs de lis, or.* fourth, *ar. two flaunches sa., each charged with a leopard's face, or.* Crest, *on a chapeau vert, turned up erm. a demi peacock, wings expanded and elevated ppr.* The Dennes resided here for many years, but the property was ultimately sold by them; and in 1848, was bought by Mr. Legg, who now occupies this mansion.

Opposite to this house, and in the nineteenth quarter, are the ruins of a building formerly called ***Trojan's or Jews' Hall:*** a door-way and window alone remain; but whence it derived its name, or for what purposes it was used, we have neither an authentic nor traditional account.

The Court Hall or ***Water Bailiff's Prison*** is situated at the north-west corner of the eighth quarter, and shows remains of considerable antiquity: the niches and arched door-way are evidently older than the present building, which

would seem to have been re-built in the Tudor days, from the materials of the older building. Until the grant of Henry VII to the Guldeford's, it was in the king's hands, and a regular rent was paid to the crown.[1] It passed with the office of Bailiff from them through the Ashburnhams to the family of Curteis, to whom a rent is now paid by the Corporation.[2]

Statistics.—The population in 1801 was 627: in 1811 it was 652: in 1821 it had increased to 817: in 1831 it was 772: but in 1841 it had gone back to 687, with only 127 inhabited houses, and 24 uninhabited. The annual value of real property assessed to the property tax in 1815, was £2,230. The poor's rate in 1776 was £160 1s.: in 1785 it was

[1] In the accounts of the town, 1 Hen. IV, (1400) entries of payments of 6s. 8d. a year will be found. See Corporation History, post.

[2] See further as to the descent in our account of the manor of Higham.

£282 15s.: in 1803 it had risen to £722 8s.: in 1813 it reached £998: in 1821 it was £995 10s.: in 1833 it had been reduced to £715. Under the Poor Law Amendment Act the town forms part of the Rye union.

There are no charities, and no National or British school within the town.

BAILIFFS OF WINCHELSEA.[1]

6	John	Manassah de Winchelsea. Rot. Pat., m. 14.
51 to 3	Henry III } Edward I }	Matthew de Hastings.[2] Prynne's King John. Carlt. Ride MSS.
5	"	Bartholomew Godard during pleasure. Rot. Orig., Ro. 7.
10	"	Matthew de Horne and John le Grit, rendering fifty marks yearly. Ib. Ro. 8.
12	"	Matthew de Horne, rendering the same. Ib. Ro. 4.
21 to 23	"	Sampson Heved. Carlt. Ride MSS.
25 to 34	"	Thomas Alard. Ib. and MSS. in Chapt. Ho. West.
34 to 8	" } Edward II }	Henry Paulin. Carlt. Ride and Dering MSS.
8	"	Alard, son of John 'de Wynchelse, during pleasure. Rot. Orig., Ro. 7.
14	"	Robert Paulyn. By virtue of his office he seized lands and tenements of the value of £100 in the town of Winchelsea and marsh of Iham, which escheated to the King on the death of John, the illegitimate son of John de Rakle, and was charged with collusion with Walter, the illegitimate son of Geoffry de Rakle of Berghershe, to lay claim as heir. Rot. Parl., vol. 1, p. 373.
3	Edward III[3]	*Robert Alard and *Gervase Alard. They were summoned before Robert Clynton, Constable of Dover Castle, to account for the arrears of the dues. Cal. Rot. Orig., vol. 2, p. 40.

[1] Those marked * are also described as Bailiffs of Rye; until temp. Hen. VII the Bailiffs of Winchelsea were also Bailiffs of the King's manor of Iham.

[2] In 8th Edw. II, Thomas de Hastings, son and heir of William de Hastings, prayed that he might be exonerated from a distress, touching the accounts of his grandfather, Matthew de Hastings, if it should be found that he had fined for the same. Rot. Parl.

[3] Among the Carlt. Ride MSS. is an account (2 and 3 Edw. III) of Richard Bat and Stephen de Padiham of the Customs, of the Port of Winchelsea: the vessels that entered and sailed were principally small ships from the French ports, with cargoes of wine, fish, &c.

4	Edward III	*Richard de Grofherst. Ib. p. 43.
6	"	*Stephen de Padiham during pleasure. Ib. p. 69.
11	"	The same.[1] Carlt. Ride MSS.
15	"	*Paul Marchant of Rye and *John Glynde of Winchelsea. Cal. Rot. Orig., vol. 2, p. 144.
Same year and to 18th June, 17	"	*John Glynde.[2] Ib. p. 146, and Carlt. Ride MSS.
17 to 20	"	*Stephen de Padiham during pleasure. Cal. Rot. Orig., vol. 2, p. 158, and Carlt. Ride MSS.
23	"	*John Longe of Winchelsea. Cal. Rot. Orig., vol. 2, p. 200, and Cal. Inq., p. m., vol. 4, p. 446.
24	"	*Paul Marchaunt of Rye. Cal. Rot. Orig., vol. 2, p. 211. He died in office, and Adam Skipsey, rector of Pleyden, his executor, rendered the account. Carlt. Ride MSS.
25 to 30	"	*John de Longe[3] of Winchelsea. Ib., and Cal. Rot. Orig., vol. 2, p. 216.
30 to 32, and 36 to 40	"	*Vincent Finch. Carlt. Ride and Dering MSS.
42 to 46	"	Benedict Cely. Carlt. Ride MSS.
50	"	*William de Well. Rot. Pat. pt. 2, m. 29.
1	Richard II	Philip Alard. Batt. Abb. Rec.
13	"	Thomas Truerhyn. Bat. Abb. Rec.
7	Henry IV	Robert Fyschlake. Batt. Abb. Rec.
3 to 8	"	William Catton. Batt. Abb. Rec. and Rot. Parl.
9	"	William Pope, who had the office granted to him by act of parliament for life, to hold in the same manner as William Catton had done. Rot. Parl., vol. 374 a. And on 9th January, 20 Hen. VI, (1441) he had a grant of the messuages, lands, tenements, and rents which appertained to his office, and which had come into the King's hands by the dissolution of alien Priories.[4] They consisted of a house or tenement occupied by Cesse Beremakere in right of his wife; a house or tenement occupied by Alan Pikard, by permission of John Beremaker; a house or tenement on the Keye, which William Allard

[1] In the same MSS. (11 Edw. III) is an account of the expenses of Stephen de Padiham for fitting a new ship for the King's service, and leading her from Winchelsea to London; without any details.

[2] In 19 Edw. III, he was committed to the Fleet as a defaulter in this office. Lord Treasurer's Memoranda Roll, m. 7.

[3] In 1354, Thomas Lend was his Sub-bailiff, Rot. Parl., vol. 2, p. 263 a.

[4] Pat., 20 Hen. VI, pt. 1, m. 17.

occupied by permission of the said John; a house or tenement occupied by Floure Benet; a house or tenement occupied by Hugh Couper; a house or tenement occupied by Richard Lucas, Irishman; and a house or tenement occupied by John Mynsing, together of the value of £7 per annum.[1]

36	Henry VI	John Treberbyn, Esq., for life. Lord Treasurer's Memoranda in Carlt. Ride MSS., Michas. 20 Edw. IV, m. 16. On his death
	Edward IV	Simon Colyde. Ib.
14	"	Thomas Cowpyldyk. Batt. Abb. Rec.
	"	Thomas Markham. Pat., 1 Rich. III.
	Richard III	John Elrington, Knt., ob. on 14th June, 1414. There is a pardon for all arrears of accounts to Margaret widow of John Elrington, Knt., he being (inter alia) bailiff of the town after the death of Thomas Markham, which Margaret Elrington was one of the daughters and heirs of Thomas Echingham, a justice of sewers, &c. Pat. 1 Rich. III, m. 24, (1) No. 1.
2 (Aug. 2nd)	Richard III	Nicholas Rigby, one of the yeomen of the crown, to whom the office was granted; vice John Elrington, Knt., deceased. Pat. 2, Rich III, pt. 2, m. 3, No. 169. On the same day he was appointed Constable and Keeper of Bodiam Castle, forfeited by Thomas Lewknor, the rebel. Ib. pt. 3, m. 24, No. 10.
1	Henry VII	Henry Auger, Esq., who was also Constable of Tunbridge, and Receiver of Fowey, and to whom the patent of this Bailiwick was reserved out of the King's Act of Resumption. Rot. Parl., 1 Hen. VII.
2	"	Sir Richard Guldeford, Knt., by grant from the crown, in whose family it remained till the the alienation by Edward Guldeford.
15	Charles II	John Carryll; and his family until sale to
3	George III	Charles Earl of Egremont; and his family until the exchange made with
27	"	Sir William Ashburnham, Bart., Bishop of Chichester; and his family until alienation to
4	William IV	Herbert Barrett Curteis, who dying,
11	Victoria	Herbert Mascall Curteis, his only child, succeeded.

[1] These were afterwards granted by Elizabeth to the Corporation. See ante p. 108.

Fairs and Markets.—A part of the perquisites of the office of Bailiff, was, formerly, the receipts at the Fair and Market. The fair produced, in Henry VI time, two marks. The proceeds were afterwards granted to Syon Monastery;[1] and after the dissolution of that religious house, they came into the hands of the Corporation. In the Chamberlain's accounts in 1754, we find that he collected at the fair £1 2s. 5d., and paid for removing the polls, &c., 2s. 8d. The fair is held on 14th May; but has dwindled to a small pedlarly and gingerbread affair.

The market day is Saturday: it is almost disused.

Yarmouth Fishery.—The town held the same relative importance with respect to other towns in this fishery, as it did in the supply of ships for the navy: and whilst Rye and other smaller places sent only one Bailiff to Yarmouth to superintend the rights of the Portmen, Winchelsea, as a larger port generally sent two, until the time of Elizabeth, when by an arrangement, the Cinque Ports elected the bailiffs in turn. Nor were the men of Winchelsea behind their fellow-portmen in their attacks upon the Great Yarmouth men. In King John's days there was a complaint by the men of Yarmouth against the men of Winchelsea and Hastings.[2] In 25th Hen. III, the Earl of Hereford, Keeper of the Cinque Ports, was commanded to distrain the Barons of Winchelsea for one hundred marks, forfeited to the king for injuries done in the fair at Yarmouth.[3] And there is no doubt, that in the depredations, burning of ships, &c., done to the men of Yarmouth by those of the Cinque Ports, the Winchelsea men were active participators. These depredations were carried on to a frightful extent. Among the MSS. in the Chapter-house, Westminster, there is a return[4] of the mischief done in the

[1] Lord Treasurer's Memoranda, Carlt. Ride MSS., Michaelmas term, 20th Edw. IV. Rot. 16.

[2] Cal. Rot. Orig., vol. 1, p. 76.

[3] Ib. p. 113. [4] Norfolk Box, a, No. 27.

15th, 26th, 31st, and 34th, Edw. I; and it appears that in these four years 206 Yarmouth men were killed by the men of the Cinque Ports, in the Swiney, and 144 out of it; and that the total damage done to them amounted to £3,022 1s. 6d., besides £233 4s., of the particulars of which there was no account: that 280 Suffolk men had also been killed, and there had been £4,976 6s. 4d. damage done to them: and that 387 Norfolk men had been killed by the Cinque Port men, and the damage to the men of that county amounted to £9,004 1s. 8d. During the same years the Cinque Ports had lost, in the whole, 306 men; and of this number 99 were from Sussex, and 122 from Kent. In the same MSS.[1] is an inquisition taken at Great Yarmouth, in 31st Edward I, by which it is returned that in 22nd Edward I, Jacke Paulyn and Benedict Seman of Winchelsea, with the men of their ship, seized at Plymouth the ship of Robert Wych and William de Stokesly, belonging to Yarmouth, and killed the captain and crew: and by another inquisition[2] taken at Yarmouth in 26th Edward I, it is returned that the men in the ship of Henry Hathelard of Winchelsea took the ship of William de Colkyrk of Yarmouth with eighty tons of wine, of the value of £180. It was during one of the quarrels between the portsmen and the men of Yarmouth that a bailiff of the Cinque Ports was killed by one of Yarmouth, for which the latter was hanged. Edward I used his utmost exertions to compose these differences, and with the aid of his council he issued the ordinance for regulating the trade, given in Holloway's Rye (p. 79.)

We refer those, who wish for a full account of the mode of conducting the great fair and the fishery at Yarmouth, to Swinden's History of that town, whence[3] we extract the names, which have been preserved of the bailiffs sent by Winchelsea.

[1] Norfolk Box, a, No. 54. [2] Ib. No. 25. [3] Swinden, p. 181.

BAILIFFS FROM WINCHELSEA TO YARMOUTH.

13	Edward I	William Maynard,	Thomas Adland
17	"	William Pacy,	William Burgeys
18	"	The same,	John Azelard
19	"	Benedict Pomsade,	William Burgeys
20	"	John Allard,	James Fitz Thomas.
21	"	Thomas Fitz Godfrey,	William Pacy
22	"	John le Clerk,	The same
23	"	John Langinogh,	John de Wherst
24	"	Benedict Pomsade,	John Ineherst
27	"	William Pace,	John Fitz Robert Paulin
31	"	The same,	Matthew Horne
34	"	The same,	James Grike
1	Edward II	Benedict Karite,	John de Wherst
2	"	The same,	James Grike
3	"	William Pace,	Robert Achelard
4	"	The same,	Robert Batail
5	"	Robert Fyckeys,	The same
6	"	The same,	Benedict Karite
7	"	The same,	The same
11	"	James Grike	John Burgeys
12	"	The same,	John Scroyl
13	"	The same,	The same
14	"	The same,	Stephen de Padyham
15	"	The same,	The same
16	"	The same,	The same
17	"	John Long,	The same
18	"	The same,	The same
19	"	Benedict Alard,	Robert Fickeys
20	"	Peter Swysh,	Henry Long
1	Edward III	Stephen de Padyham,	John de Folk
16	"	Peter Fisch,	John Fitz Henry Finch
18	"	The same,	John Henes
19	"	John atte Glynde,	John Batte
20	"	Richard Battle,	James Horn
21	"	Benedict Cely,	John Panham
22	"	Richard Batte,	Thomas de Clavering
23	"	John Heved,	John Salerne
24	"	Thomas Clavering,	John Paulin
25	"	Theobald Alleyn,	John Sandych

26 Edward III	Theobald Alleyn,	Richard Brustelere
27 "	The same,	John Sandich
28 "	John Allard,	John Peytenyn
32 "	Vincent Fynch	
35 "	John Peytenyn	
37 "	The same, and for Rye	
43 "	Henry Sely, and for Rye	
44 "	Thomas Talyour, and for Rye	
45 "	Thomas Sybbe, and for Rye	
23 Richard II	Thomas Tayllor, and for Rye. (Dering MSS.)	
13 Charles II	Roper Bamford, for Hastings, Rye, and Winchelsea	

MANUFACTURES.—The town was not well situated for manufactures, even in the time when the Weald abounded in wood. It was separated from the wood and iron districts by the marshes on the north and west: nevertheless, attempts have been made to introduce manufactures.

SALT was a product, which could be readily manufactured; and we have already seen that salt pans existed in Old Winchelsea at the Conquest, and that others were in use in the ground between Modern Winchelsea and the ocean, in Henry VIth's time (1422 to 1461:) how much later they were worked we know not.

CHARCOAL.—This article was largely manufactured here, and the burning was carried so far that it became dangerous to the shipping; so that in 28th Edw. III there was a proclamation[1] for charring wood at a certain place called Le Sloghdam, within the port of Winchelsea and not elsewhere.

IRON.—There were a few furnaces for the manufacture of Iron; and Strype tells us[2] that the first trial to find out the mode of transmuting iron into copper, was made here, on account of the plenty of wood. The work was carried on by one Medley, who had engaged Sir Thomas Smith and others in the project. The manufacture was soon moved to Poole and elsewhere, but at last the project proved abortive.

[1] Pat., 28 Edw. III, pt. 1, a tergo. [2] Life of Sir Thomas Smith.

CAMBRICS, LAWNS, &c.—About the year 1761 a manufacture of Lawns and Cambrics was introduced into England, and a manufactory established here; but it being doubtful whether it was consistent with the laws then in existence to sell such articles in England, and the adventurers desiring to be incorporated, a public act was passed (4 Geo. III, c. 37) 1763, by which it was enacted that any person might make and sell cambrics and lawns in this country, and the promoters, viz.:—The Earl of Verney, the Rt. Hon. Charles Townshend, Sir Geo. Colebrooke, Bart., Sir Laurence Dundas, Bart., Arnold Nesbit, Esq., Peregrine Cust, Esq., Geo. Prescott, Esq., Barlow Trecothic, Esq., Gilbert Heathcote, Esq., Moses Franks, Esq., Master Edward Bridgen, Master Ben. Barnett, Master Wm. Grace, and Master Tho. Bidewell, were incorporated by the title of the "English Linen Company," with liberty to buy lands not exceeding the annual value of £500, and to raise a capital of £100,000: the ends of each piece were to be sealed by the Excise and the lengths marked upon them. For a few years the trade flourished:[1] it was superintended by two Frenchmen, Mr. Mariteau, who has left a record of his name in the house he built for his own residence; and Mr. Corbeaux, who subsequently returned to France, but came back to end his days here.

When the manufacture of Cambrics was abandoned an ITALIAN CRAPE manufactory was established by Mr. P. Novaille, through whose ingenuity the manufacture arrived at great perfection; but owing to local disadvantages it was, in 1810, removed to Norwich.

TANNING was the last manufacturing process carried on in the town; the tan yard, however, has been disused for the last quarter of a century.

[1]In the book of Chamberlain's accounts is an item, 1764,—Received of the agent of the manufactory for cutting brambles at the waste, 1d.

ECCLESIASTICAL FOUNDATIONS.

THE CHURCH OF ST. THOMAS, built between 1288 and 1292, is situated in one of the squares, between the thirteenth and fourteenth quarters, near the centre of the town. It was originally dedicated to St. Thomas à Becket, otherwise St. Thomas the Martyr, but is now called St. Thomas the Apostle. The choir and chancel, with some portions of the transepts, alone remain. It was originally a cruciform structure of large dimensions. The nave has long since disappeared, and no traces of the foundations, after a recent and very diligent search could be found, excepting those of the central great piers, and a small portion of the wall at the south-west angle, of what was the southern aisle. The general arrangements and dimensions of the choir, with the remains of the transept walls, enable us to form some approximation to the arrangement of the original structure, as will be seen in the ground plan below, furnished by Mr. Gough, the architect under whose direction the repairs of the chancel, undertaken entirely at the expense of Thomas Dawes, Esq., have been recently carried out. The building originally consisted of a nave and side aisles, north and south transepts, and a central tower, most probably surmounted by a tall shingled spire, like old Fairlight, to serve as a land mark to mariners.

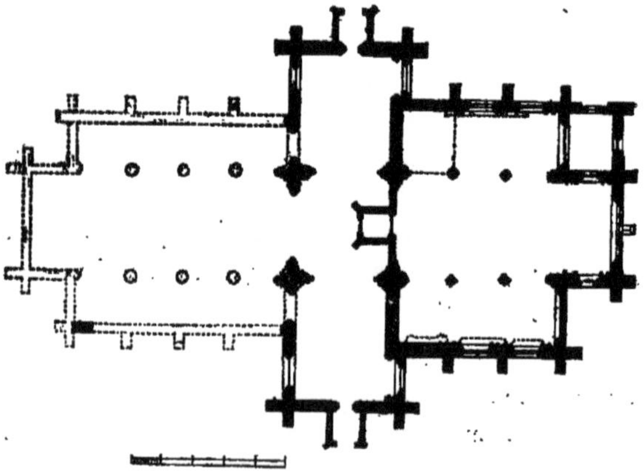

PLATE V

CHURCH OF ST THOMAS,

FROM NORTH WEST & SOUTH EAST.

The nave appears to have been of less importance than the choir. The side aisles were not so wide as those in the choir; and in all probability a single roof, like the roof of the adjoining church of Icklesham, spanned the nave and its side aisles.

The arches at the west end, which originally opened from the side aisles of the choir into the transepts, have been filled in, and a small porch of the later perpendicular period, has been added.

The choir is in length, from east to west, 56 feet; and in width, between the piers, 28 feet. The south aisle, formerly the chapel of St. Nicholas, and wherein was situated the Alard chantry, is 20 feet wide; and the north aisle, formerly the chapel of the Blessed Mary, in which was the Farncombe chantry, is 18ft. 6in. wide.

The choir is divided from the aisles by three lofty arches, supported on either side upon massive piers, consisting of fluted and banded shafts of Caen stone and Sussex marble. The distance from centre to centre of each pier is 18ft. 3in.

The chancel is 14 feet in depth by 28 feet in width. Until the present restoration the ancient Ecclesiastical fittings were entirely concealed by most unsightly old framing and pewing, put up to support what was once the dignity of the mayor and jurats of the place. On the removal of these obstructions the sedilia and piscina, much mutilated, were brought to view, consisting of four richly canopied and recessed compartments, surmounted with croketted gables and pinnacles. The easternmost forming the piscina, and the remaining three the sedilia. The piscina had also in the upper part a richly carved stone shelf as a credence table; the water-drain below, projects from a continuous string, which, together with the shortened shaft on the eastern side of the piscina, is supported upon foliated corbels. The entire lining of this compartment is richly diapered.

The sedilia are continuous: the three seats being of equal elevation; the piers of separation are composed of clustered shafts supported upon a projecting moulded string, terminating with foliated corbels; the central shafts are of Sussex marble; and the inside wall lining, as high as the springing line of the canopies, is diapered, but above that line it is filled in with plain ashlering. These have been entirely restored.

The remains of a small bracket, much knocked about and disfigured, were found attached to the wall westward of the sedilia. This bracket, in all probability, sustained the figure of St. Thomas, the patron saint of the church. Upon the removal of an accumulation of earth within the ruins of the ancient sacristy, the body of a mutilated stone figure was discovered: the head, arms, and feet were gone, the trunk alone remaining. The drapery of the figure is extremely graceful and delicate, and evinces a very high order of excellence in mediæval art. The bracket has been restored.

The windows on the north and south sides of the chancel had been bricked up and plastered over. Upon opening them out, the shafts and tracery were found in a very decayed state, but sufficiently distinct to exhibit a very peculiar and handsome tracery of foreign, rather than English character: quatre foils are worked within the square with perpendicular and transverse mullions rising thereout, thereby giving the form of the cross. These windows are within slightly recessed arcades, composed of slender shafts of Sussex marble upon a continuous string of the same material, supporting tracery heads and hood mouldings on either side: they correspond, generally, with the arrangement of the window arcades in the north and south aisles. The nearest approach to these windows is to be found in a window at Chartham, Kent, engraved in Rickman's Architecture, (p. 142) and in Bloxam's Principles of Architecture, (p. 225.)

Beneath the northern window, on the removal of his worship's pew, was found the doorway to the sacristy. Mutilation had completed its work on the corbel heads; but the jambs remained entire with the hinge hooks: hung upon these original hinge hooks a new door has been placed, and the sacristy has been restored.

On the following page we give a woodcut of the northern window, engraved by Mr. Childs, from a drawing made by Mr. A. D. Gough. This window has been restored exactly in its original form, and as much of the original stone as could be used has been preserved.

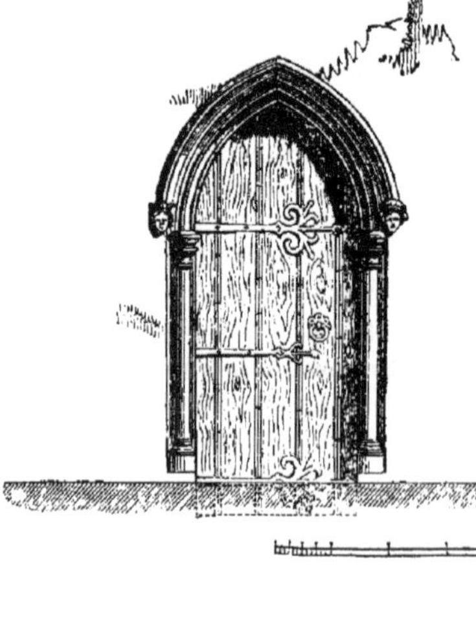

The eastern window of the chancel had been filled in with late perpendicular work, at variance with the general character of the church and chancel; it was probably altered temp. Hen. VI, when the last chantry was founded. This window was much decayed, and the restoration has been in strict accordance

CHUDS.

with the style and character of the original tracery as exhibited in the side windows. Its effect would be improved if filled up with stained glass.

The great eastern windows of the aisles are still in a delapidated and mutilated condition: the inner tracery of the window heads having entirely disappeared. The two easternmost windows on the north and south sides of the aisles are in better condition, requiring but little to restore them to their ancient beauty: the western-most side window in each aisle, however, is blank, and should be filled in with windows corresponding in character with the windows towards the east, which, in their tracery, are varied from those of the east end of the respective aisles, and also from the chancel.

Upon the removal of the chancel flooring, and about six inches below the then level of the modern flooring, were discovered a few of the original tiles, and being made distinct enough, by the junction of parts, to define the pattern clearly, new tiles have been made from Mr. Gough's drawings, by Messrs. Minton, and used in the restoration.

A dwarf stone screen with Sussex marble capping, has been introduced to enclose the altar, and the flooring is laid with encaustic tiles, ornamental and plain alternated, and laid diagonally, which intermediately form the same into compartments. There are ornamental marginal tiles and Sussex marble risers to the steps; the whole corresponding with the ancient tile and marble-work found in the church. In connection with the restoration of the church, a new stone pulpit is to be placed on the north side of the chancel steps, and an oak lectern on the south side,[1] and if funds permit, a new organ is to take the place of the present grinder.

The font is modern.

The north-western angle of the choir has been long parted off for a vestry, with rough brick and lath and plaster, which has cut off and mutilated a very fine monument, presently described. Some remains of the old screen-work of the chantries appear to have been roughly worked in for this filling up.

The transept walls form a very picturesque ruin, and are richly overgrown with ivy, as is much of the choir. Upon the removal of some ivy on the north aisle, a portion of the original parapet presented itself. It had formerly been

[1] Of the present internal fittings it may be observed, that the pews, like sheep pens of modern churchwarden construction, equally prevent the seating of such as would attend divine worship, and the due attention to the church services of those who do attend: and the pulpit, reading, and clerk's desks, one above the other in a central position, obstruct the entry to the chancel. The latter are in a transition state, being removed temporary on either side to admit of the completion of the works connected with the chancel. The old pewing, &c., is to be entirely re-placed by low open oak benches with carved ends. The perfect and complete restoration of the several monuments, with which the church is so richly endowed, should speedily follow, together with the restoration of the windows, nave, piers, arches, and roof timbers, which happily have been already relieved from lath and plaster. The entire removal of the unsightly excrescence, forming the present vestry and way up to the belfry, (a portion of the wall of which is barbarously built through the centre of a monument) should follow: the clock and bell turret should be rendered independent of so cumbersome an arrangement, and every thing else done, which may be requisite to sustain these venerable remains, externally, as a truly picturesque and interesting object, while the interior should exhibit a consistent and careful restoration, combined with a judicious regard to the requirements of a Protestant parish church.

open and richly carved. Projecting from each transept, north and south, are the foundations of entrance porches: these are unusual, and would appear to be of later introduction than the transepts, though not so late as the western porch; giving an appearance that the nave was first lost in the early French attacks, and that the transepts were abandoned, when the church was finally altered, about the time of Edward IV or Henry VII.

At the north-east angle of the sacristy is a fine massive flying buttress, built, it would seem, to meet a contemporaneous subsidence in the foundation of the original building, but adding much to the picturesque effect.

Beneath the chancel is a vaulted crypt; into it there were originally recesses for lights, which would have permitted its use for a penitential chapel.

Near the south-western side of the church yard stood, until 1790, a campanile or bell tower.

When it was removed, the foundations of the nave were also taken up, and the stones used for the repair of Rye harbour.

ALARD'S CHANTRY.—Neither the date of the foundation of this chantry nor the particulars of its endowments have reached us. The sedilia and piscina remain. They are on the same plan as those in the chancel, but of somewhat later date. They adjoin immediately upon the principal monument, and formed part of the same design. From them the foundation of the chantry may be assigned to the close of the reign of Edward I, or the commencement of his successor's. The chantry was called indifferently St. Nicholas' or Alard's. Among the Dering MSS. the four Capellans of the Chantry of St. Nicholas are named. In the Valor Ecclesiasticus it is called Allarde's Chantry. The patronage was in the Abbot and Convent of St. Martin at Battle: and among the seals found in the town, is one, which seems to have belonged to a priest of this chantry in the fifteenth century. The device is

the same as the seal of Dover, St. Martin dividing his cloak with the beggar, which connects the priest with the great house of that saint at Battle: the legend is,—IEHAN POUPART: PRESTRE.

In the Valor Ecclesiasticus (temp. Hen. VIII) we have this valuation of

> The chantry, called "Allarde's Chantry," in the chapel in Winchelsea; Richard Cresseweller, chaplain there, worth clear per annum, in glebe lands, houses, a water mill, and certain other lands, and returns with all profits and emoluments to the same chantry belonging, in the counties of Kent and Surrey, £13 6s. 8d.
>
> In the same work, among the payments of Battle Abbey, was an annual pension to William Culpeper, in respect of Allarde's chantry, of 66s. 8d.

And in 1553, we find that Oliver Stacie, incumbent of Winchelsea chantry, had a pension of £6 13s. 4d. per annum.[1]

GODFREY'S OR FARNCOMBE'S CHANTRY.—This chantry, which was originally called the Chantry of Saint Thomas, was

[1] Willis' Hist. of Abbeys, vol. 2, p. 240.

founded (temp. Hen. VI) in the chapel of the Blessed Mary, by John Godfrey,[1] who was member for this town in 1441 and 1448: for this purpose it was not necessary, by the custom of the town, for a freeman, giving land within the town, to have a royal license. The chantry was, however, richly endowed by his daughter, Maline (that is, Matilda) who married and had become the widow of Simon Farncombe. As her endowment included lands without the town, we find all the usual preliminaries. Her husband had, as we have seen, employed his vessels in the export of pilgrims to the shrine of St. James, and out of the wealth so accumulated, his widow made no unfit appropriation by adding to the endowments of her father's chantry. In 17 Edw. IV, (1477) an inquisition[2] ad quod dampnum, was held for her in respect of this chantry: it related to six messuages, a windmill, 175 acres of land, and 17s. 4d. rents, in the several parishes and places of St. Thomas and St. Giles' Winchelsea, Westham, Horsey, Mankesey, Haylesham, and Langloy; and after the return of the inquisition, the king, on 27th Nov., 1477, granted[3] her his license to found a perpetual chantry in the chapel of the Blessed Mary in the church of St. Thomas in Winchelsea; the prayers to be for the souls of the King and his dear consort the Queen Elizabeth, for the souls of the said Maline, and of Simon Farncombe her late husband, the souls of John Godfrey and Alice his wife, and of Simon Godfrey and Joan his wife, &c. And on 24th February, 1478, the queen consort granted her that she might give a messuage, called Haukham, and 180 acres of land, in Westham, for the perpetual maintenance of a chantry priest in this chantry,[4] and the king

[1] Battle Abbey Charters, p. 121. [2] Cal. Inq., vol. 4, p. 387.

[3] See Esch., 17 Edw. IV, pt. 2, m. 26. 18 Edw. IV, pt. 2, m. 20, and 21 Edw. IV, pt. 1, m. 15, and pt. 2, m. 5.

[4] Battle Abbey Records, p. 121. She had given a power of attorney to John Convers of Winchelsea, to receive seizin of the land, windmill, and two tenements in Winchelsea, and the other land in Westham, &c.

confirmed his former grant. In 1481 she still further endowed the chantry with tenements, called the Beerhouse and the Wharf, in Winchelsea. The patronage was in the Abbot and Convent of Battle.

In the Valor Ecclesiasticus is this valuation:

> The chantry, called "Godfrey's Chantry," in the church of St. Thomas in Winchelsea, Thomas Edwards, clerk, chaplain, worth clear per annum, with all profits and emoluments, £11 6s. 8d.

After the dissolution of this chantry, the tenements within Winchelsea were granted to the mayor, jurats, and commonalty: and the land called "the Godfrey's," situated at Haukham, in the parish of Westham, became the property of the Sackvilles, but a large portion has been lost by the accumulation of beach.[1]

Monuments.—In the aisles of the choir are five fine monuments: three are canopied tombs of cross-legged secular warriors: one of a young man, who had not been knighted, usually, though erroneously, called a priest: and the fifth of a lady in the dress of Edward the Third's time, often mistaken for a nun. The three warriors are in mail armour, and their legs are crossed in token that they had assumed the cross and taken a vow to march to the defence of the christian faith in Palestine. The figures resemble those in the Temple church, London, and like them have been erroneously supposed to be monuments of the Knights' Templars. The Templars were always buried in the habit of their order, and are represented in it on their tombs.[2] This habit was a long white mantle with a red cross over the left breast; it had a short cape and hood behind, and fell down to the feet, unconfined by any girdle.

Two of these tombs are in the southern aisle. The most easternly, of which we give an engraving, has been ascribed by Mr. Blore and his editor, Dr. Bliss, with every appearance

[1] Burrell MSS. Addl. MSS., 5697. [2] Addison's Hist. of the Templars.

Drawn by Edw[d] Blore.

Engraved by H Le Keux

MONUMENT OF GERVASE ALARD, ADMIRAL OF THE CINQUE PORTS.

IN THE CHURCH AT WINCHELSEA.

Published July [illegible] by Harding, Triphook & Lepard, Finsbury Square London.

of certainty to GERVASE ALARD, who is declared by Leland to be buried in Winchelsea. As we have seen,[1] he was admiral of the Western fleet, 31 and 34 Edw. I; he was living at the time the church was built; and a memorial of his own person was, doubtless, added, as was the custom at that time with reference to benefactors to a church. In describing this monument, Mr. Blore[2] says, that "it is composed entirely of stone, wrought with extraordinary nicety; but now (1826) so thickly plastered over with repeated coats of white-wash, as nearly to have obliterated some of the minuter ornaments. The effigy is of stone, lying with its face somewhat inclined towards the church: it is cross-legged and armed, according to the style of figures of the same age, with the hands elevated, enclosing a heart, and having a lion at the feet. That it was originally painted is very clear, although the colours are now so nearly effaced as to render the decorations on the surcoat unintelligible. It is without a shield, and has the mutilated remains of two large angels supporting the double cushion on which the head reposes. The painted pattern on the cushions remains in some parts tolerably perfect; that of the upper cushion consisting of a blue ground, on which are drawn dark lines, forming lozenges, enclosing quatre-foils; and on the lower are the same with the exception of the quatre-foils, instead of which small roses are inserted at the intersection of the lines. The sword belt has been decorated with painted ornaments, now nearly effaced, if we except two dark lines, running parallel to the sides. The knee-cap, which terminates in a fringe, and is decorated with a row of rich raised escallops surrounding the knee, has the centre of each escallop enriched with a lozenge in colour, with a semicircle inscribed on every face." The whole is surmounted by a recessed canopy, and filled up with diapered work. The tomb stands upon a raised plinth, and is flanked by canted

[1] See ante, p. 60. [2] Blore's Monumental Remains.

ends with projecting buttresses and narrow arched openings between them, surmounted with crocketted gables and pinnacles. The front of the tomb is filled in with small niches, the arched heads of which are filled in with tracery, and have crocketted gablets and finials. The arched canopy of the tomb springs from slender clustered shafts with foliated capitals. The arch is cinque foil with feathered tracery, and its spandrils are richly ornamented with foliage: the main gablet of the canopy springs from sovereign heads, beautifully carved, the expression of the Queen being most dolorous. Traces of coloured embellishment are discernible in parts throughout the monument: a wreathed band or pennant, twisted in a spiral form round the clustered columns, is clearly defined.[1]

The western monument differs in some particulars from the preceding. The figure is in stone, and the feet rest upon a lion; the figure is encased in mail armour, but the arms, which are folded on the breast as if in prayer, do not enclose a heart; and there is a shield bearing arms. It is evidently of somewhat later date, is less elaborate, and of somewhat inferior execution to the monument last described. The arms, *A lion rampant between escallop shells*, were worn by OXENBRIDGE, of Brede; but they married an heiress of the Alards, and Leland says, assumed their arms. From the arms, the tomb has been usually ascribed to one of the Oxenbridges. We are, however, more inclined to the belief that it is the tomb of Stephen Alard, who was

[1] Mr. Gough suggests that this monument may be the work of Johannes Lemovicencis, who, in 1276, came over to this country to construct the tomb of the Bishop of Rochester, and afterwards of Aymer de Valence, Earl of Pembroke.

admiral of the Cinque Ports' and of the Western fleet in the time of Edward II (1324.) The date of the monument is about 1340, and it was not till 1393 that we find an Oxenbridge mentioned as a person of importance in the district. The tomb stands upon a raised moulded plinth within buttresses, which originally terminated in crocketted pinnacles, and the intermediate compartments terminated with ogré gablets, crockets, and finials, which are now entirely lost. The front of the tomb is divided into five niches with semi-hexagonal gabled and crocketted canopies. From richly carved heads within the buttresses springs a cinque foil arched head like that of Gervase Alard; but the inside lining of the canopied recess is plain and not diapered. The monument has been decorated with gilding and colour: azure and gules being most conspicuous.

On the three tombs in the northern aisle the effigies are all of Sussex marble, polished and not coloured: they lie within sepulchred canopies, with ogre feathered tracery heads. The end compartments of support to each agree in general with the western-most monument in the south aisle, but are smaller and inferior in design and execution. The tombs of the two male figures are alike; but in that of the lady, there is some slight variation of detail. They have all been decorated with colour.

The figure of the western-most monument is that of a cross-legged warrior in mail armour, the head resting upon cushions; the surcoat is clearly marked and would appear to represent leather: it is open in front and exhibits the left thigh, which has an oval knee-cap over the mail: the left leg crosses the right; and both rest on a lion. A strap over the shoulder supports a shield, without any armorial bearings. The right hand grasps the hilt of a sword, upon the knob of which is the cross and sacred monogram I.H.C. The canopy has been most copiously treated with white-wash, but the successive efforts for ages of the local Goths, have been unable to conceal the bold relief of the leaves and flowers.

The middle monument is that of the lady. The head dress is close, confining the hair, and, passing over the chin, produces a nun-like appearance; but the dress is open at the neck and bounded by a narrow fillet. The left hand lies on the breast and seems to have held a crucifix: the right grasps a portion of the dress, which falls from the hand in graceful folds. A short mantle presents itself over the shoulders. The feet rested on a hound.

The eastern-most monument is that of a young man dressed in a long robe in flutes, with tight armlets, confined at the wrist with small buttons. The hair lies in flat curls upon the forehead, and from behind is turned in curls over the ears. The head is supported upon cushions, and the hands are elevated over the breast, and closed as if in prayer. The feet rested upon some animal. The shoes were confined by a strap and buckle.

By the position, following each other from west to east, and from the character of the three tombs, which seem to be of the same age and date, we are induced to believe that they represent a warrior, his wife, and a son, possibly an only son, who had died before he had borne arms. They are of the time of Edward III; and the best conjecture would ascribe all three to the Alards, and perhaps to Nicholas Alard, whose daughter, Parnel, married (temp. Edw. III) Henry Herbert, alias Finch.

Brasses.—In the choir is a slab, formerly inlaid with brass, which has long disappeared. The stone has the indent of a fleuried cross: the following marginal inscription remains, each letter being indented separately.

Reynaud Alard, Qi Morust le xv d'April l'an m.cccliiii, gist icy. Dieu de s alme eit merci. Qi pur sa ame priera X jours de pardon avera.

The slab was removed within the last half century from the Alard chantry. Beneath it were found the bones and a glass bottle.

In the choir is also the brass of an Ecclesiastic, 2ft. 4in. in length, in the attitude of prayer. The inscription-plate at the foot is missing, as are also the shields on either side of the head.

INSCRIPTIONS.—On a grave stone in the choir:

H: S: E: Willielmus Willes, A.M., Rector hujus Ecclesiæ; qui obiit 12°. die Decembris, anno, 1751.

On another grave stone in the choir:

Here lyeth ye body of Margeret Iorden, late wife of Ieremy Iorden of Winchelsea, who had Isve by him 3 daughters, Margeret, Alse, and Martha. Shee departed this life the 2d of Aprill, 1636; ætatis suæ, 63.

Tis not (deare sainct) a stone can deck thy hearse,
Or can thy worth lodge in a narrow verse.
No, (pious matron) this engraven breath
Is not to speake thy life, but weepe thy death;
And is here laid by the ingenious trust
Of a sad husband, in honor to thy dust.

On a stone adjoining:

Sara Iorden, eldest daughter to William Iorden, and Ann his wife, of Edimvre in Svssex; who deceased ye 18 of Febry., 1633; aged 7.

On the east wall of the south aisle:

Memoriæ sacrum. Obdormit hic Margareta, filia Gvilielmi Lambard de Westcomb in comitv Cantii Armigeri et Cancellariæ; magistri viri pietate et prudentia spectatissimi; uxor autem Thomæ Godfreii, Generosi, ot hvivs villæ Ivrate; cvi Lambardvm et Thomam filios peperit; obiit die 29° Ivnii, anno Sal', 1611. Cvm Christo æternvm victvra. Conjvgi charissimæ Maritus moostissimvs cvm lachrymis posuit.

To the memory of Edwin Beresford Dawes, eldest son of Daniel Butler Dawes, Esqre. of this place; born 18th April, 1808; died 15th February, 1835. And of Amelia, daughter of the said D. B. Dawes, Esqre.; born 24th September, 1816; died 16th June, 1836. Their mortal remains are deposited in the family vault beneath this church.

On the south wall:

In the vault beneath this marble are deposited the remains of John Stewart, Esqre., late commander of the Mount Stuart, Indiaman; fourth son of Charles Stewart, Esqre. of Ard Sheal in Argyleshire, North Britain. As a mark of their love and a tribute due to his great worth, his mother, brother, and sisters, have caused this monument to be erected. He died October the 3rd, 1780; aged 40 years.

Beneath this tablet are deposited the remains of Sophia Dyne, one of the daughters of Wm. Dyne, Esqre., and Effield Dyne, of Milton, near Sittinbourn, in the county of Kent. She died the 24th Decr., 1809; aged 38 years.

On the south-west wall:

Sacred to the memory of Drake Hollingbery, clerk, M.A., late rector of this parish, and for upwards of forty years Chancellor of the Diocese of Chichester. He died December 31st, 1821; in the eightieth year of his age.

Sacred to the memory of Elizabeth, widow of the Revd. D. Hollingbery. She died August 28th, 1826; in the seventy-first year of her age.

In the family vault, near this place, are deposited the remains of Ann Hollingbery; who died Nov. 21st, 1843; aged 62. John Hollingbery, her only brother; who departed this life 21st March, 1844; aged 63; the remaining children of Drake and Elizabeth Hollingbery.

In memory of Richard Denne, Esqre., late of this town; who died on the 25th of January, 1819; aged 68 years; and whose mortal remains are deposited in a vault in this place. Also of Mary, widow of the above-named Richard Denne, Esqre. She died on the 15th July, 1827; in the 66th year of her age.

To the memory of Richard Greenland Denne, late of the Inner Temple, London, Barrister, youngest son of the late Richard Denne, Esqre., and Mary his wife; he died on the 5th Decr., 1839; aged 44. His remains are deposited in the family vault in this church. Also to the memory of Mary Jane, wife of Robert William Newman, of Mamhead, in the county of Devon, Esqre., and youngest daughter of the said Richd. and Mary Denne. She died on the 28th July, 1834; aged 42; leaving 4 sons and 5 daughters surviving her. Also of the above-named Robert William Newman, (late Sir R. W. Newman, Bart.) formerly representative for Bletchingly, and subsequently in two successive parliaments for the city of Exeter. He died on the 24th Janry., 1848; aged 72.

To the memory of three sons of Nathaniel Dawes, Gent., late of this town, and Elizabeth his wife: namely, of Captn. Nathaniel Dawes; who died at the seige of Bangalore, in the East Indies, on the 24th of March, 1791; aged 40 years; of Ensign James Dawes; who fell at Penin-bar-cum, in the battle between Hyder Ally and Coll. Baillie, on the 10th of September, 1780; aged 23 years; and of Lieutt. Richard Dawes; who was mortally wounded in the engagement betwixt the English and French fleets on the memorable 1st of June, 1794, and died on the 5th; aged 34 years; this marble as a tribute of sincere affection is inscribed. Also to the memory of Walter Dawes, another son of Nathaniel and Elizabeth Dawes; who died at Macassar, in the autumn of 1804; aged 40 years.

Sacred to the memory of Jane, the wife of Edwin Dawes; who died the 17th May, 1820; aged 83 years; and whose remains are deposited in a vault in the front of this church. In the same vault are deposited the remains of George Dawes; who died on the 17th November, 1820; aged 59 years. Also, in the same vault, are deposited the remains of the above-named Edwin Dawes; who died on the 30th of Septr., 1824; aged 75 years.

Sacred to the memory of Richard Maliphant, Esqre., late of this place; who departed this life October 8th, 1823; ætat. 68.

To the memory of Mrs. Baldwin, wife of Captain Baldwin, of the King's Own Infantry, and daughter of General Prescott, Governor and Commander in Chief in British North America; who died 22nd June, 1798; in the 24th year of her age; to the memory also of their Infant Son; this monument is erected as a mark of grateful affection by her husband, who, in all situations in life, must deplore their loss.

Tablets outside the church:

In a vault beneath this marble are deposited the remains of Richard Stileman, Gent., late of this town; who died the 8th of April, 1795; in the 56th year of his age. And of Mrs. Katharine Stileman, wife of the said Richard Stileman; who died the 17th January, 1795; in the 56th year of her age. In the same vault are deposited the remains of Robert Stileman, Gent.; who died 5th October, 1802; aged 56 years; and Mary, relict of the above-named Robert Stileman; who died 2nd January, 1830; in the 88th year of her age.

Sacred to the memory of Richard Stileman, Esqre., late of the Friars; who died the 10th of October, 1844; aged 57 years. Also of Sarah Curteis, his wife; who died the 29th of September, 1844; aged 50 years.

In a vault under this marble are deposited the remains of Jane, wife of D. Hollingbery, clerk; who died Jany. ye 26th, 1776; aged 27 years.

In a vault beneath this tablet are deposited the remains of Eliza Frances, wife of Thomas Richards, clerk; who died the 29th June, 1819; aged 39 years. Sacred also to the memory of the Revd. Thomas Richards, clerk, B.A., of St. John's Coll., Cam., Vicar of Icklesham; who departed this life Decr. 0th, 1843; aged 53 years. His remains lie beneath the communion table in Icklesham church. This stone is erected as a filial duty by the Revd. T. W. Richards, M.A., Sid. Coll. Cam., and the Revd. J. Richards, M.A., University Coll. Durh., only surviving children of the above Eliza Frances Richards.

In a vault beneath this stone are deposited the remains of Charles Terry, late Jurat of this corporation; who died the 17th of January, 1818; aged 70 years. Also Mary, wife of the above Charles Terry; who died the 1st of May, 1818; aged 60 years.

In a vault under this stone are deposited the remains of Rachel, wife of Richd. Ade; she departed this life Febr. 2d, 1787; aged 72 years. And also of Richard Ade; he departed this life Feb. 15th, 1802; aged 81 years.

The Living of St. Thomas is a rectory in the Deanery of Hastings, and within the Archdeaconry of Lewes and Diocese of Chichester. In Pope Nicholas' Taxation (1291) it stands:

Eccl'ia de Thomae de Winchelsee, £10 13s. 4d.
p't bre de xxxvs. vijd. Rector.

In the Valor Ecclesiasticus (temp. Hen. VIII) the value is thus given:

In the church of St. Thomas in Winchelsee, Edmund Atkynson, clerk, rector, there worth clear per annum, with all profits and emoluments, beyond 18d. paid annually to the bishop, "pro sinodal." and 2s. 2d. annually "pro procuracione," and 10s. to the archdeacon for the same, £6 13s. 4d.

In the King's books it is valued at the clear yearly sum of £28.

In the 2 Henry IV, (1400) there was a grant confirmed by Henry VI, (1426) to the Rector of St. Thomas, of a tenth of the fishery there, called Christ's share.[1] An award for the commutation of the tithes was made on 7th March, 1842 and the apportionment was confirmed in the same year. The annual sum, for which the tithes were commuted, was £235 9s. 3d.: and the estimated quantity of titheable land, included in the apportionment, was 720a. 3r. 9p., which was cultivated thus: 112a. 1r. 22p. arable; 477a. 3r. 26p. meadow or pasture; 16a. 3r. 20p. woodland; 108a. 2r. 1p. sandbanks, roads, or waste lands; and 5a. 0r. 20p. as gardens, exclusive of gardens[2] occupied with dwelling houses: the gardens so attached and occupied are exempt from payment of tithes in kind, by reason of a payment calculated on a proportion in the pound on the value.[3] This proportion is 2s. in the pound on the actual value.

The parsonage house has fallen to ruin. On 10th August, 1349,[4] a commission was directed to John Longe, then the King's Bailiff of Winchelsea, to enquire the value of a house seized into the king's hands, in which John Glynde, late rector of St. Thomas' church, died; and in return to the writ, the Jurors said that the messuage was worth 5s. per

[1] Pat., 2 H. IV, pt. 3, m. 31; and 4 H. VI, pt. 2, m. 18.

[2] In 1837 there were 10 acres of hops. Parl. Return.

[3] Apportionment in office of Tithe Commissioners. The rental in the poor rate for the whole parish in 1849 was £2,286 15s.; and the rate at 5s. in the pound for the year ending 25th March, 1850, (see ante, p. 114) amounted to £571 13s. 9s.

[4] Inq., 23 Edw. III, pt. 2, (1 nrs.) No. 173.

annum, and not more; that it contained in length 80 feet, and in width 40 feet; that it was formerly held of the king by the rent of 4d. per annum; and that it came into the king's hands by the death, without heirs, of Matilda, the daughter of Jacob Licotyn. The house was situated on the eastern side of the church yard, and was in the same year and on the return of the inquisition, granted by the king[1] to John de Scarle, then rector of St. Thomas, for the inhabitation of himself and his successors, rectors of the said church.

The patronage of the church was in the Abbot of Fischamp until the town was taken into the king's hands by Henry III: who took also the patronage of the churches. The Crown continued to present[2] until the grant by Henry VII to the Guldefords. From that time the patronage followed the same descent as the manor of Higham, until sold by the Ashburnhams, in 1834, to James Eldridge West, Esq.

Rectors of St. Thomas.

			PATRON.
1 Edw. I	-	- — Warner. See ante, p. 15.	The Crown
23 Edw. III (1349)		John de Glynde late rector. Cal. Inq., p. m., vol. 4, p. 446 -	Same
	..	John de Scarle. See above -	Same
INSTITUTIONS.[3]			
1405.	April 16.	William Tyrell - -	Same
1412.	June.	John Wade - -	Same
1438.	Oct. 8.	Walter Peytewyn - -	Same
1478.		Richard Mayew,[4] (Story's Visitation;) resigned -	
1482.	Dec. 12.	David Parsons - -	Same

[1] Cal. Rot. Orig., vol. 2, p. 206.

[2] In the confirmation, 1 Edward IV, (1461) of the Rape of Hastings, to William Lord Hastings, among other things granted, are the advowson and patronage of the churches of St. Clement and All Saints, Hastings, and of the churches of St. George of Brede, and of the Saints, Thomas the Martyr, Giles, and Leonard, at and within the town of Winchelsey. MS. belonging to the Earl of Chichester, ex. inf., John Phillips, Esq. The Crown, however, presented in 1482.

[3] From the Bishop's Registers, ex. inf., J. B. Freeland, Esq.

[4] He is called Thomas Mayhew in Batt. Abb. Rec., p. 120.

1500.	Aug. 18.	John Haddenham - -	The Crown
		Robert Wode, died - -	
1527.	June 15.	Richard Darell, resigned -	Sir Edw. Guldeford
1529.	Feb. 18.	Edmund Atkynson -	Same
		Henry Strensham, resigned -	
1543.	Oct. 5.	Thomas Chapman - -	Sir John Gylford
		Peter Danyell - -	
1555.	Oct. 24.	Robert Jordan, on deposition of Peter Danyell - -	The Bishop (jure devoluto)
		Peter Danyell was restored by Bishop Barlow,[1] (died) -	
1565.	Dec. 2.	Richard Roberts - -	Thos. Guldeford, Esq.
1587.	March 29.	Robert Poole - -	The Crown (by lapse)
1612, to 4th July 1620.		Robert Thomson[2] - -	
1640.		Martin Fist - -	
1671-2.	Nov. 19.	Richard Acton - -	The Crown
1686.		Edward Matthews; ind. 7th June[3]	
1690.	Dec. 16.	John Harris,[4] A.M., afterw. D.D.	The Crown
1707.	Feb. 27.	John Prosser, curate 1700, rector on resignation of John Harris; bu. 30th April, 1722 -	Thos. Muchell
1723,	Aug. 24.	William Willes, A.M., ob. 12th, bu. 20th Dec., 1751 -	Trustee for the Carylls[5]
1752.	June 5.	Richard Tireman, A.M. -	Thomas Paine
1767.	Oct. 21.	Drake Hollingbery, A.M. He was curate in 1764, succeeding the Rev. John Rudd; ob. 31st Dec., 1821	Earl of Egremont
1822.	Jan. 14.	John William Dugdell, A.M., exchanged for Kington-Magna Dorset, with - -	Sir W. Ashburnham and his mortgagees
1829.	Nov. 19.	Hans Sanders Mortimer, A.M.	The same
1831.	Oct. 20.	James John West, A.B. He was curate in 1829 - -	The same

[1] In 1563 there was no rector or curate resident. See certificate of Bishop Wm. Barlow. Harl. MSS., No. 594, 109.

[2] Harl. MSS., No. 703. [3] Parochial Register.

[4] The Historian of Kent and Secretary of Royal Society. In the Parish Register is this entry: "Sept. 7, 1690, John Harris, clerk, vicar of Icklesham, entered on the cure of this parish by virtue of the especiall order and licence of the Rt. Rd. Father in God Symon of Chichester, and of a sequestation from the Chancellor Dr. Briggs, bearing date Sept. 6, 1690: and February the 15th following (having institution from the said Bishop) read his articles: and having induction the day before, given him by Mr. Brian of Gestling."

[5] The Carylls were Catholics and could not present.

The earliest register commences only in 1655; and until 1690, that is only a compilation made by Dr. Harris.

THE CHURCH OF ST. GILES was situated at the western side of the town, between the twentieth and twenty-first quarters. It consisted of a nave, chancel, one aisle, and a small tower, with one bell.[1] The walls were standing in Lambard's time, 1570, but it was described by Thomas Godfrey in 1608-9 as ruinous. The walls have since been removed. The foundations may, however, be traced in dry summer weather. In the winter of 1399-1400, a large tree, which contained no less than 632 feet of timber, (probably a wych elm) was cut down in the church yard, and converted into shields.[2]

The original church was built at the same time as the foundation of the new town, to accommodate the inhabitants of a small portion, the north-western side of this town. It suffered great damage during the French attack in 1359, when the parsonage house seems to have perished: for not only is there a patent[3] for enlarging the church yard, which had been rendered too small in consequence of the burial of those, who had been slain in the conflict, but there was a license in the same year[4] to Robert de Brembre, clerk, to assign a messuage near the church of St. Giles, to Robert the parson of the same church, for a habitation for him and his successors for ever. This residence was also allowed to go to decay, and the site of the parsonage and church yard was a pasture field until 1849, when the present rector commenced rebuilding a parsonage house for the two parishes of St. Thomas and St. Giles, on a part of St. Giles' church yard.

In Pope Nicholas'. Taxation, 1291, the church of St. Giles is rated at £6 13s. 4d. In the Valor Ecclesiasticus, 8th April, 35 Henry VIII,

The rectory was worth, clear of all reprisals, per annum, £1 6s. 8d.

[1] Corporation Accounts 1388. Dering MSS., post.
[2] Corporation Accounts 1399-1400. Ib.
[3] Rot. Pat., 33 Edw. III, m. 4.
[4] Rot. Pat., 33 Edw. III, pt. 1, m. 4, and Cal. Rot. Orig., p. 255.

No name of any rector is given.

The patronage has followed the same descent as that of St. Thomas; and since the year 1500, when the last institution of a separate rector of St. Giles took place, the two rectories have been held together, though not united, and though no formal presentation to St. Giles has been made. We have the names of three rectors preserved.

Rectors of St. Giles.

1483.		Robert Seggeforth. Dering MSS.
		William Wightman. Bishop's Registers.
1500.	July 25.	Lawrence Pike, on resignation of W. Wightman. Ib.

RELIGIOUS HOUSES.

The Gray Friars.—The house of the Friars Minors, which had been founded in Old Winchelsea soon after the establishment of the order in England in 1224, was moved to the hill on which the new town was about to be built, and one of the best sites was selected for the new building.[1] It was not enumerated in the quarters, but was on the east side of the town, bounded on the south by the twenty-seventh quarter, on the west by the twenty-third, and on the north by the seventeenth quarter. That the order was at once re-established here, is clear, for we have seen, in the assignment of places in the new town, 16-20 Edw. III, an allotment in the second quarter to Andrew of the Monastery: and about 1290 a dispute having arisen between the Convent of Westminster and the Friars Minors, about the restoration of William Pershore, one of their order, the Pope directed the Convent to pay 100 marks for costs, which were afterwards commuted to 60 marks, and were paid for the help of two poor houses of these

[1] In Sliford's Collections Lansd. MSS., No. 906, p. 69, his house is said to have been founded by William de Buckenham, (temp. Edw. II) and that King Edward III confirmed the possessions. This must be an error.

friars, Winchelsea and Lichfield.[1] Peckham, then archbishop, had been a member of their order, and would naturally be desirous of favoring the brothers.

By degrees they received other benefactions; and their house and chapel dedicated to the Virgin Mary, were large and handsome.

The choir of the chapel is still standing, and with its apse and its lofty arch, of a span of 26 feet, forms a most picturesque ruin.

[1] Widmore's Wesminster, p. 79. The house at Lichfield was founded about 1229. Shaw's Staffordshire, p. 320.

The lithograph view, from a drawing made by Buck in 1737, shows the position of the cloisters and cells, which have since been removed.

Of the piety or learning of the brethren, little record remains. The only trace we have, is, that one brother, Thomas of Wynchelsey, D.D., was a large contributor to the library founded by the renowned Whittington in 1429, in the house of the Gray Friars in London, and a generous benefactor to their new church;[1] in which he was buried in February, 1436. John de Winchelsey, canon of Sarum, was a noviciate of the Gray Friars.[2] The benefactors to the Winchelsea house included the most eminent of the merchants and land owners of the town. In 1413, the Convent of the Friars Minors granted prayers and masses to their special benefactors, Vincent Finch and Isabella his wife:[3] by his will, dated 1st Dec., 1432, Sir Thomas Sackville, knt., bequeathed to these brothers Minors 10s.:[4] and this house is mentioned as the third house in the custody of London in the old catalogue of the Franciscan order.[5]

The house fell with the other houses of this order. The ornaments and furniture were removed, but the cells and chapel were not wholly destroyed. Richard Bishop of Dover, writing to Cromwell, Lord Privy Seal, and giving an account of the destruction of religious houses, says, "[at] Wynchelse according to yower commandment I have sold the stuff: the house is at the king's commandment and yowres."[6] The

[1] By the procurement of B. Thos. Wynchelsey, D.D., in 1420, the new church, in London, was wainscotted at the expense of 200 marks, and painted at the expense of 80 marks. He also procured other convenient buildings for the brethren. The whole expense of furnishing the library with books was £556 16s. 9d., whereof Richard Whittington gave £400, and Dr. T. Winchelsey gave the other £156, and also 100 marks for transcribing the works of Nicholas de Lyra in 2 vols., to be chained there. Dugd. Monas., vol. 6, pp. 1514-20.

[2] Cotton MSS., Vitellius XII, p. 227-236.

[3] Dering MSS.

[4] Collins' Peerage, vol. 2, p. 705.

[5] Tanner's Not. Mon., p. 564.

[6] Suppression of Monasteries. Camden Soc. Publications, p. 200.

buildings were placed under the custody of Capt. Philip Chowte, at that time captain of Camber Castle.

On 19th March, 1545, (36 Hen. VIII) the king, in consideration of £756 11s. 10d., paid into the Augmentation Office, by George Clyfford, gentleman, and Michael Welbore, gentleman, gave and granted[1] to them (among other estates in different counties) and to their heirs, &c.,

> All that house or scite of our house, lately the Priory of the Friars Minors, commonly called the Greye Freyers of Wynchelsey, in our county of Sussex, together with all other houses, edifices, messuages, tenements, cottages, orchards, gardens, closes of land and foundations, with the appurtenances, now or lately in the tenure or occupation of Philip Chowte or his assigns, situate, lying, and being in Wynchelsey aforesaid, and lately called the House or Priory of Friars Minors, in Wynchelsey, lately dissolved, and rents there, then of the clear annual value of 20s.

The grantees acquired in the same grant the King's Green, which adjoined the Gray Friars; and the two properties having thus become united have since passed together. The house was occupied as a farm house, and the chapel converted into a barn. The Millners would seem to have been owners at the close of the sixteenth century, as their arms, granted by Camden, as Clarencieux, (1597 to 1623:) *Erm. three wolves heads, couped ppr.*, and crest, *A wolf's head couped ppr., pierced with a javelin ar. and az.*, were in the windows of the house, now taken down.

In the early part of the seventeenth century this estate became the property of John Plumer, gent., whose widow, marrying John Weekes of Westfield, carried the estate to him. Their son and daughter, John Weekes and Mary Weekes, sold it to William Alderton of Winchelsea, who died S.P., 1687. On 30th Nov., 1695, Thomas Alderton of Winchelsea, barber-surgeon, his nephew, sold to Thomas Farnham of Beckley, yeoman, his reversion in

[1] Pat. 36 Henry VIII, m. 15, (32) in Rolls Chapel.

All that scite or mansion house of the late dissolved Priory of the Friars Minors, commonly called the Gray Friars, in the ancient towne of Winchelsea, one barne, commonly called the Stone Barne, with the cellar or vault under the same, one stable, and the orchards, cherry ground, &c., and seven pieces of land, with the pendents of the hill thereto belonging, called by the names of the King's Garden, otherwise King's Green fields, the two small meadows, Barne field, Hop Garden field, Long field, Monday's Market field, and Pendents of the Hill, then in the tenure of John Padiham, which William Alderton, the uncle, before 1687, had purchased of John Weekes.

In 1713, Mary Farnham of Udimar, only daughter and heiress-at-law of Thomas Farnham, for considerations amounting together to £660, sold the same property to Samuel Newman, jurat of Winchelsea; and in 1731, Robert Newman, his son, and Elizabeth his wife, sold this (inter alia) to Thomas Fuller of this town. In 1739, his trustees, among whom was Samuel Jeake, aliened to Nathaniel Pigram of Rye, gent., who, most probably, repaired and improved the house; and who, in 1754, devised these premises to his son Nathaniel: and he, in 1764, devised them to his nephew, Nathaniel Pigram Beaver, for 99 years if he should so long live, with remainder to his heirs, and in default thereof to the testator's own right heirs, who were his two sisters, Jane, the wife of Thomas Halford of Rye, surgeon, and Eleanor the wife of —— Beaver. The nephew died without issue, and the estate passed to the coheiresses. In 1773, Mr. Holford and his wife, and Jane the daughter of Eleanor Beaver, conveyed the premises to Mr. Holford and his wife, who, in 1797, in consideration of £3,710, sold to Richard Barwell, Esq., these and other estates, containing together 46 acres. Mr. Barwell made a good bargain, for, in 1803, he sold the same 46 acres in consideration of £12,000 to William Henry Earl of Darlington. In 1804 the Earl sold them for £10,000 to Thomas Lloyd, whose property was sold in 1819 under a decree of the Court of Chancery; and the house, with the Chapel, Cherry Garden, Monday's Market, King's Green, &c., was purchased

PLATE VIII

A.D. 1819.

R. Stileman, del. A.D. 1843. J. Bayley sc.

THE FRIARS.

FROM THE EAST.

by the late RICHARD STILEMAN, Esq.,[1] who pulled down the old house and erected the present mansion. In his family the estate still remains. They bear for their arms: *Sa. an unicorn passant, or. on a chief of the second three billets of the first;* and for their crest: *A camel's head erased az. collared, lined and ringed, or.*

The remainder of the property belonging to this house consisted of half an acre near Monday's Market; two messuages and two gardens in the thirteenth quarter; a tenement, orchard, and garden in the fourteenth quarter; a messuage, garden, and orchard in the eighteenth quarter; and a messuage, garden, orchard, and one acre in the nineteenth quarter. These were retained in the hands of the Crown until 1586, when, as we have seen,[2] they were granted by Queen Elizabeth to the mayor, jurats, and commonalty of the town.

Eagles have not unfrequently been shot at Winchelsea: one, winged near Camber in the early part of the spring of 1837, has been kept in the grounds of the Gray Friars, and is still alive there.

THE BLACK FRIARS.—The house of the Friars' Preachers or Black Friars, was founded by Edward II, in the year 1318. It was first established in the place called the King's Green, containing twelve acres, which was then vacant, and which, together with the Pendents of the Hill thereto contiguous, was granted by the King, 19th March, 11 Edw. II,[3] to his beloved in Christ, the brothers of the order of the Preachers, for the purpose of building a church for the celebration of divine

[1] Deeds in possession of R. Stileman, Esq. [2] Ante, p. 109.
[3] Pat. Roll, 11 Edw. II, part 2, m. 29.

worship, and houses and buildings for the habitation of the brethren of the order. This grant was confirmed by Edw. III, in the thirteenth year of his reign, 1339. The order had become popular in the town: in the same year as this confirmation, William Bacon of South Iham, obtained the King's license[1] to grant to this house six acres of land near Winchelsea. Subsequently the King granted to them another site near to St. Giles church; and the townsmen conveyed other property to them. On 18th February, 1358, the King issued his patent,[2] wherein he recited the return to an inquisition ad quod dampnum, that it would not be to any one's damage if he granted to his beloved in Christ, the Prior and brethren of the order of the Preachers in the town of Wynchelse, one acre of land with the appurtenances, lying near a certain windmill in the parish of St. Giles, in the same town; and if he permitted Robert Cely to assign one messuage, Richard Baddyng one messuage, William the son of John Long one messuage, Robert Treignon and Stephen Treignon one messuage, and John Tighlere one messuage, with their several appurtenances, in Winchelsea, held of the King, to the said Prior and brethren to hold, together with the said acre of land, to them and their successors, to build a new oratory there, and also certain houses for their own habitation: the King made the grant of the acre accordingly, and gave the license to R. Cely and the others to assign, the statute of mortmain non obstante.

The Prior and brethren built a new and commodious house and oratory on their new land, and thither they removed. All that remains of this house, is to be found in a few walls and five spacious crypts at the east side of a field, now called Chesnut field. The arches were groined, and on the south side of the entrance, which was at the eastern end, there is a piscina.

The order in this town met with equal favor from Henry VI, who, on 18th November, 1429, granted to them an In-

[1] Pat. 13 Edw. III, pt. 1, m. 22. [2] Pat. 32 Edw. III, pt. 1, m. 23.

speximus Charter,[1] in which he recited the Foundation Charter of Edw. II, and a charter of Edward III, dated 26th November, 1372, wherein the King forgave to the Prior and convent of the house of the order of the Brothers' Preachers 5s. 8¾d., (being the King's rents of the five houses given to them in 1358) theretofore paid for the site of their house by the hands of the mayor and bailiffs for the time being; Henry VI confirmed these grants and privileges to the then Prior and convent and to their successors; and Sir Thomas Sackville, who was, as we have seen, a benefactor to the Gray Friars, by his will, dated 1st December, 1432, (11 Hen. VI) bequeathed 10s. to these Friars Predicants.[2]

This house of Black Friars fell with the lesser houses, and on 19th March, 1545, (Henry VIII) by the same grant that he conveyed the site of the Gray Friars to George Clifford and Michael Wildbore,[3] granted to them and their heirs, executors, and administrators,

> All that house or site of one house or late Priory of the Friars' Preachers, commonly called the Black Freyers of Winchelsey aforesaid, in our county of Sussex, with all other the house, edifices, messuages, tenements, cottages, gardens, &c., with the appurtenances then or then lately, also in the occupation of Philip Chowte, and rents then of the clear value of 5s.

No attempt seems to have been made to preserve the building, of which only the few walls are standing, and now form part of a barn and shed. The vaults beneath have served the good purposes of the smugglers: and there was much superstitious and illicit mystery hovering round these crypts when we visited them in the autumn of 1849, and fixed the site beyond all doubt.

For many years after the grant we have found no traces of the owners of the house or land: but the property passed through the hands of Mr. Chesson about 1680,

[1] Pat. 8 Hen. VI, pt. 1, m. 19.
[2] Collins' Peer., vol 2, p. 705.
[3] Pat. 36 Hen. VIII, m. 15 (32.)

from a corruption of whose name the field is called Chesnut field. The site is now owned by THOMAS DAWES, Esq. The arms are: *Ar. on a bend, az. cotized, gu. three swans, or. betw. six battle axes, sa.* Crest, *A halbert erect or. on the point a flying dragon (or wivern) or. without legs, tail nowed sa. bezantée, vulned gu.*

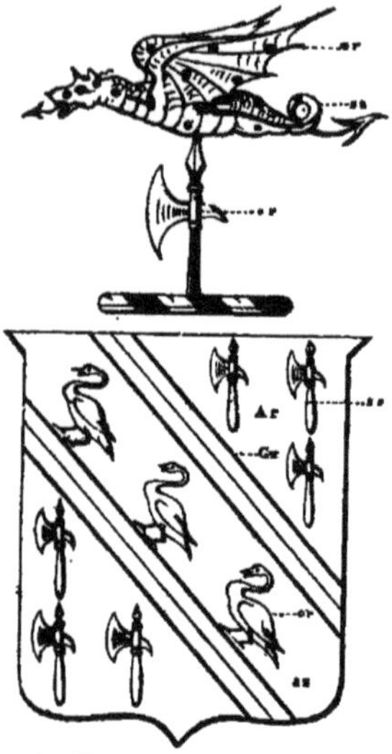

The remainder of the possessions of the Black Friars within the town, were granted, as we have seen,[1] by Queen Elizabeth in 1586, to the mayor, jurats, and commonalty of the town.

A PRECEPTORY dedicated to ST. ANTHONY existed here; but of its situation or endowment we have no knowledge. A brass seal of the house was found in the town, representing a monk, holding in one hand a book, and in the other a lanthorn to St. Anthony, who is followed by his emblem, the Pig; with the following legend: S: PRECEPTORIE: S: ANTONII. DE GRATÆNON. This may have been a cell of the Abbey of Grestein, in Normandy; they had a house at Wilmington. The arms at the foot of the seal are those of De la Pole, a family connected with the Cinque Ports from the time of Edw. III. The seal itself is of the period of Hen. VI.

[1] Ante, p. 108.

HOSPITALS.

There were places assigned, on building the new town, for three hospitals, all of which were situated on the south side of the town, where it was entered from Fairlight by the New Gate.

St. John's Hospital was situated at the north-eastern corner of the thirty-fourth quarter, at the junction of the present road leading to Icklesham and the road to Pett. The gable end of the building is still standing, and the field retains its name of St. John's or Chapel field. This hospital was for both brothers and sisters. It had, at its dissolution, a house and ten acres of arable land within the town; and also rents payable out of some houses in Great Yarmouth.[1] It ceased to exist in the time of Henry the VIII, and probably fell with the two houses of the Friars.

The Holy Cross or Holy Rood was situated in the thirty-ninth quarter, where one acre of land was assigned for it under the yearly rent of 3s.: subsequently an addition was made to its possessions in the thirty-eighth quarter; and it had, at its fall, 6a. 2r. 27p., which were granted by Elizabeth to the mayor, jurats, and commonalty. The master of this hospital confirmed the tenths of Stonmersh, in Icklesham, to the Abbey of Battle.[2]

[1] Swinden, in his History of Yarmouth, p. 18, says, "there is great reason to believe that the first founders of Great Yarmouth were portsmen, and for several centuries afterwards came and resided here; became seized of lands and tenements; and at their deaths, in memory from whence they came, bequeathed some portion thereof to their countrymen. Among the annual rents payable to the Cinque Ports, out of lands and tenements in Great Yarmouth, from time immemorial, were: To the hospital of St. John of Winchelsea. In the reign of Edw. I, John de Romeney, the attorney of the brothers' and sisters' hospital of St. John of Winchelsea, received of Richard Randolf half a mark, of Richard Carleton 17s. 8d., of John de Beccles, and Benedict, his brother, 7s., for annual rents belonging to the same hospital. Total, 31s. 6d."

[2] Addl. MSS., No. 6344, p. 245.

St. Bartholomew's was also situated in the thirty-ninth quarter, at the extreme south of the town, and close to the New Gate. Two acres of land at the annual rent of 6s. were assigned for it; and, within the town, there was no more when the land was granted by Elizabeth to the mayor, jurats, and commonalty. The foundations may still be traced; and until a few years since some of the walls were standing.

The two last hospitals were for brothers and sisters, who were required to be members of the commonalty of the town. These two hospitals seem to have been united before the time of Philip and Mary: and they existed after the dissolution of the religious houses in the town. The mayor was visitor, and the mode of election is prescribed in the Customal, compiled in 1557; but they must have been dissolved soon afterwards, for when Elizabeth, in 1586, granted the toft, &c., they are described "as parcel of the dissolved Priory of St. Bartholomew," and as being then occupied by Francis Bolton.

Wesleyan Chapel.—The Wesleyan Chapel, erected in 1786, near the old church of St. Giles, is the only place of worship at Winchelsea, besides the established church. Mr. Wesley himself preached in this chapel; and on 7th October, 1790, he preached at Winchelsea his last sermon in the open air.[1] The following is the entry in his journal:

> I went over to that poor skeleton of Ancient Winchelsea. It is beautifully situated on the top of a steep hill, and was regularly built in broad streets, crossing each other, and encompassing a very large square, in the midst of which was a large church, now in ruins. I stood under a large tree on the side of it, and called to most of the inhabitants of the town: "The kingdom of heaven is at hand," repent, and believe the gospel. It seemed as if all that heard were, at the present, almost pursuaded to be Christians.

The tree still stands on the west side of the church yard.

[1] In the Christian Miscellany for February, 1849, p. 33, there is an interesting notice of this sermon, from a record of the Rev. Robert Miller, who accompanied Mr. Wesley. Mr. Wesley dined with Mr. John Haddock, and preached at Rye that evening, and at five o'clock the next morning.

FAMILIES.

Alard.—This family, which was of Saxon origin, was settled in Sussex before the Conquest. The name, Adlard or Alard, is a corruption of the Saxon name of Æthelwald. It is stated in Doomsday[1] that Ælard held Treverde (Treyford) of Earl Godwin: and Collins adds, that the "name flourished in Winchelsea[2] from the Conqueror's days. Their monuments in the (old) church inscribed with Saxon characters, are testimonies of their antiquity; and their deeds sealed fairly with their arms, show their gentry." The chief seat of the family, was a place bearing their name, situate in the parish of Biddenden,[3] Kent; and they were also owners of the manor of Snergate,[4] Kent, which was anciently held of the manor of Aldrington by knight's service, at one quarter of a knight's fee. One of the family, who was an Abbot,[5] and the anniversary of whose death is January 2nd, on which day is his festival, is a Venerable in the Roman Catholic church.

The Kent branch of the family bore for their arms: *Ar. three bars gu. on a canton az. a leopard's head, or.* The Sussex branch bore the arms, emblazoned on the shield of the Knight in the monument.[6]

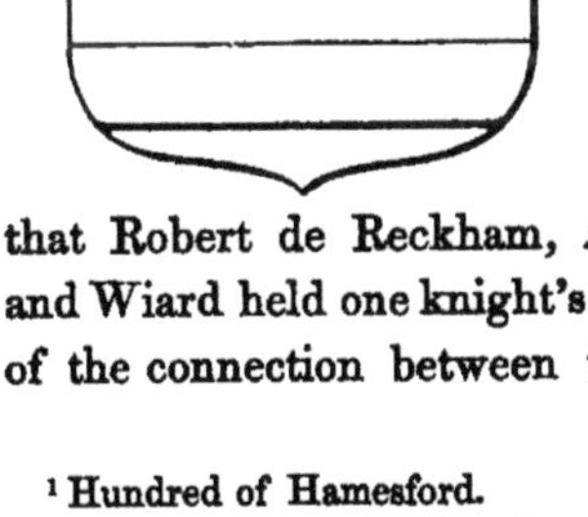

In 12 Hen. II, (1166) Hilary, Bishop of Chichester, enumerating the feoffments of the knight's of his church, says,[7] that Robert de Reckham, Anketel, William son of Alard, and Wiard held one knight's fee: but the first direct evidence of the connection between this family and Winchelsea, is in

[1] Hundred of Hamesford.
[2] Collins' Peer., vol. 2, p. 302.
[3] Harris, p. 41, and Hasted, vol. 3, p. 64. There are memorials to the family in Biddenden church.
[4] Hasted, vol. 3, p. 484.
[5] Nicolas' Chronology of Hist., p. 125.
[6] See ante, p. 134.
[7] Madox' Firma Burgi, vol. 1, p. 576.

1242, (26 Henry III) when William Alard of Winchelsea is described as owning the manor of Snergate, except Capenesse, and the lastage of Winchelsea, together with the customs of the port.[1] In the same reign, 38 Hen. III, (1253-4) we find a warrant[2] directing Robert de Cryoll, keeper of the Cinque Ports, to summon Gervase Alard (no doubt the son of William) and Alice the wife of Paulinus of Winchelsea, to answer the complaint of John Page and Petronilla his wife, in the Court of Shepway. In 1273, (2 Edw. I) we find that Roger Alard was a merchant of the town;[3] and we have already seen,[4] that when, in 1288, the new town was founded, places were assigned to Gervase Alard, sen., and his sons Gervase and John; to Reginald Alard, sen., and Reginald and John his sons; to Colin Alard; to Nicholas Alard; to John and Justin Alard, brothers; to Thomas Alard; and to Henry son of John: and from the quarters in which was their property, it is evident that they were among the principal merchants. The two sons of Gervase Alard, sen., were, however, the most distinguished members of the family. Gervase Alard, the son, in 21 Edw. I, (1292) became bail for Benjamin Seman, Benjamin Carite, and John de Pistons, of Winchelsea, who were charged with murder on board a Yarmouth vessel.[5] In 1294, he accompanied Edmund, the king's brother, to Gascony; and he served in the wars in Flanders, Scotland, and Normandy, for which he received as a reward, only £4 from the hand of Ralf, the cofferer, at the Rose in Galway, and a horse from Edward I.[6] In these wars he seems to have distinguished himself: for in 1303, (31 Edw. I) he was made[7] captain and admiral of the Cinque Ports' fleet: and, in 1306, he was appointed captain and admiral of the Cinque Ports, from

[1] Inq. ad quod dampnum, 26 Hen. III, m. 1.
[2] Cal. Rot. Orig., vol. 1, p. 142. [3] Prynne's King John.
[4] See ante, pp. 44 to 53. [5] Plac. de Parl., vol. 1, p. 98, a.
[6] Ib. p. 174, a; where he petitioned for a further reward for his services.
[7] Rot. Pat., m. 39.

Dover, westward, including the coast of Cornwall.[1] He was directed to proceed to Skymburnesse, there to lend all aid against the Scotch rebels. He died soon afterwards, and according to Leland, "lyeth buried in Winchelsea." His monument in the chantry, which bore the name of his family, and of which he was probably the founder, we have already described. John Alard, his brother, was an eminent Brabant merchant.[2] We have already seen, that during Edward the First's reign, other members of the family were bailiffs of the town and to Yarmouth, and masters and constables of ships.

In the following reign, (1307) Henry Alard held lands of the king in Westham, called Yland, containing 36 acres, a salt marsh there, containing 400 acres, and the Honor of the Eagle.[3] In 1318, Robert, son of John Alard of Winchelsea, received a feoffment from Robert le Mareshal of Westminster, of land in Pevensey, which, in Dec., 1322, he was directed to assign to the Abbot and Convent of Battle,[4] being at that time the attorney for the abbey, and as such he received land in Camberwell, and East Greenwiche and Lewisham.[5] Stephen Alard, who seems to have been son of the admiral, was, in 1315, a commissioner for embanking the marshes of Tillingham and East Wytenham:[6] and 1324 he was appointed captain and admiral of the Cinque Ports and of the King's fleet of the western seas.[7] In the following year, Benedict Alard was bailiff to Yarmouth.

In the days of Edward III, this family again commanded ships, and filled the office of bailiff: and in the various accounts relating to the town, we find many members of the family named. In January, 1341, James, son and heir of Gervase Alard of Winchelsea, enfeoffed land in St. Thomas', adjoining the messuage of Henry, the son of Richard Alard.[8]

[1] Spelman's Glos., p. 16.
[2] See ante, p. 59.
[3] Inq. ad quod dampnum, 1 Edw. II, No. 100.
[4] Batt. Abb. Rec.
[5] Inq. ad quod dampnum, 14 Edw. II, No. 176.
[6] Dugd. Imb., 9 Edw. II.
[7] Rot. Pat., 18 Edw. II, pt. 1, m. 22.
[8] Batt. Abb. Rec.

In the Non. Inq., (1341) we have seen[1] the names of Robert and Stephen, sons of Stephen; Robert Alard, who married Lucy de Wigsell, and she being his widow, re-married John Finch, and became the mother of John Finch, Lord Prior of Christ's Church, Canterbury;[2] Alan Alard; and Reginald Alard, the latter of whom died in 1354, seized of 20 acres of land and Farlegh, held of the manor of French Court;[3] and the slab, containing the inscription to his memory, yet remains in the church. In the Bailiffs' Roll[4] of 16 and 17 Edw. III, (1343) are the names of Richard Alard and John Alard: and the roll, 40 Edw. III, (1366) records the names of Robert Alard; John Alard; Roger Alard; Reginald Alard; Richard Alard; Nicholas Alard, whose daughter Parnel married Henry Herbert, otherwise Finch; Justin Alard; Stephen Alard; and Gervase Alard. In the following year, 41 Edw. III, Agnes, the wife of the latter, died seized of the manor of Snergate.[5] He was grandson of the admiral, and seems to have died without male issue; for Leland, speaking of the admiral, says,[6] "Oxenbridge of Southsex is heire by descent to this Alarde, and bearith his armes." The estate in Biddenden, however, remained in the Alard family till the reign of Charles I, when Francis Alard died, leaving an only daughter Elizabeth, who, marrying Terry Aldersey, carried the estate into his family.[7]

In 1423, (Dec. 17) there was an assize of novel deseizin between the Abbot of Battle and Gervase Alard, concerning a free tenement in Guestling.[8]

In 1428, 1429, 1436, and 1444, William Alard was member for the town,[9] and resided here:[10] and John and William Alard were non-resident freemen of Winchelsea, living at

[1] Ante p. 87. [2] Collins' Peer, ed. 1779, vol. 3, p. 370.
[3] Cal. Inq., p. m., 28 Edw. III, vol. 2, p. 192. [4] Carlt. Ride MSS.
[5] Inq., p. m., 42 Edw. III, No. 1. [6] Itin., fol. 53.
[7] Hasted, vol. 3, p. 64. [8] Batt. Abb. Rec.
[9] See list of members, post. [10] See ante, p. 115.

Pelsham,[1] 23 Hen. VI, (1445:) but soon afterwards the connection of the family with this town seems to have ceased, though they still resided in Sussex. The will of Thomas Alard, who married the heiress of John Bourne of Aldingden, in Sandhurst, Kent,[2] was (1491-2) proved in the Prerogative Court next after the will of Elizabeth, Queen of England; they were also resident and acted as bailiffs of Pevensey; and from the Battle Abbey Records it appears that Henry Alard was bailiff of their manor of Wye and the liberties of Battle, from 1498 to 1506.

The family is not extinct, but yet exists in Kent.

THE HERBERTS OR FINCHES were also merchants of importance at the founding of New Winchelsea, (1288:) in which Vincent Herberd[3] had places assigned to him in the 9th and 37th quarters. We have not space to enter into the claim of the Finches to the descent from Fitz Herbert, the Lord Chamberlain, through Herbert, son of Matthew, a younger son of the Chamberlain.[4] Matthew was summoned to parliament, 1234, (Selden's T. H. 722,) and killed at Margam, 1245. (Math. Paris, p. 590.) Collins has a strange blunder: he makes Herbert, son of Herbert, under

age in 1300, to be the grandson of Matthew, although he never bore the name of Finch. The intervention of a generation gets rid of this difficulty. We have seen (ante, p. 59)

[1] Carlt. Ride MSS. [2] Hasted, vol 3, p. 75.

[3] See ante, pp. 46, 52. In another copy of the same MS. the name is written Herbert.

[4] See Gent. Mag., vol. 67, p. 648.

that Vincent Herberd was the name at Winchelsea in 1306; and the evidence furnished by the MSS. relating to this town seem to add weight to the Finches' claim to the name of Herbert, if not to the descent. The assumed name of Finch, as connected with Winchelsea, does not appear before the time of Edward III. The name of Herberd or Herbert, alone occurs until 15 Edw. III; in 1342 John Fitz-Henry Finch[1] was bailiff to Yarmouth; and in 1355 we find Vincent Finch bound in £40 to Robert Arnold and others.[2] In the following year he was bailiff of the town;[3] and in 1358 bailiff to Yarmouth. Leland says,[4] "the name of Finches hath beene of auncient tyme in estimation in Southsax, about Winchelsey, and be al likelyhood rose by some notable marchaunte of Winchelsey: for it is written that Alarde and Finche Herberte were capitaines at the batel of Trade,[5] and that Finche was sore wounded there. The Finches that be now say that theire propre name is Hereberte, and that with mariage of the Finche heyre, they tooke Finche's name, and were caulled Finch-Herbert, joining booth names." The Finches seem to have been, indeed, "sore wounded," for Henry Herbert, alias Finch,—who, in 15th Edw. III, (1341) held a knight's fee in the rape of Hastings worth 100s., being lands in Ewhurst, Morehall, Whatlington, Sedlescombe, Salehurst, and Buxle, under John Duke of Brittany,[6] and acquired the lands formerly of the De Denes,[7] in Icklesham, through the heiress of Nicholas Heringod and Sybella his wife, (herself the heiress of the De Denes,)—married for his

[1] See ante, p. 119. [2] Dering MSS.
[3] See ante, p. 115. [4] Itin. 6, p. 57.
[5] Pennant, in his Tour, (vol. 2, p. 27) mistakes this expression, and assuming it not to be a metaphor, says, "does he mean the battle of Terrocene in 1522?" The context (as Mr. Bolton Corney points out) means that the two families were rival merchants.
[6] Inq., p. m., No. 43.
[7] The Denes claim to have been Cup Bearers to Edward the Confessor. They were the founders of Otham and Bayham Abbeys.

second wife, Parnel, daughter of Nicholas Alard, and ob. 8th Rich. II; whilst John, the brother of Henry, married the widow of Robert Alard. Vincent Finch was a commissioner of embankments in 1393-4; he served the office of mayor in 1400; he was M.P. in 1395, 1397, 1402, and 1419; and to him and his wife Isabella the convent of the Gray Friars, granted, in 1413, the prayers and masses, as being their special benefactors.[1] William Finch was member for the town in 1432. Other members of the family[2] represented the town at different periods until 1642, when Sir John Finch, then M.P., died.[3] On 12th July, 1628, Elizabeth, daughter and heir of Sir Thomas Heneage, Knt., widow of Sir Moyle Finch, and Viscountess Maidstone, was advanced to the title of Countess of Winchelsea.

The Finches bear for their arms: *Ar. a chev. betw. three griffins passant, sa.;* and for a crest, *A griffin passant, wings endorsed, sa.*

Henry Fynch, who died 1493, is buried in the south chancel of Icklesham church: his plain altar tomb of Sussex marble, remained till the alterations made in 1849, when it was removed; although he had been a benefactor to the repairs of the church, and had caused an altar to be built in the chapel of St. Nicholas at his expense.

Miss Strickland has thrown an air of romance upon the life of Mary Finch, daughter of Sir William. In her youth,

[1] Dering MSS., and ante p. 146.

[2] We had hoped to have been able to give some unpublished particulars of this family; but the Rev. Heneage Finch of Oakham, informs us that few, if any, of the early documents of the family descended with the title to the second branch, and of those few the late Earl of Winchelsea, not long before his death, burnt, with the more modern papers, as many as would have filled a chariot, and under circumstances which forbad Mr. Heneage Finch's attempting to rescue them, although he was present. It is possible that there may be some papers among the archives at Longleat, carried there by an heiress; from some of whom, as well as from dowagers, the family have sustained great ravages.

[3] Journ. of Ho. of Com., vol. 2, p. 967.

(accompanied by her father and mother) she was in attendance on Catherine of Aragon at the Field of the Cloth of Gold. Queen Mary seems to have relied on her in her difficult succession to the throne. She rode with her to Cambridge, to the Huddlestones, and to Framlingham; was her mistress of the robes; and appears on all occasions up to the time of the Spanish marriage: not approving that, she retired, and her name never appears again: nor is it in the list of ladies to be rewarded with jewels for supporting Philip's views.

Strype (Annals of Reform., c. 32, pp. 330-1) relates the following disastrous death of Sir Thomas Finch, near Winchelsea. "1563, March 29. A lamentable chance happened to Sir Thomas Finch, being appointed to the Marshal of Newhaven, (in France) in the place of Sir Adrian Poynings; taking ship at Rye with thirty gentlemen, whereof two were brethren to the Lord Wentworth, and some others of his name, were lost with the ship beside ye Camber, coming (driven to return upon foul weather) before ye tide was full to serve him. The loss was esteemed great, and he as much lamented as any man of his degree in any part of England."

The Oxenbridges were not originally a Winchelsea family. They resided at a place bearing their name in Iden. The first mention of their name occurs in 1329, when John de Oxenbridge was a juror on the inquisition between Simon de Echingham and John de la Beche;[1] but they do not seem to have been of importance till 1393, when Robert Oxenbridge was a commissioner of embankments for Farlegh, &c. Having married an heiress of the Alards, they assumed the arms of that family, and settled in Brede, at a place formerly belonging to the Atte Foards, called after them Foard Place, but more recently named Brede Place. From 1329 to 1581 they occupied an important position in the county, and built the chancel of Brede church, over which they had exclusive rights; but

[1] Hall's Echingham, p. 11.

they do not appear to have taken any prominent part in Winchelsea affairs. They were, however, freemen of the town to escape contribution to the subsidies.

THE LONDENEYS were in the eighteenth quarter of the new town at its settlement in 1288.[1] When Edward III conferred the right of returning members to parliament upon the town, Robert Londeneys was one of the first returned; and he was re-elected in 1373. The family remained in Winchelsea until about 1400, when the head of the family married an heiress of the Oxenbridges, and removed the chief residence to Brede. We have already referred to them and given a cut of their seal.[2] They bore for their arms: *Gu. a lion rampant, ar. within a bordure, erm.*: and their pedigree is in the Visitation of 1634, p. 321.

THE GODFREYS were also among the families, who existed in the old town, and to whom places were assigned at the settling of the new town: where we find Juliana, the relict of Alan Godfrey; Thomas Godfrey, and Jacob his son; Richard Godfrey; and John Godfrey. In 3 Edw. II, (1309) Godfrey the son of Alan Godfrey, of this town, released to his brother Theobald, in Wales, his land and all his right and services belonging to the manor of Sieltelond.[3] The family flourished in Winchelsea, and also at Lydd; where a branch settled, and were many times mayors. From the year 1300 till 1313, Robert Godefray represented Horsham. In 1332, John Godfrey was member for that town: and in 1441 and 1448, another John Godfrey was M.P. for Winchelsea. In 23 Hen. VI, he was among the non-resident freemen, living at Ore.[4] And on 27th Nov., 1477, he obtained a license to found the chantry in St. Thomas' church.[5] He seems to have died before his good intentions were perfected; and they were, as we have seen,[6] fully carried out by his daughter and and heiress, Matilda, widow of Simon Farncombe. From his

[1] See ante, p. 48. [2] See ante, p. 39. [3] Cal. Rot. Orig., vol. 1, p. 108.
[4] Carlt. Ride MSS. [5] Batt. Abb. Rec., p. 121. [6] Ante, p. 131.

death until the year 1609, no branch of the Godfreys appears to have resided in Winchelsea; but in that year, Thomas Godfrey, the father of Sir Edmund Berry Godfrey, whose assassination in 1678, caused a great sensation,[1] came to reside in the town. During his residence here, he kept a diary and an account of his expenses, (preserved in the Lansd. MSS., No. 235) in which he gives some curious particulars of the town, and of the price of provisions at that period.

By reason of my marriage on Assention Day, being ye 5th of May, 1609, in St. Catherine's by the Tower, with Margarett, the sole daughter of Wm. Lambard of Greenewich, Esqr., one of the Masters of the Chancery, I retired myselfe into the country and lay for one yeare at sojourne wth Mr. Robt. Boteler of Winchelsea, in the county of Sussex, gent., in whose house my first child, being a son, was borne in anno, 1609, March ye 29th, being Munday, betweene 4 and 5 in the afternoone, and was christnd the the ninth of Aprill, being Palm Sunday, in ye forenoone; the witnesses were my wife's brother, Sr. Multon Lambard, Knt., and my father, and my mother, and my brother Peter's wife: he was named Lambard, after Sr. Multon's sirname. Memdm., that my son was nursed by Mr. Boteler's son's wife, in the Camber Castle. My father sent 3 of us his sons successively to St. John's in Cambridge, where we were all of us Fellow Comoners; we gave a white silver pott to ye College, of about a 12 pound price, our arms engraved upon it, with this Ænigma: "Petrus, Thomas, et Richardus Godfrey, cujus Colegii allumni, oreundi De Lidd in agro Cantiano, quorum pater est Tho. Godfrey, armigr., cui horum alter vter est primo genitus." I came from Mr. Boteler's to housekeeping, in a house that I took of Mr. Raynold's in Winchellsea, who had it in right of his wife, who was Mr. Thomas Egliston's widdow, the 29th of January, 1609. Wm. Bing, Capt. of Deale Castle, who was also formerly my bedfellow in my Lord Privie Seal's house, and myself, was chosen burgess' by the town of Winchellsea, for ye parliament begun to be held at Westminster, 5º Aprillis, 1614, and 12 of Jacobus. The which Parliamt. was desolv'd and nothing done, and concluded to be no sessions. My second child, being a son also, was borne the 4th of Octor., being Thursday, in anno, 1610, between the hours of 1 and 2 in the night, and was christnd the 10th of the same month: his godfathers were Mr. John Egliston, gent.,

[1] For very interesting particulars see Gent. Mag. for Nov. 1848, and March, 1849; and Nichols' Topographer.

one of the jurats of the town,[1] and Mr. Thos. Isted, gent., common clerk of the same town, who gave him his name: his godmothers, Mrs. Mary Clynton, (one of the daughters of Sr. Tho. Clynton, second son to ye Erle of Lincoln, that was Lord Admirall,) his other godmr. was my sister Eliz. This son departed this life ye 8th of Febr. following, 1610, and lieth buried in ye south isle of the church of St. Thomas, at ye upper end of ye isle, just under the great window of ye east end. My most loveing wife, Margaret Lambard, departed this life in a most comfortable manner; her last words being these: (viz.,) My soul is in heaven with the angells; and soe most patiently gave up the ghost between 2-3 and 3-4 of the clock in the morning on a Saturday, being St. Peter's Day, the 29th of June, 1611, after that we had been married three years and almost two months, and was buried close by her son Thomas, the 4th of July, in ye south isle of the church of St. Thomas in Winchellsea, under the great window of ye east end of ye isle.[2] I had taken a house at Canterbury, without St. George his gate, whither my first wife and I intended to have removed from Winchellsea, but all things being ready for our departure, it pleased God to take my said wife away, so that I put that house away. And having married again he took another house at Halling, Kent.

There are several items in Mr. Godfrey's expenditure which are worth preserving, for the prices of food, clothing, and labour.

Michas., 1608, *to Michas.*, 1609.	£	s.	d.
To a pillion and furniture	0	50	0
It. ye outside of a suite for me	4	2	0
My wife at the faire	0	40	0
The nurse	0	0	xii
My freedom	0	40	0
For 72 rods of ditch, at 8d. the rod	0	48	0
Washing my sheep	0	2	0
The use of the turne and pound	0	1	0
Shearing at 12d. the score	0	8	8

	£	s.	d.
It. To the winders and helpers	0	2	8
Mending my bowe	0	2	0
Three loads of broome faggotts	0	11	6
One load of charcole	0	24	0
Qr. at the Rye Ferry, from our Lady-day to Midsummer	0	2	0
To Mr. Evans for a vomitt	0	8	0
Pd. my Cosn. Wymond for 6 load of loggs, and 6 load of faggotts, at 8s. per load	3	12	0

[1] The Egglestones or Ecclestones of this town, bore for their arms, *Ar. a cross sa. in the first quarter a fleur-de-lis gu.*, the same as the arms of the Ecclestones of Ecclestone, county of Lancaster. A short pedigree is in the Harl. MSS., Vis. Suss. 1562. Thomas Eccleston was M.P. for Winchelsea in 1586.

[2] See inscription, ante p. 137.

	£	s.	d.
It. Pd. the collectors for the poore of Winchelsea, for half a yeare - - -	0	3	4
To Robin for 9 ells of Holland - -	0	22	0
To James Appleton for 36 ells of coarse canvas - -	0	42	0
Pd. Mr. Whitton, July 29th, for 4 acres of grass, at 23s. 4d. the acre, and two over	4	15	0
Pd. for carrying of 5 loads and an half of hay - - - -	0	6	6
Shoeing my horse -	0	0	8
For 1 great glass bottle and 1 small, of Mr. Reynolds -	0	0	8
Aug. ye 8th, bought of Mr. Evans, 1 white salt and 1 white beaker, (glass) weying 21 oz. 1 drachm	0	5	11
Gassing the kitchen	0	2	8
A pint of wine -	0	0	6
A pair of kersey hose	0	4	6
Michas., 1609, to Michas., 1610.			
A cess for the bell -	0	20	0
The clarke's quarterages - - - -	0	0	6
For 1 pr. of bootes, 4 pr. of shoes -	0	16	0
For 4 Venis glasses -	0	2	6
For cleving 50 rails and 6 posts -	0	2	0

	£	s.	d.
It. For a handsaw -	0	1	6
For a cleaver - -	0	1	4
An ax - - -	0	1	4
One tonn of timber -	0	9	0
A quart of sack -	0	1	0
Two ounces of lace -	0	6	0
For 24lb. of butter -	0	12	0
The mason and his boy for a day -	0	0	18
One bushell of salt -	0	0	18
A qr. of veale -	0	2	6
A legg of veale -	0	1	0
Pr. of gloves - -	0	3	0
Two cloakes - -	3	13	4
An hatt - -	0	12	0
Goeing to the play (he was in London) -	0	1	6
Boetius in English -	0	0	12
Two chees - -	0	0	14
For mowing two acres of grass - -	0	5	0
A seam of wheat of 9 gall. measure, at 3s. 3d. pr. bushell	0	28	8
Lost at bowles -	0	4	0
2lbs. of cherries -	0	0	8
For a cow - -	3	6	8
One dozen of glass plats - -	0	2	6
For 5 Welch runts, Uherst faire, at 4 marke a bullock	13	6	8
The players - -	0	18	0
Three bushells of oats	0	3	0
A gallon of barberryes	0	0	10
For 6 chicken -	0	0	18

The bowling green, where Mr. Godfrey lost his money, had been established at Cook's Green, and was continued till the close of the last century. The new bell, for which a cess was made in 1610, yet remains.

The Godfreys bore for their arms: *Sa. a chev. bet. three pelican's heads, erased, and vulning themselves, or.:* crest; *A demi-negro, ppr. holding in the dexter hand a cross crosslet, fitchée, ar.* The pedigree is in Berry's Kentish Geneal., p. 146.

THE FARNCOMBES are a Saxon family, taking their name from Varncombe, an estate in the parish of Patcham, Sussex. In the 15th Edw. III, Henry de Farncombe of Blatchington, made the return of the ninth sheaf, &c., for that parish.[1] In 1402, Roger Farncomb was M.P. for Shoreham: and in the same century (1456) Simon de Farncombe was a merchant in Winchelsea,[2] and his widow, the heiress of John Godfrey, endowed the Farncombe chantry.

The family have continued to occupy the station of yeomen in the county. At the election in 1705, William Farncomb of Heathfield, Joseph Farncomb of Patcham, and Richard Farncomb of Bexhill, voted as freeholders: and in the present year, 1850, Alderman Thomas Farncomb, who was born at Hollington, and who was, in early life, a banker at Hastings, is Lord Mayor of London; bearing for his arms: *Vert, on a cheveron engrailed between three cinque-foils, or. as many gryphon's heads, erased, sable:* and for his crest, *A cockatrice's head couped sable, combed and wattled, or. between two wings of the first, each charged with a cinque-foil of the second:* motto; *Leges ac jura servare.*

A large majority of the other families, to whom places were assigned at the foundation of New Winchelsea, cannot now be traced, and the names of many have become extinct. Some, however, such as the Austins, the Colyns, the Coopers, the Dawes, the Martins, and the Mots, have remained in connection with the town down to a recent period; whilst others, such as the Beneyts, the Campions, the Crouches, the Lambs, the Melewards, the Popes, the Pennifathers, and the Wytings, are still to be found in the neighbouring towns and parishes of Sussex and Kent.

[1] Non. Inq.

[2] See ante, pp. 99 and 131.

MANOR OF HIGHAM, AND CASTLE AND HAVEN OF CAMBER.

HIGHAM.—The manor of Higham, which was obtained by Edw. I from Wm. de Grandison and Isabella his wife, extends into the several parishes of St. Thomas, Winchelsea, on both sides of the modern harbour of Rye, St. Leonard, Winchelsea, and into parts of Icklesham, of Broomhill, and Pett. It is intimately mixed up with the history and prosperity of Winchelsea. The kings usually held it in their own hands; and the King's bailiffs of the manor of Higham were bailiffs of Winchelsea, and generally of Rye. The manor and the royal dues of the town of Winchelsea were, however, granted by Edw. I, as part of her appanage, to his wife Eleanor.[1] Edw. II granted them to his Queen Isabella for her life.[2] And, in 4th Edw. III, there were granted (inter alia) to Bartholomew de Burghersh, Lord Warden of the Cinque Ports, for his life,[3] the marsh of Iham and the town of Winchelsea, worth in the whole, £95 a year, for the maintenance of a chaplain, of the watch, and of a carpenter in the castle of Dover. In the reign of Henry VII, however, the king's property was alienated from the Crown to Sir RICHARD GULDEFORD, Knt., who was one of the Chamberlains of the Exchequer, Master of the Ordnance and of the Armory, Keeper of the King's Manor of Kennington,[4] and one of the King's Counsellors.

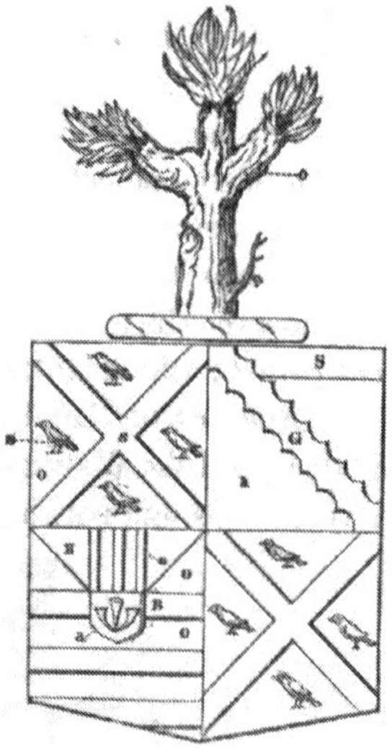

[1] Bliss in Blore's Monuments.
[2] Cal. Rot. Orig., vol. 2, p. 36.
[3] Ib.
[4] Rot. Parl., vol. 6, p. 354 b.

By letters patent, 6th Oct., 2 Hen. VII, (1486) and 17th Jan., 21 Hen. VII, the grant[1] was made to Sir Richard Guldeford, Knt., and the heirs male of his body lawfully begotten, of the lordship or manor of Higham; and also the office of bailiff of the town of New Winchelsea, of which town the ground and area were anciently parcel of the aforesaid lordship and manor of Higham, otherwise Iham; and the rents of assize of all and singular free tenants and bondmen, residents and non-residents; and with the custom of ships and fishing boats, called shares; and with the custom of divers merchandizes, as well arriving by water as brought by land; and also the custom of wood for tanning, corn, &c.; and also lastage, stallage, &c.; and also fines, forfeitures, and amerciaments of bakers, maltsters, and other victuallers whatsoever; and for trespasses against the peace; and the chattels of felons, &c.; waifs, strays, and all fees, &c., to the office of bailiff belonging; also the creek called the Camber, otherwise Wenway; and all those marshes, fresh and salt, and lands, &c., called the Camber Marsh, and the Camber Salts, and the Camber Beach, and the Camber and Wenway Sands; and the creek, called the Puddle; and the advowsons and free dispositions of the churches of St. Thomas and St. Giles; and also all and singular messuages, mills, &c., with all the rights, members, and appurtenances to the lordship or manor, office of bailiff, messuages, &c., belonging.

On 10th April, 1610, (8th James) in consideration of £20, Sir Henry Guldeford, Knt., and his heirs male, had a grant[2] of the same estates, to hold in as ample a manner as Sir Richard Guldeford, deceased, had held them, yielding yearly a fee farm rent of £20 to Queen Anne for her life, and after her death into the public Exchequer. The Guldeford family had their principal seat at Hempstead, in Kent. They bore for their arms:[3] *Or. a saltier, between four martlets, sa.*

[1] Holloway's Romney Marsh, p. 154, where there is a full description of the lands, &c., granted.

[2] Charter, Penes W. D. C.

[3] See wood cut, ante p. 168.

Their pedigree is to be found in the Harl. MSS., 5507, p. 250. On the 8th January, 1662, (13 Charles II) Edward Guldeford, Esq., obtained a grant of these estates to himself and his heirs and assigns, without the limitation to his heirs male, to hold as of the manor of East Greenwich in free and common soccage, and not in chief, at a fee farm rent of £20.[1] And in 1663, he sold the whole, with the exception of Camber farm,[2] to JOHN CARRYLL of Harting, who bore for his arms: *Ar. three bars sa. in chief as many martlets of the last:* and for a crest, *On a mount vert, a stag, lodged, reguardant, ar.* His grandson, John Caryll, sold and spent all his property. In 1762, he joined with his mortgagees in selling this Higham and Winchelsea estate, including the office of the bailiff, the patronage of the churches, &c., to Charles O'Brien Earl of Egremont: and, in 1787, his son, George O'Brien

[1] This fee farm rent is now the property of the Hon. — Herbert, and is paid in the proportions following: Mr. William Longley, Camber farm, £6 12s.; Rev. T. S. Curteis £2 18s.; Mrs. Curteis (late) £1 10s.; the same £3 8s. 4d.; devisees of the late Mr. William Croughton £2 4s.; Mrs. Curteis, Mr. John Stonham, Mr. Mortimer, and Mr. Thomas Mills, £3 7s. 8d. Total £20. Holloway's Romney Marsh, 162.

[2] Among the private acts of 10th Anne, 1711-2, No. 15, is an act for the sale of the manor of Hempstead and other lands in the counties of Kent and Sussex, the estate of Sir Robert Guldeford, Bart., for the payment of debts, and for settling Camber farm and other lands in the county of Sussex, to the same uses as Hempstead manor then stood settled. Camber farm was subsequently alienated, and is now the property of Mr. William Longley.

Earl of Egremont, exchanged them for the manor of Wiggonholt with SIR WILLIAM ASHBURNHAM, Bart., then Bishop of Chichester, whose family property was at Broomham, in Guestling. The Ashburnham estates in Winchelsea have been since sold to various persons. The manor of Higham, with all its rights and royalties, together with the Castle of Camber, the office of Bailiff of the town, the Kings rent's there, the town hall, &c., was purchased in 1834 by the

late HERBERT BARRETT CURTEIS, Esq., and is now the property of his only son, Herbert Mascall Curteis, Esq. They bear for their arms: *Ar. a chev. sa. betw. three bulls heads, cabossed, gu.:* and for their crest, *A unicorn, passant, or. betw. four trees proper.*

A new church in the early English style was built in 1848-9, in that part of the manor of Higham and parish of Icklesham, which lies on the west side of the mouth of Rye harbour. The architect was Mr. Samuel S. Teulon.[1]

[1] Under his direction the chancels of the old church at Icklesham have been restored, and two new eastern windows put in.

Bounds of Camber Beach and Salts.—The bounds of the Camber beach and salts were fully ascertained in 1590, under a royal commission issued to Sir Thomas Pelham and others, and are fully set forth in an exemplification made 4th July, 1666, (18 Charles II) after the sale to Mr. Carryll.[1] It recites a certain record before the Barons of the Exchequer of the 39th Queen Elizabeth: vizt., Among the records of Easter Term, roll the first, on the part of the remembrancer and treasurer, being a commission dated 30th June, 38 Elizabeth, to Thomas Pelham, James Thetcher, George Chewte, Edward Pelham, Henry Cupesley, and Edward Henden, Esqrs., or any five, four, three, or two, to look over and perambulate a certain great quantity of salt marsh and lands called the Camber Beach and Camber Salts; and to enquire as to the quantity and number of acres, and of the ancient metes, limits, and bounds, and within what liberties, parishes, and manors lying; and by sufficient metes, limits, and bounds, to separate and divide from all other manors, &c., lying contiguous; and to make a plot or map. It then goes on to give the return of Thomas Pelham, James Thetcher, and Edward Pelham, three of the commissioners, with the following inquisition, and a plot or map to the same annexed.

Sussex. An inquisition indented, taken at Rye, in the county aforesaid, the 23rd day of September, in the 38th year of the reign of our Lady Elizabeth, by the grace of God, Queen of England, France, and Ireland, defender of the faith, &c., before Thomas Pelham, James Thetcher, and Edward Pelham, Esqrs., commissioners of the said Queen, by virtue of a certain commission of the said Queen, issued out of her Court of Exchequer, and to them and others from thence directed, and to this inquisition annexed, by the oaths of Richard Portriffe, Thomas Fisher, John Fisher, William Mellowe, John Benbricke, Edward Seringe, John Robinson, John Osborne, John Dowce, William Sharpe, Thomas Young, John Allen, Thomas Shether otherwise Stace, Richard Fribody, Richard Sheather otherwise Stace, Francis Iordan, William Davye, Christopher Edwards, Thomas Bennett, Thomas Harwood, John Holman, Nicholas

[1] Pat. Penes Mr. E. N. Dawes.

White, Richard Gossepp, and Henry Walter, who, upon their oaths, say that the marsh and lands in the said commission specified, called the Camber Beach and Camber Salts, contain in the whole, 1,368 acres, of which 135 acres only are enclosed within a certain wall there, among other lands, now or late in the occupation of one Thomas Godfrey. And that the said marsh and lands, called the Camber Beach and Camber Salts, in the said commission specified likewise, lie near and abut on a certain place called the Camber Head, by the sea shore on the east, towards Lydd, bordering upon Bowcliffe, otherwise Beach Cliffe; and from thence beyond the said marsh or lands below the aforesaid wall, in a straight line northward as far as a certain creek or river called Camber Haven, otherwise Wayne Way Water, towards a certain limit or boundary hundred of Goldspurr, called Kent Dike; and from thence abutting by the aforesaid creek or river, called Camber Haven, otherwise Wayne Way Water, as far as to the Camber Head aforesaid; and also that the said marsh and lands called Camber Beach and Camber Salts so abutting as aforesaid, lie between the high sea, called the Main Sea, on parts of the south and west; and lands called Bates Lands, and lands now of Richard Smith, Esquire, on the part of the east; and the aforesaid river or creek called the Camber Haven, otherwise Waine Way Water, on the part of the west; which limits and bounds aforesaid are the ancient limits and bounds of the marsh and lands aforesaid, called Camber Beach and Camber Salts. And that the said marsh and lands called Camber Beach and Camber Salts, are and, from time whereof the memory of man is not to the contrary, have been parts and parcels of the manor of Igham, otherwise Heigham, in the county of Sussex aforesaid, and for all the time aforesaid have been and did lie, and as yet are and do lie, within the liberties of the town of Winchelsea, one of the ancient Cinque Port towns of the lady the Queen, and within the parish of Saint Thomas the Apostle, in Winchelsea aforesaid. And they further say, that for the separation and division of the aforesaid marsh and lands, called the Camber Beach and Camber Salts, from all other manors, lands, and tenements lying contiguous thereto, they have placed two posts of wood in the same lands on the day of taking this inquisition, vizt., one near the sea shore, not far off (in English, a little too short) from the view of Bowcliffe, and the other on a part of the river or creek aforesaid, called Camber Haven, otherwise Waine Way Water, towards the aforesaid boundary hundred of Goldspurr, called Kent Dike. And they further say, that the print or description (in English, the map or plot) to this inquisition annexed, is a true and perfect print (in English, a plot or map) of the same marsh and lands, called Camber Beach and Camber Head. In testimony whereof to both parts of this inquisition, as well to the aforesaid commission as to the inquisition aforesaid, they have affixed their seals on the day and year, and at the place abovesaid. The exemplification is stated to be at the instance and request of the mayor and commonalty of the town of Winchelsea, one of the ancient Cinque Port towns.

The beach has continued to increase; and the accumulation of land has been much facilitated by planting the grass named *Ammophila Arundinacea*, sea reed, marum or mat-weed. It was brought from Holland by Mr. Sotherden, when tenant of Camber farm, and planted on the east side of the harbour. In Holland, as well as in Norfolk, Cleveland in Yorkshire, Durham, Cheshire, and other places in England, it is extensively employed in forming the banks of sand, which preserve the land against the encroachments of the sea. This it does by means of its extensively creeping roots, which meet together and spread far and wide. The seeds drop into the sand, which gathers round the roots, vegetate and collect more sand until banks are formed. It only grows in the very driest sandy soils. It is common as far north as Orkney, and is found as far south as the Mediterranean.

Castle.—Winchelsea or Camber Castle is in that part of the manor of Higham, which is in the parish of Icklesham.

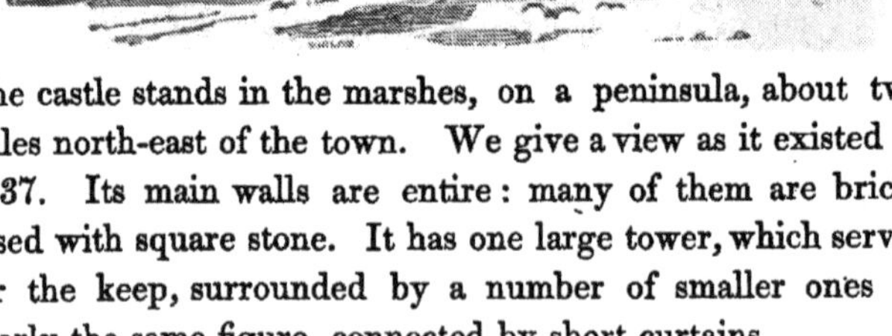

The castle stands in the marshes, on a peninsula, about two miles north-east of the town. We give a view as it existed in 1737. Its main walls are entire: many of them are brick, cased with square stone. It has one large tower, which serves for the keep, surrounded by a number of smaller ones of nearly the same figure, connected by short curtains.

S & N Buck, delt. J. Basire, litho

CAMBER CASTLE.

WEST VIEW.

1737

These buildings clearly evidence the very low and imperfect state of military architecture in this kingdom in the time of Henry VIII, for of all others, round towers were the least capable of actual defence. Round about the large tower or keep, there was a very low battery or place with chinks for firing out of, so low as now to be below the surface, though it is shewn in the engraving of 1737. On the moulding round the keep, are some devices, particularly the cross and rose:[1] and there are several specimens of the Tudor badge of the rose and crown.

This castle was built by Henry VIII, in 1538 or 1539, to defend the coast against invasion, on the ruins, according to Grose, of a more ancient building. It cost £23,000.

The history of the building of the several castles on the coasts of England and Wales by Henry VIII, is thus quaintly given by Hall in his Chronicle, (p. 828:)

The Kynges highnes, whiche never ceased to stody and take payne, both for the avauncement of the common wealth of this his realme of England, of the which he was the only supreme governour and hed; and also for the defence of al the same, was lately enfourmed by his trustie and faithfull frendes, that the cankerd and cruel serpent, the Bishop of Rome, by that arche traitor Reignold Poole, enemie to Godes worde and his natural contrey, had moved and stirred diverse great princes and potentates of Christendome to invade the realme of England, and utterlie to destroy the whole nacion of the same: Wherefore his Majestie, in his awne persone, without any delay, tooke very laborious and paynefull iourneys towardes the sea coastes, also he sent dyvers of his nobles and counsaylours to view and searche all the portes and daungiers on the coastes, where any meete and convenient landing place might be supposed, aswell on the borders of Englande as also of Wales, and in all soche doubtfull places his hyghnes caused dyverse and many bulwarkes and fortificacions to be made.

The castles of Camber and of Walmer, seem to have been the largest of the fortresses which were thus constructed by the king.

[1] Gent. Mag., vol. 67, p. 9, where a print is given of the view on entering the gate as it existed in 1797.

Leland, in his *Cygnia Cantio*, where his swan is singing and recounting the castles raised by King Hen. VIII, on the sea coasts,

> Prudens continuo per alta passim
> Artes littora confici jubebat,

Expresses that at Winchelsey, in the two following verses:

> Winchelseya suos sinus tuetur,
> Quà Limênus aquas agit profusas.[1]

"His Hyghnes" selected a very eligible position for Camber Castle. At the time it was built it was probably immediately adjoining on the sea shore, and must have been a strong guard against an enemy's entrance, either into Rye haven or Camber haven.

"At this time," (1540) says Mr. Holloway, "the sea flowed very close to the walls of this castle on the south-east and north sides, and having passed the latter, it formed a large bay, running back to the westward as far as Winchelsea, and covering the whole expanse between the east side of this town, and the west side of Rye, which constituted one general harbour for the two ports. It was for the general defence of the coast, and the particular one of this chamber or harbour, that this fortress was erected."[2]

Grose tells us, that "in the year 1541, this and all the other castles, block-houses, and bulwarks, in Kent and Sussex, were, by an act of parliament then made, put under the care of the Constable of Dover Castle."

On 21st July, 1544, (36 Hen. VIII) Captain Philip Chowte was appointed for life,[3] Captain of this castle, and Superintendant of the Camber and the Puddle creek, with a salary of 2s. a day, and power to appoint eight soldiers and six gunners, to be paid sixpence a day each out of the Treasury. In 1550, Robert Lucy was his deputy, and there were for the

[1] Lel., vol. 9, p. 21, v. 546, 547, 564, 565. [2] Hist. of Rye, p. 304.
[3] The letters patent are among the Dering MSS.

defence, seventeen gunners and ten soldiers.[1] Captain Chowte was continued in his office by Mary.

In 1553, 1 Mary, 1st August,[2] the following charges appear for this castle: 'Captain Philip Chowte captain there,

	£	s.	d.
For his wages, after the rate of 2s. ye daie by ye yeare .	36	10	6
Under capn. there, at 8d. ye daie by ye yeare	12	3	4
Porter, John Henbury, at 8d. ye daie by ye yeare . .	12	3	4
Under porter, Henry Gardiner, at 6d. ye daie by ye yeare .	9	2	6
Nine soldiers for their wages, at 6d. ye daie, every of them, in all by ye yeare	82	2	6
Seventeen gunners, at 6d. ye daie, every of them, by ye yeare	155	2	6
	£307	4	2

In 19th Elizabeth, (1576) Thomas Wilford was Captain.[3] The annual expense of the castle in her time,[4] was,—"captaine, fee per diem, 2s.; porter, fee per diem, 6d.; soldiers, four, fee do. a peece, 6d.; gunners, do. a peece, 6d."

In her time, a strong mount was cast up on the north side of the Camber, and formed an excellent road, to which ships repaired when they could not lie at Dover.[5]

In 1584, Thos. Wilford was still Captain;[6] and the following was "the proporsyon of repearations bestowed uppon the castells and forts wth in the v ports in anno 1584 and 1585:[7] Cambar castell, 1584, in money by warrant, clxxj*l.* j*d.* ob q." A heavy sum for the repairs of a castle built only forty years previously. And, in 1586,

The chardge wch Her Matie shal be at in furnishinge the castelles and fortes, wth in Mr. L. Wardein's chardge, he hath been accustomed in time of warre. Cambre Castell. The capitaine there hathe the Queen's Mats lres. patentes wth a certain nombre of gonners and soldiers, for

[1] Dering MSS. Chowte's name also appears in the Benevolence, granted 36 Hen. VIII. MS. Carlt. Ride.

[2] MSS. in Dulwich College Library.

[3] Dering MSS.

[4] Peck's Desiderata Curiosa, 1, p. 65.

[5] Harris' Hist. of Kent, p. 103.

[6] Addl. MSS. Hayley, 6344, p, 610.

[7] Lands. MSS, 48, art. 30.

the keeping thereof,—standing fee. And yet the capitaines doe make requeast, as in times past they have doen, for a supply of gonners and soldiers.[1]

Thomas Wilford was knighted, and was still Constable[2] there in 1596.

In 1610, (James I) there is a roll indented of the names of the captain and soldiers of the Castle of Camber, to receive pay from the 29th of September, 1610, mustered before Sir Thomas Waller. The following names appear: Captain Peter Temple, per diem 2s.; the captain's four men 6d. each per diem, Thos. Marshall, Marke Conney, Antny. Courtenden, Edmund Packson; Lieut. Robt. Butler, for himself and his men, per diem, 1s.; soldiers 6d. per diem each, Wm. Fox, Saml. Fish, Jno. Gallop, Wm. Dowland, Edmd. Collingwood, Thos. Boteler, Thos. Allen, Laurence Adams. This roll is signed by Robt. Butler, gent., Lieut. of the Castle. The orders of the captain were thus given:

These are to will and require you to take charge and care, under me, of several soldiers and gunners above-named, appertaining to the garrison of the castle, as well for the due ordering of them as for the performance of their several duties, in keeping wardes and watches, as other services there to be performed according to his majesty's behoof, according to the statutes and ordinances of ye said castle; and if any of ye said garrison shall be found disobediente or negligente in the performance of their dewties herein, you are to certifie the Lieuts. of Dover Castle thereof in my absence, or else unto myself, that I may see reformation therein as the case requires. Signed, Peter Temple, captain.[3]

The castle had, however, already become useless for defence; and in 2 Chas. I, (1626) we find a commission[4] directed to Lord Tufton, the Lieut. of Dover Castle; Sir N. Knatchbull; and Sir P. Haymond, knight, and the mayors of Dover, Romney, Hide, and Lid, mentioning,

[1] Lans. MSS. 48, art. 33.
[2] Dering MSS.
[3] MSS. in Dulwich Coll. Library, and Burr. MSS.
[4] Ib.

That the King having been informed that "our Castle of Camber, in or county of Sussex, is grown into great decay, being forsaken by the sea and left distant from ye water two miles at the least, so as the same is now of no further use for defence, but of continual charge unto us;" and "being humbly advised that our said castle should be demolished and the materials thereof sold to our use, and the value thereof employed for the fortifying of some other neighbouring castles and forts of more importance for our service and the safety of our kingdome," &c., &c. "We do give full authority unto you, or any five or more of you," to sell the materials of the said Castle of Camber. Witness ourself at West., 15 Nov., per ipsum regem.

The demolition was not effected; and by patent, 8th October, 9 Chas. I, (1632) the king granted to Thomas Porter, Esq., the custody, and office of Constable during life.[1]

On 26th August, 1642, it was ordered by the House of Commons that Mr. Morley do prepare an order for removing ye ordnance, musquets, powder, and other warlike ammunition from ye Castle of Camber, between Rye and Winchelsea, to the town of Rye.[2]

29 Aug. Whereas ye —— and commons in parliament have received information that divers pieces of ordnance, with powder, and other warlike provisions are now remaining in the Castle of Camber in ye Cinque Ports of ye county of Sussex, wch castle being altogether unguarded and no way useful for defence of ye sd county, ye ordnance and other provisions are exposed to the surprise of any ill-affected or malignant persons who may thereby be enabled to disturb ye peace of ye sd county; for prevention thereof and to ye intent they may be disposed of into a more safe place, ye lords and commons in parliament assembled, do order and appoint Captn. Richd. Cockeram, with ye assistance of ye inhabitants of the ancient town of Rye, in ye same county of Sussex, to seize, take, and remove ye ordnance and other ammunition from ye sd Castle of Camber unto ye said town of Rye, there to be reserved and kept for the use and service of ye sd county, and not to be delivered to any person or persons without special direction and allowance of both houses of parliament. Ordered: That this order be carried up to the House of Lords for their concurrence.[3]

[1] Rym. Fœd., 19, p. 528. [2] Journ. of Ho. of Commons, 2, 742.
[3] Ib. p. 746.

This order for dismantelling was fully carried out, and the walls were left to decay. So rapid was this, that, in 1664, (14 Charles II) we find a petition from Lieut. Wm. Carr for a lease of the site for 31 years, with the correspondence[1] which thereupon ensued. On 3rd June, 1664, the King referred the petition to the Lord Treasurer, (Southampton) who, on 14th June, sent it to Sir Charles Harbord: he, in his turn, on 18th June, forwarded it to Sir Denny Ashburnham, who was instructed to view the site, calling to his aid such magistrates of the town as he should think fit, and a carpenter and mason. Sir Denny reported that this ruined castle, and the ground whereon it stood, was of so inconsiderable a value that a grant to the petitioner would be worth just nothing; but Sir C. Harbord reported that if the petitioner desired it, the Lord Treasurer might do well to grant him a lease for thirty-one years, at 12d. rent, with power to take down and make sale of the old materials for his own use, without accompt: and a constat for such a lease from the preceding Michaelmas-day was made out accordingly. Notwithstanding this lease, the walls again escaped destruction. They became the property of the Carylls, and have since passed with the manor of Higham, in which they are locally situated.

The area is about three acres; and during the late war it was used for military reviews. In the beginning of 1795, the Duke of York reviewed here a brigade, consisting of the 14th regiment, then stationed at Winchelsea, and the 69th, then stationed at Silver Hill barracks, near Robertsbridge.

Camber Haven.—At the beginning of the reign of Henry IV, (1399) the state of this harbour attracted the serious attention of the king, who, in the first year of his reign, issued his patent for surveying the harbour of Winchelsea: viz., from a place called the Camber to Bodiam.[2] And in the following reign, 2 Henry V, (1414) a patent was issued[3] for

[1] Addl. MSS. 5705, p. 12. Lord Treasurer's Warrants, fol. 195.

[2] Rot. Pat., 1 Hen. IV, pt. 8, a tergo. [3] Ib., 2 Hen. V, pt. 2, a tergo.

walling and ditching between the port of Rye and Bodiam bridge. For some time the harbour remained good; but before the end of Henry the Eighth's reign the accumulation of beach at the mouth of this haven, and the want of back-water, caused by the inning of the marshes, gave cause for uneasiness, and various attempts were made to prevent the ruinous effects, which had been already produced upon Winchelsea, and were threatening Rye. On 29th January, 1548, the Commons read a first time, a bill for the Amending of Camber, and the Havens of Winchelsea and Rye,[1] and, as it is afterwards called, for Casting Ballast into the Camber. It was read a third time and passed in the Commons on the 19th February: it seems to have been lost in the Lords; and the evil was allowed to continue until 25th May, 1562, (4 Eliz.) when an inquisition was taken at Rye,[2] to enquire into the decay and ruin of the two havens of Rye and Camber; and the return showed that the injury had been sustained by the inning of the marshes, begun since 1532; and by Sir John Guldeford's inning since 1542, in Guldeford marsh (in his second inning) three great creeks; and by his lately new inned marsh, which being two foot lower than the salts, held a great quantity of water, which was then stopped and let off its course. But instead of opening the said creeks and laying forth the low marsh lands again, Sir J. Guldeford not only kept what he had inned off himself, but his heirs continued to in and embank more lands from the said haven, till at last, to complete the ruin of it, in 1719, Sir Robt. Guldeford, Bart., caused a wall or dam to be erected over the mouth of it at Camber point. Thus, in less than 187 years, after the inning of the marshes began, was this ancient haven, called Le Camber, alias the Waining Creek or Channel, totally stopped and destroyed, and a new church and parish erected on its ruins, called Guldeford, or East Guldeford.

[1] Commons Journals, p. 7-8.

[2] Burrell MSS., Brit. Mus., 5679, p. 486; and printed by Horsfield, vol. 1, p. 503.

Notwithstanding the evils thus produced before 1562, we find that the mischief was augmented. In 1570 there is, among the papers in the State Paper Office, (undated 1570) a petition to Cecil, for a grant on the payment of a fee farm rent of the Camber salts, for the purpose of inning them.

We have already seen the proposal,[1] made in the same year, on behalf of the town of Winchelsea to the Council, for cutting a new mouth, to be protected by stone piers and jetties. And in the year 1573,[2] the mayor, jurats, and commonalty of the town of Rye petitioned the Council for aid in the repair of the Puddle and Creek of Rye, and desired £3,000 towards the same, and her Majesty's Commission of Sewers for cleansing the watercourses from Newenden.

In 1582, the harbour and town of Winchelsea had gone to such decay that Thomas Digges, the excellent mathematician, when writing of Dover harbour,[3] says, "If we search the very cause of the flourishing estate of London, which, almost alone, in quantity, people, and wealth, in this age and realm is so increased, and contrary-wise of the poverty, or rather beggary and decay of Winchelsea, Rye, Romney, Hide, Dover, and many other poor towns, we shall find the decay of those havens, and preservation of the Thames, the only or chief occasion." Then he goes on to tell the Queen, that if her renowned father, in his time, found how necessary it was to make a haven at Dover, (when Sandwich, Rye, Camber, and others were good havens) how much more was the same then needful or rather necessary, those good havens being extremely decayed, and no safe harbour left in all the coast, almost between Portsmouth and Yarmouth.

Nevertheless, in the instructions for resisting the Spanish Armada,[4] in 1588, we find this direction:

Hastinges, whose members be, and are to fynde for the transportation

[1] See ante p. 106.
[2] MSS. in State Paper Office, No. 107.
[3] Arch., vol. 11, p. 214-5.
[4] Harl. MSS., 168, p. 115.

of the Kinge xxj shippes, of xx tonne the peece. Winchelseye, Rye, Deleaupenmey, Bulverhide, Bekesborne, and Guanshe.

In the names of "the chiefe portes, townes, and creeks in the maritime partes of the realme,"[1] we have mentioned, "Chichester, Shorham, Brighelmston, Hastinge, Rye, Dover, and Sandwich." And in the names of the forts and castles along the sea coast, with the names of the counties wherein they are,[2] we have "the castell of Camber, the port Rye, the port of Winchelsea, the port of Hastinges, the castell of Pemsey, the towne of Bishopston and Bleecherton, the towne of Esborne, Cutmere haven, Birlingate, the towne of Shrafford, Newhaven, Brighthemston, Shoram, Little Hampton, the haven of Arundell, and Chichester." Chichester was then the port, of which all the ports thence eastward to, and including Folkstone, were members.[3]

Norden, speaking of the haven of Winchelsea, tells us, that "within the memory of many yet living, (1724) there have been anchored above 400 sail of the tallest ships of all nations in a place called the Camber, near Rye, where now sheep and cattle feed." But in 44 Eliz., (1601) Sir Walter Raleigh[4] had declared, "there be many havens which have been famous, and now are gone to decay as Winchelsey: Rye is of little receipt."

We gather other interesting particulars of the state of the harbour at various times, from the government surveys which have taken place, and from the records of the efforts made at the commencement of the 18th century to restore the harbour to its former uses. The same cause of the decay is in every instance agreed on. In a survey[5] of the ports on the south-west coast of England, from Dover to the Land's End, by Edmund Dummer,

[1] Harl. MSS., 168, p. 116. [2] Ib. p. 117.

[3] Ib. In 1596, the inhabitants of Sandwich contributed to Rye harbour, in consequence of letters from the town of Rye and the Privy Council. Boys' Sandwich, p. 700.

[4] Townsend's Coll., 309. [5] Addl. MSS., 3233.

surveyor, and Capt. Thomas Wiltshaw, commissioners of his Majesty's navy, together with Capt. James Connaway, and Capt. William Crust, masters of the Trinity House, at Deptford, delineated in July and August, 1698, and addressed to the principal officers and commissioners of her Majesty's navy; it is said, that

The Commissioners came to Rye on 5th July, 1698, and were assisted by the informations of the most ancient and best observing persons dwelling there, who acquainted them in how much better condition the haven of Rye was known to be in former times within memory, and what they esteemed to be the reason of the great decay of it at that day, and having viewed it, the Commissioners add, that, upon the whole of what they saw and observed of the circumstances of this place, they were easily induced to make this determination in their opinion. That it was in no case proper for a safe harbour to resort to, nor capable to be improved by any tolerable charge for any services of the navy, for the following reasons. First:—There was a very high sand westward of the entrance of the haven, which ran above two miles in length without the mouth thereof. The channel or gut towards the haven lyeth on the east side, and is, for the whole length of the sand, one continued bar of not above four and so to two foot depth at low water, and made it impracticable for the smallest vessels to venture in, but when the tide was aloft or lifting and smooth water. Secondly:—The harbour within, likewise, at low water times, was all dry, except some gleeting of freshes from the country; and all the space of water that was therein, when the tide was out, lay in the very entrance of the haven and just within it, capable only of floating a few fisher boats. Thirdly:—The encroachments and inning of the lands upwards in the country, and the infinite mass of matter that floated in the troubled sea, with which all weathers and tides were constantly working to fill the same, had almost shut the sea out of this haven: and the Commissioners doubted it would be very difficult to propound effectual means to remove it, unless it might be possible to be brought to pass to give the sea the same freedom of flux and reflux as it was presumed, by ancient tradition, to have had for near thirty miles into the country, though then confined to less than three miles course that way. But the propriety of sundry persons, and the policy of the sewers in several ages past, had wholly dammed it out: and doubtless would be very unwilling to abandon the wast, which had been, from time to time, taken in at great expenses. Therefore, the Commissioners looked upon this haven as entirely lost; at least, in no condition to be esteemed for any services of the navy. They then give a map of the harbour as it then was, and after describing other ports, the Commissioners wind up their whole report by saying, that the havens and rivers of Rye, Pemsey, Cookmere, Newhaven, Shoreham, and Arundell were then (whatever they had been) no proper subjects of improvement for the navy, for want of that benefit, all useful ports had, namely, a sufficient indraught of the sea suitable to the rise of tides upon the same coasts, that there (on springs) were observed to be 19 or 20 feet upright: for industry, by enclosing waste on the one hand, and nature on the other: by the plenty of sullage the sea washed from the higher shores, and carried about in motion to lodge again in places more confined and quiet, which had, by degrees, not only filled vast spaces, once, doubtless, possessed by the sea with firm ground, but had likewise choked up almost the very passages of the land fresh, which naturally tended to it, so that in these, as in the decays of natural things in general, the conduits and channels of their being, were destroyed with themselves, and the Commissioners doubted without hopes of recovering.

Notwithstanding this unfavorable report, the inhabitants of Rye and Winchelsea made a vigorous, though fruitless, effort to obtain the sanction of the Legislature to an amendment of the haven, by the restoration of a good supply of back-water. A committee of enquiry was appointed by the House of Commons at the instigation of the members for Rye; and on 4th January, 1699-1700, a petition[1] was presented from the mayors, jurats, freemen, and chief inhabitants of Winchelsea, setting forth,

"That Rye is the only harbour for ships upon the coast of Kent and Sussex, from Dover to Portsmouth; lies opposite to Diep and other considerable French ports, and was a sufficient reception for the whole navy royal; but now the harbour is so choked up with slub, by the inning of land, and making flood-gates and walls across the same, that not more than twenty small ships can now lie there; and if some speedy care be not taken, a ship of burden will not be able to get in there, the harbour, yearly, growing worse and worse, to the great discouragement of navigation and trade:" and praying "that some course might be taken to restore the said harbour to its ancient goodness, which was for the benefit of the whole nation."

[1] Journals of Ho. of Com., vol. 13, p. 95.

The petition was referred to the committee, to whom a like petition from Rye, presented on the 16th Dec. preceding, had been referred. In the Rye petition, it was said that the mouth of the harbour was but sixty fathoms wide, so that a fort might be built there at a small charge, which would hinder an enemy from coming to annoy the ships riding in the harbour. Petitions in favor of the harbour were also presented from Poole, Liverpool, Portsmouth, Limington, Weymouth and Melcem Regis, and New Romney.

Mr. Robt. Colepepyr gave information as to the removal of obstructions, which were referred to the surveyor of the Navy Board, and having been favorably reported on, the report was sent to this committee. It was given in evidence,[1]—That at the time of the Beachy Head fight, (1690) Capt. Stone came into the harbour with a fire ship that drew eleven feet of water, and two or three other fire ships: that the St. Andrew had rid there in 21 feet of water, and a Dutch man-of-war of forty guns, rid afloat with loaded guns: that forty-five years before, in Oliver Cromwell's time, a hundred sail of ships could ride in the harbour, and that ships could ride against the town of Rye, then having two fathoms and a half of water: that even during the then late war with the French, twenty sail of ships might come and ride within a mile of the town: that recently four ships, of about sixty tons each, had put in there without anchor and cable: but that the tide then flowed, at spring tides, four fathoms, and at low water, not more than a foot and a half; two miles without the town being a flat: that about forty-five years before, a ship of 100 tons was built at Appledore, six miles above the town: that fifteen or sixteen years before, a hoy of sixty tons, which drew nine feet of water, went to Blackwall and unloaded there: and that a ship of 100 tons was known to have gone up to Stone, in the Isle of Oxney, and loaded there. It was also proved that the evil had

[1] Journals of Ho. of Com., vol. 13, p. 315.

arisen from erecting flood-gates, stops, and cross walls, across the river Appledore and the channel through Wittersham marsh, which were made at Blackwall about 1646, and continuing to be made till 1695, took away the strength of the water from the harbour, hindered the efflux and reflux of the tide, and caused all the sullage that came in to rebound back and settle in the harbour, so that it was choked up. Upon which the Committee, on 6th April, 1700, reported, "That the cross walls, stops, and flood-gates set up in the river Rother and chanel through Wittersham levell, and inning the said river and chanel, and making land of the same; and likewise inning of sea wastes, which draw a constant influx and efflux to scour the harbour of Rye, have wholly injured the navigation of the said river and chanel, and are the cause of stopping up the said harbour. That if the stops in the chanel through Wittersham level shall be taken away, and inside walls made on both sides of the chanel, it will restore the ancient navigation of the river Rother, and make the harbour of Rye a good harbour again."

Parliament was prorogued on the Thursday following, and no further steps were that year taken on this report. In the new parliament, however, (15th Jan., 1701-2) a bill was presented for restoring the harbour to its ancient goodness, for the benefit of the nation, which was opposed by the Earls of Leicester, Chesterfield, and Thanet, Sir Robt. Guldeford, John Hales, Geo. Pearce, John Shelley, Thos. Frewen, Esqs., and other land owners, and by the Commissioners[1] of Sewers for the upper levels, and defeated.

Had the works, under the act of 1722, for making a new harbour, with the mouth near Cliff-End, succeeded, Winchelsea might have been benefitted; but when those works were abandoned, this town lost its last hope of becoming once more a port.

[1] Their case is given in Holloway's Romney Marsh, p. 168. They stated that 10,000 acres had been inclosed.

The state of the harbour and its defects are fully pointed out in the report of the Commissioners on the Harbours on the South-Eastern Coast, made in 1840.[1] They agree with the former commissioners as to the causes of the decay. Since their report, however, a sum of £10,000 towards the improvement of the harbour has been paid by the South-Eastern Railway Company, for leave to make their bridge across the river.

PARISH AND LIBERTY OF ST. LEONARD.

The Parish and Liberty of St. Leonard of Iham, as it is called in the Hastings Corporation MSS., lies at the north-west corner of the town of Winchelsea; of which, however, it never formed part. It has always been, and still is, a liberty of the town and port of Hastings, for which place the occupiers of tenements, &c., have the right of voting. Like the manor of Brede, this parish remained the property of the Abbot of Fischampe until the dissolution of alien monasteries, (temp. Hen. VI) and then it was granted to Syon monastery. The best description of this liberty is to be found in the following survey, made in 1748, preserved among the records of Hastings, which, together with a copy of the map, was communicated to us by Mr. John Goldsworthy Shorter.

A survey and representation of the parish of Saint Leonard, situate and adjoining to the town and corporation of Winchelsey, in the county of Sussex, which said parish belongeth to and is under the jurisdiction of the worshipful the mayor, the jurats, and commonalty of the town and port of Hasting, in the said county. Herein are exhibited not only all the sought or known boundaries and limits, but the whole parish: consisting of thirteen pieces or parcels of pasture and wood land, the shattered remains of St. Leonard's church, a windmill, and the miller's house contiguous, as did appear on the said premises to Samuel Cant, the appointed and authorized surveyor thereof, taken from the best informations that could be obtained from the worshipful Edwin Wardroper, Esquire, mayor of Winchelsey in 1747, and from William Marten, gent.,

[1] Report, Parl. Papers, Session 1840, No. 368.

and John Baker, and also, and more especially and particularly, from intelligence afterward had from the Revd. Mr. Willes, minister of the parish of St. Thomas the Apostle, in the said corporation of Winchelsey, who formerly has gone the bounds of St. Leonard's, as well as those of St. Thomas', abutting thereto on the south and south-east, being confines to each other. He also well remembers (nearly, if not to exactness) the procession line went from the mark stone near St. Leonard's church, (see the following tables) cross a corner of Mr. Odiarne's field, to a point in the eastern-most hedge thereof, between a corner thorn bush and a shrub ash; and that the next limit extended cross the next field more east, to a point in the northern-most hedge, near to a round stone conick building, called the Roundle, in St. Thomas' parish; and to confirm these limits, saith, that about a quarter of an acre in Mr. Odiarne's field always paid tithes annually to him, the present incumbent of St. Thomas'; and that about the same quantity, or a little more, in the Roundle field has ever been exempted from the payment of the tithes to him as being in St. Leonard's. From this last point, he saith, that the limit goes in a straight line under the hill, almost impassable to the bottom. And that to avoid a precipice and other steep descents, they used to go down a footway near the Roundle, into the common highway, fetching a compass to that point, which circumambulation of the processioners might induce Mr. Wardroper, &c., to imagine that the Ferry marsh was in St. Leonard's parish: whereas this marsh has paid tithes (time immemorial) to St. Thomas'. The said Mr. Willes saith the limit, from this point, goes along by the ditch, bounding Ferry marsh on the west and north-east, into the corner of Rushy marsh, near a bridge over the channel. That the channel is the north boundary; that the point of concourse or meeting of the waters of the channel and the common sewer, running southward, is the western boundary. That, from this point, the limit goes up the hedge eastward, to the remains of an old stone house in St. Thomas' parish. That passing close by this old foundation, go along the brow in or by a green deepish ditch, where formerly was an hedge and trees, as appears from stems and roots, northward to the corner of St. Leonard's church yard. Lastly, from this point go eastward, through the church yard to the mark stone above-mentioned, in the lane or street leading into the town of Winchelsey, and you will have the limits of St. Leonard's parish according to the afore-mentioned declarations.

The map, which follows, is inaccurate as to the square in which St. Thomas' church stands.

EXPLANATIONS OF MAP.

References.			Rods.
a	Is a known mark stone near St. Leonard's church yard, and the remains of the parish church, marked (H,) distance - -		15
b	Is a sought point in an hedge eastward, cross Mr. Odiarne's field, between a thorn bush and shrub ash, and distant from -	*a*	20
c	Is a sought point in an hedge more eastward, cross the Roundle piece, being near to it, and at the distance from - -	*b*	24
d	Is a sought point in an hedge north-westernly, cross the Hanging piece, over a precipice and some descents, and distant from -	*c*	42
e	Is a known point in the eastern-most corner of Rushy marsh, going along the ditch boundary, Ferry marsh, near a bridge, distant from	*d*	56
f	Is a known point along the channel in Rushy marsh, westernly, in the corner, and meeting of the channel and sewer, distant from	*e*	112
g	Is a sought point along the sewer, southernly, going through this marsh, St. Leonard's marsh, and Brewer's marsh, and distant from	*f*	108
h	Is a known point up an hedge at the Barr's, easternly, near a stone foundation of an house in St. Thomas' parish, distant from -	*g*	28
i	Is a known point at the end of the ditch, northward, under St. Leonard's church yard fence, being post and rayl, and distant from	*h*	22
a	Is the first and only mark stone above-mentioned and described, situate in a lane or street leading to the town, distant from -	*i*	17
	Total		429
	So that it appears, and is found by computation, that the extent from point to point around the entire parish of St. Leonard's, near Winchelsey, amounts to one mile, one quarter, and twenty-nine rods.		
	OTHER OBSERVABLES.		
1	From the mark stone (*a*) going the St. Leonard's church yard, along the way (the dotted line to *h*) you come to St. Leonard's well, which supplies almost all the inhabitants of Winchelsey with good water; 'tis under the southern-most hanger, and is distant from	*a*	65
2	The Roundle is supposed to have been a watch tower or a windmill: (*l*) is the north gate, near one mile distant from the south gate: (*m*) is a public house, (Mr. Parnell's) a corner house, entering the street leading to St. Leonard's church: (*n*) is a part of St. Thomas' church, or rather 'tis the chancel, the body of the church being in ruins, the walls having no roof.		

The bounds thus given, coupled with an examination of the lithographed map, will give an accurate view of this liberty; but Mr. Cant goes on to set out the names of the thirteen different pieces, with the quantities in each piece, and the names of the several owners and tenants.

Plate X

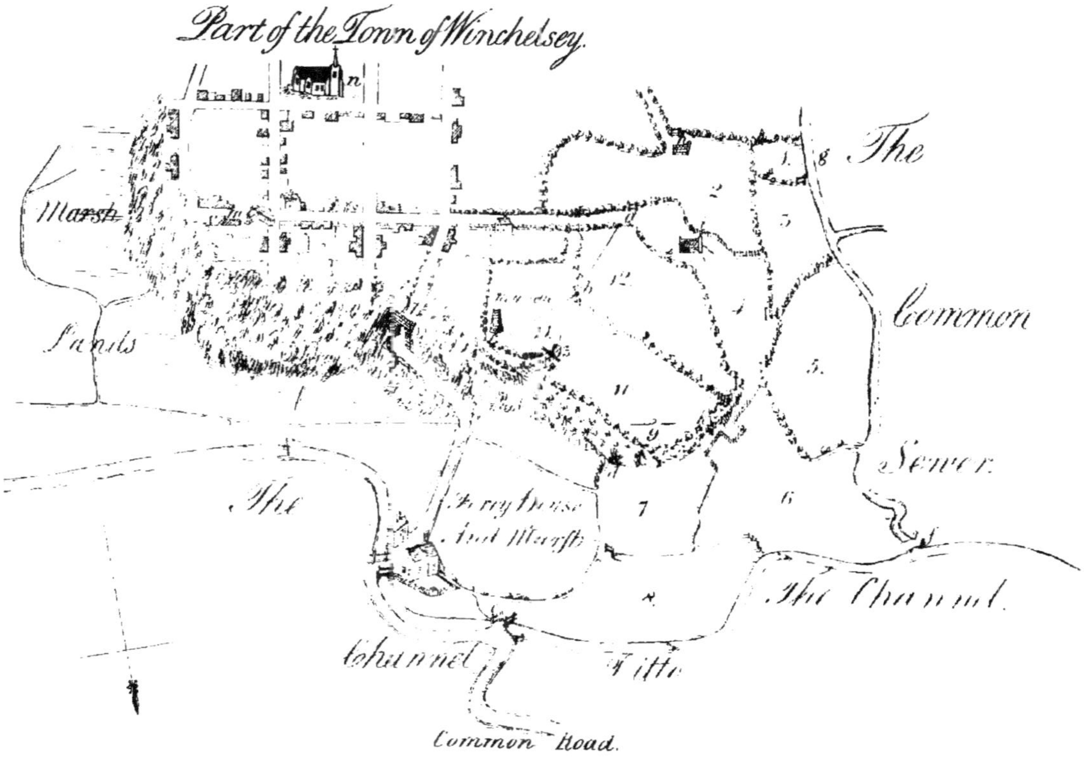

Part of the Town of Winchelsey
The
Common
Sewer
The Channel
Marsh
Sands
The
Channel
Ferry House And Marsh
Common Road

	NAMES OF PIECES.	THE OWNERS' NAMES.	THE TENANTS' NAMES.	Acres, more or less
1	Nameless, or the Short Acre field -	Captain Pigram, of Rye -	John Brown -	1
2	Nameless, or the Hilly field -	Lord Viscount Donerayle	John Knight -	2½
3	Brewer's marsh - - -	Ditto, late Newman's -	Francis Cruttenden	2½
4	Nameless, or St. Leonard's church field - - - -	Lord Donerayle - -	John Knight -	4
5	Saint Leonard's marsh - -	William Stone, Esq. -	Francis Cruttenden	6
6	Rushy marsh, southern-most -	Lord Donerayle - -	John Knight -	7½
7	Rushy marsh, middlemost -	Ditto - -	Ditto -	3¼
8	Rushy marsh, northern-most, eastern-most - - - - -	Ditto - -	Ditto -	7
9	The two hangers, wood land, rough	Ditto - -	Ditto -	3½
10	The Mill field - - -	Ditto - -	Edward Catt -	5
11	The Roundle piece - - -	Ditto - -	Ditto -	0½
12	Nameless, or the Street field -	Edward Odiarne, gent., of Winchelsey -	Joseph Tree -	5¾
13	The garden, the bank, the house, the mill - - - -	Mr. Newnham or Mr. Staffield, of Rye -	Thomas Taylor -	0½
			Total by Estimation	48¾

N.B.—Number 1, 2, 4, and 12 are feigned names, by me assumed, and so called from No. 1 being something short of an acre; No. 2 is a rising ground or hilly; No. 4 is under or below St. Leonard's church yard; and No. 12 is adjoining to the lane or street. The course of the channel from *(f,)* westward, and from the Ferry house, eastward, is only feigned by way of ornament. Also the marshes and ditches in the level the same. Together with the plan of the town, which, notwithstanding, seemed to me necessary by way of illustration and ease in finding the premises.—*Samuel Cant*, 1748.

CHURCH, &c.—The Church was formerly an object of considerable interest. In it, says Lambard, " stood the image of St. Leonard holding a fane, or rather Eolus' mace, in his hand, which women and others of like infirmities used to turn (after offering made) toward such coasts as they desired the wind to serve for the speedy return of their friends or husbands."

The living was a rectory thus valued in Pope Nicholas' Taxation.

Ecclesia de Yham non excedit, £4 13s. 4d.

The last institution of the rector to be found in the Bishop's Registers, is

1484, Dec. 18. Thomas Bate, Canon regularis, on the decease of John Grafton, and on the presentation of the Abbess and Convent of Syon.

From this time the church was allowed to fall to decay, and all traces have now disappeared.

CORPORATION.

The most accurate account of this Corporation is to be found in the report made in 1835, by the Commissioners for enquiring into the Municipal Corporations in England and Wales; and that report we must take as our guide. The title of the corporation is, "The Mayor, Jurats, and Commonalty of the Ancient Town of Winchelsea."

The officers appointed by the Corporation are, or should be, a Mayor; twelve Jurats; Town Clerk; Chamberlain; Sergeant-at-Mace; Town Serjeant; Water Bailiff; Gaoler; six Constables; and a Pound Driver. The number of Freemen, (in 1834) exclusive of the jurats, was three: it has been increased since to thirteen, the present number including the jurats. The mayor is elected annually, on Easter Monday, from the freemen, at what is called a Hundred Court, by the mayor, jurats, and freemen. In order to form this court, there must be present, the mayor or his deputy, and at least two jurats, and two freemen. It had been always customary for the corporation and town clerk to meet together the evening before the election, and arrange who should be mayor for the following year. Such person had been then proposed the next day and elected, as a matter of course. For many years the mayor had seldom been resident. The duties had generally been performed by a deputy, except on the day of election, when the mayor had usually attended. The office, until 1832, had been for some years confined to three individuals, one of whom had always been elected. The object of the system pursued in this election, and that of the jurats, as well as in the admission of freemen, may be briefly stated. Previously to the Reform Act, the freemen had the exclusive right of voting for members of parliament for the town. For many years the patronage of the borough was considered to be entirely in the hands of one individual; all the elections, therefore, had been made with reference to his parliamentary interest. Most of the persons elected jurats, had been on first coming into the corporation, strangers to the town. There can be no doubt that some of them had taken up their residence there, solely for the purpose of keeping up the patron's interest. In order to preserve the borough as close as possible, the number of electors had been kept as low as would secure the existence of the corporation. By this means, one or two individuals could prevent any valid meeting of the corporation taking place, by merely staying away from it. One object of always electing a personal friend of the patron to the office of mayor, was, that of having him for Returning Officer in case of an election. Additional security was also obtained by it. The mayor has the appointment of his own deputy, whom he can displace at pleasure: and the presence of one or other of them is necessary for every corporate meeting. These two would have been able to prevent any admission into the body, even if all the other members of it had combined to open the corporation. No election took place at Easter, in 1833, and the mayor of the preceding year continued in office. The town clerk and other inferior officers, with Mr. John Tilden, went into the hall on the day of election, but, as neither the mayor or his deputy attended, no Court could be held. Another attempt was made the following day, pursuant to the statute, with the same success. The deputy mayor stated, that the reason of his non-attendance was his having had no instructions from the mayor to attend. He admitted, however, that it was understood before hand that no election should be come to. There seemed to be no doubt that this proceeding had been agreed upon between the patron and his friends, purposely to cause a dissolution of the corporation, the disfranchisement of the borough having taken away all inducement to them to take any further trouble in the affairs of the town.[1]

A deputy mayor is annually appointed by the mayor, to officiate for him in his absence during the year. The appoint-

[1] Commissioners' Report.

ment is made after that of jurats has taken place; one of whom is always appointed. The deputy mayor has always been resident.

The jurats are appointed annually, by the mayor, out of the freemen. As soon as he has taken the oaths, he calls upon such freemen, not exceeding twelve in number, as he thinks proper, who then take the oaths of Justices of the Peace. It is not necessary that they should be present at the time, as they may take the oaths at any time during the year. It has been usual to re-appoint all who have ever been jurats. Of late years, four or five have generally been appointed.

All the other officers are elected annually, on the same day as the mayor. The right of election of all of them, except the serjeant-at-mace and constables, is in the mayor, jurats, and freemen, jointly.[1] The appointment of constables is probably in the justices only. The sergeant-at-mace is appointed by the mayor.

The freemen are admitted at a common assembly, consisting of the mayor, jurats, and freemen. There have seldom been more than twelve at one time, including the mayor and jurats.[2] The members of parliament have generally been admitted, pursuant to the resolution of a Guestling, temp. Elizabeth, but

[1] As long as the freemen of 1834 had been acquainted with the corporation, all the elections had been merely matters of form, the selection of the officers having been made by those members of the corporation who had the principal management of the borough. As soon as the deputy mayor and jurats were appointed, a list was handed to the mayor, containing the names of the officers for the following year. Persons who wished it were continued in office: when any one had signified a wish to resign his office, the name of his successor was inserted instead of his. The mayor then read over the list, and proposed each person. No opposition was ever made, and the officers were severally sworn into their offices.

[2] Although the Corporation refused to admit the inhabitants to their freedom, they did not scruple to fine non-freemen for exercising their callings within the town. In the Chamberlain's book there is this entry: "1762. To received for fines of Messrs. Johnson, Christopher Clarke, John Clarke, Thomas Atwell, and Colin Bridger, for exercising their trades in the town, £2 12s. 6d."

as they have not resided and paid rates, they were not entitled to any privileges.[1]

The whole number of freemen, including jurats, is now, (1850) as we have seen, only thirteen.

The Mayor, Jurats, and Freemen form the governing body of the corporation. Forty-eight hours notice of every meeting is requisite. This is given to each resident member personally, by the sergeant-at-mace, on a precept directed to him by the mayor.

The *Mayor* is a Justice of the Peace for the town and liberty. He or his deputy is a quorum Judge of the Court of Record. The mayor is also Coroner.

Formerly the mayor received 20s. every quarter, or £4 a year salary. He has now no salary nor any other emoluments.

The duties of the *Jurats* are confined to those which devolve upon them as Justices of the Peace for the town and liberty. They have no emoluments.

The *Town Clerk* attends all the meetings of the corporation, and enters the proceedings. He acts as Clerk to the Justices. In early days he had a salary of 10s. a quarter, or £2 a year: of late years he had no salary, but charged for his services in a professional bill.

The *Chamberlain* acts as the Treasurer of the Corporation. He seems to have had no salary or emoluments: he is a freeman.

The *Sergeant-at-Mace* attends at and proclaims all the courts and assemblies. He serves all the precepts and summons the juries. When the Court of Record was in operation, the

[1] The object in all the admissions was merely to keep the parliamentary borough in the hands of the patron: no one was admitted who was not either a personal friend of his, or who had not some strong inducement to promote his interest. Most of those admitted of late years, up to 1834, had come to reside within the town from a distant part of the kingdom. Some of them had a nominal residence, and were rated in the town, but had seldom gone there except on occasions of elections of mayor and of members of parliament.

sergeant-at-mace was one of the attornies of it, and the person to whom the process was directed. In practice, the sergeant-at-mace has been also goaler, crier, water-bailiff, and constable. Formerly his salary as sergeant,[1] was 7s. 6d. a quarter, or 30s. a year: now it is £3 2s. 8d. He receives from the corporation 5s. for every jury which he summons. He has an annual allowance of £1 for taking care of the court hall. Up to 1834, he had a salary as gaoler, of £25 He has the customary fees as constable for executing warrants. He has no allowance as crier, and his earnings as such are very trifling.

The duties of *Town Sergeant* are the same as those of

[1] The Chamberlain's accounts were formerly audited yearly; but between 1812 and 1834 there was no audit. In the earliest Chamberlain's book, which has been preserved, commencing 1753, there is this entry of the salary formerly paid. 1755, March 26. Pd Benjn. Tree, town sergeant, salary and two years blowing the horn, due at Easter, 1753, £1 19s. Blowing the horn was the mode of summoning all the assemblies. The horn blower took a very prominent part in the entrance into Yarmouth of the Bailiffs from the Cinque Ports, to regulate the herring fishing. In the record of the proceedings in 1833, when no mayor was elected, it is expressly stated that the corporation were duly warned according to ancient custom, by sounding the horn at the break of day. And some years since, when a riot occurred at Hastings, and the gaol was broken open by the fishermen, to release their wives and children, imprisoned for selling fish at their accustomed place, the Stade, the men were assembled by blowing the horn along the stade. The Winchelsea horn yet retains its place in the town hall. The entries in the Chamberlain's books are few, and generally uninteresting: a very few only may be worth recording.

		£	s.	d.
1755, Jany 9.	Pd for the press warrant - - -	0	2	6
1756, May 14.	Pd John Alce, spent at the declaration of war, &c.	0	19	8
1761.	Pd ditto, a bill of expences at the coronation and other times - - - -	9	2	10
	Pd Ben. Tree a bill of expences at the same time	2	16	8
	Faggots and fireworks at the same time	3	7	0
1764.	Two Frenchmen's gaol allowance - -	0	11	3
	For watching the Frenchmen at the gaol	3	2	0
	Mr. Mayor, as per bill for conveying the Frenchmen to Horsham - -	4	10	6
	For cushions for seat in the church -	0	15	2

sergeant-at-mace, for which he has his salary. He is Pound Driver, for which office his profits are very small.

The *Water Bailiff*[1] is the officer authorised to execute warrants and to make arrests upon the sea, within the jurisdiction of the corporation. There are no emoluments attending the office, beyond the usual fees for executing warrants.

The *Constables* are seldom called upon: they reside within the town of Winchelsea.

It was not known in 1834, that the Freemen had ever enjoyed any special privilege in the town beyond that of voting for members of parliament; but they are entitled to the same exemption from toll, and to the same general privileges as other freemen of the Cinque Ports.

The Quarter Sessions are held regularly before the mayor or deputy mayor, and jurats. The jurisdiction of the court extends to capital felonies; but they, and indeed all serious cases, are sent for trial at the Assizes or County Sessions. The town clerk is the Clerk of the Peace.

The Court of Record was to be held every fortnight, before the mayor or his deputy, and two or more jurats. The court days are Tuesdays.[2] In practice, during recent times, the court was never held, except when there was business to be done, but regular entries of adjournments were made in the book. It has jurisdiction over all actions, real and personal. The greatest use to which it was applied, was levying fines. The expense was about £4 each fine. Since the act, however, for the abolition of fines and recoveries, this business has ceased. The court exercised its powers for any amount, and was, in effect, a Court of Request. A court of this nature, for debts under 40s., has immemorially existed at Rye; and the constitutions of the two towns are in other respects the same.

[1] The emblem of the Water Bailiff's office is a silver oar; and, as part of Rye harbour is in this jurisdiction, his aid is needed to take offenders there into custody.

[2] Jeake.

A rate, in the nature of a County Rate, is imposed on the whole district within the jurisdiction of the Corporation, at the Quarter Sessions. It was first imposed about the year 1818. The usual rate is 6d. in the pound upon a fixed rental.[1] The rental for Winchelsea is £1,476; for the part of Icklesham within the liberty, £1,188; of Broomhill £1,248; and of Pett £127. The frequency of the rate has depended chiefly upon the number of smugglers taken. The charges upon it consist of the usual expenses of inquests and prisoners, gaoler's salary, allowance to the juries for dinners, and treasurer's salary of £3 3s.

Town Dues.—The only revenue which the Corporation possesses, is derived from the Town Rents, of which, together with the King's Rents, we give a list. Many are fee-farm rents, and are paid in respect of the houses and lands granted by Elizabeth to the town, or for buildings which have been erected on what was originally the waste land of the town.[2] An exchange was made about 1830, of the site of the public pound, for a small plot of ground, and the pound removed to

[1] Out of a Land Tax of 4s. in the pound, amounting altogether to £1,257 4s., for Hastings, Rye, and Winchelsea, the last town paid £405. Addl. MSS., 6344, p. 437.

[2] The majority of these grants was made between the years 1660 and 1690. Several are in the possession of Mr. Stileman. They were usually made in consideration of a sum of money paid at the time, and of a small reserved rent. They are only interesting now as shewing the names of places and of the then inhabitants, and boundaries of property. Among them, on 3rd August, 1675, is a grant to Richard Chesson and his attorney, Mr. Hovedon, of a piece of land called Furze Bank and Deadman's lane, containing a quarter of an acre, abutting to Saffron garden and Furze Bank field, towards the east, to land called Frayes, towards the north, to Crooked Acre and Pont's field, towards the west, and to a lane leading to Icklesham, between Gallows Hill field and Furze Bank field, towards the south, at the yearly rent of 12d. And on 21st April, there was a similar grant to R. Chesson, in consideration of £4, and the yearly rent of 6d., of several parcels of streets or lanes on the west side of the town, adjoining to a parcel of land of Chesson's, called Hammell, as far as the north-west corner of St. Giles' church yard, and towards the east

another part of the waste. The ground taken in exchange is let by the Corporation. The fee-farm rents, as stated in the report of the commissioners, amount to £19 0s. 7¼d. The whole income of the Corporation, in 1834, was only £22 3s. 7½d. During the halcyon days of nomination, the difference between the receipts of the town and the expenditure was made up by the patron: it was of no importance, therefore, to audit the Chamberlain's accounts.

SEAL, &c.—The Seal of the Corporation is as ancient as the corporate seal of any port, and is far more elaborate than the seals of most towns. For the annexed engraving we are indebted to the kindness of the Sussex Archæological Society,[1] and to the author of the paper on the Cinque Port Seals in Sussex, Mr. Mark Anthony Lower, of whose description, with some slight additions, we make a free use. The date of the seal is the early part of the reign of Edward I; the royal arms do not contain the quartering of France, which took place 14 Edw. III, (1340) and the banner bears the arms of Lewknor, *Or. three chevrons, gu.*, who was, as we have seen, one of the owners at the foundation of the new town.

The obverse is the same as that on the Pevensey seal, and "exhibits an ancient ship with a poop and an embattled forecastle, both very lofty. On the latter is a banner, and abaft the staff of it a fleur-de-lis. The crew consists of eight men, one of whom is steering; over his head, upon the poop, are two others with immense speaking trumpets, like those observable in many seals of this period; four others are engaged in drawing in a cable and squaring a yard, and the remaining man is ascending the backstay. Above the yard are a crescent and a star, and beneath it the

---

as far as the highway, leading from Pipewell gate towards Newgate, and westward as far as the bars entering Furze Bank field, and northward as far as the highway, from Petmorris upward, towards the town, all which were situate in the parish of St. Thomas, and contained one acre. Among the same deeds, we find that Crooked Acre and Soggs, two acres, were in Winchelsea; but that the piece of marsh land adjoining Crooked Acre, called Philpott's, containing one acre, was in St. Leonard's parish.

[1]Suss. Arch. Collections, vol. 1, p. 21.

royal arms of *three lions passant.* The legend is, SIGILLVM : BARONVM : DOMINI : REGIS : ANGLIE : DE : WINCHELLESE. 'The Seal of the Barons of our Lord the King of England of Winchelsea.'"

The device of the Counter Seal[1] is of a very elaborate kind: like the seals of Shrewsbury and other towns, it consists of a representation of the public buildings of the town. On the right side is the gothic church of St. Thomas, with its nave, side aisles, and central tower, and spire with crocketted gables and pinnacles: on the left side is the gothic church of St. Giles, with a nave, side aisle, and spire, also shewing crocketted gables and pinnacles. In the centre is a high embattled tower, representing, most probably, the town hall and light-house.

On the central tower stands the figure of a warden "holding out a lantern, as if to guide benighted mariners into port. In front of this personage, on a shield, are the three lions passant of England, and behind his back is a banner charged with three chevrons for Lewknor." More to the left, perched upon the spire of St. Giles' church, is a "bird, which appears to have been introduced merely for the purpose of filling up a blank space in the design." At the base of the seal, below the tower and churches, are three or four buildings, representing the religious houses of the new town, and below them waves of the sea. In the central or tower compartment is a doorway, approached by several steps: in the opening are figures, representing the Annunciation; and in a small niche above, there is a crowned or nimbed figure of the Virgin and child: on the left hand, in two niches, are "representations of St. Giles caressing that faithful hind, by whose milk his life is reputed to have been sustained. The three niches to the right of the tower exhibit the martyrdom of St. Thomas à Becket. In the central compartment the Archbishop in his pontificals is seen kneeling before an altar, while an attendant priest elevates a crucifix above his head, as if to ward off the sword of one of the assassin knights, who, from behind, is aiming the fatal blow. On the left, another is seen armed with a shield and a drawn sword; and to the right, a third is in the act of unsheathing his weapon. These representa-

[1] The Counter Seal now in use is a modern imitation of the original, which was lost during an electioneering squabble, and is now in the possession of Mr. W. J. Denne.

tions of S. S. Giles and Thomas refer to the dedications of the two principal churches of Winchelsea, and the surrounding legend contains an invocation of these joint patrons of the port, viz.:

✠ EGIDIO : THOME : LAUDVM : PLEBS : CANTICA : P(RO)ME :
NE : SIT : IN : ANGARIA GREX : SVVS : AMNE : VIA.

The precise meaning of the second verse has long been a matter of enquiry and discussion. Mr. J. D. Parry's translation, which, to the Rev. Edmund Cartwright, seemed to express the meaning as near as it can be made out, was,

'To Giles' and Thomas' praise, ye people chaunting pray;
Lest in the Angarian road their flock be washed away.'

Though this rendering is obviously absurd, it is not very easy to arrive at the true sense." Mr. Lower's attempt to do so was, that Angaria was "applied to any pressed or compulsory service, and from thence came to mean anxiety or distress of any kind. 'IN ANGARIA' then simply means, 'in a straight,' or 'in distress.' AMNE again, is 'sea,' not 'river.' These terms accepted, the whole will read thus:

Give forth, O people, songs of praise to Giles and Thomas:
Lest their flock be in distress by sea or land.

Or, more paraphrastically:

Pour forth your songs, ye people all,
To Giles' and Thomas' praise;
Lest evil should their flock befall,
By land or ocean's ways.

Mr. Lower, however, had some doubt about AMNE VIA."

The translation of Mr. Boys, in his History of Sandwich, is this: "'Address, ye people, songs of the praises *of* Thomas *to* Giles, lest *his flock* be in *danger* by water or land.' The address to the patron saints is by no means inappropriate in relation to the far-wandering mariners of Winchelsea, whose trade was in a great degree a foreign, and consequently (at the period when the seal was engraved) a dangerous one.

The Winchelsea Mayoralty Seal has the Cinque Ports' arms very incorrectly designed, and bears the inscription: SIGILLUM : MAIORATUS : VILLE : DE : WYNCHELLE, in Old English characters of the 15th century. In the intervals between the shield and the legend are three figures, which are not very intelligible, but which, on a comparison with the corresponding seal of Rye, may be intended for wyverns."

The Mayor's Seal appears to be of the age when the Pipewell gate was restored, (Hen. IV) and made to supply an older seal lost during the attacks of the French.

The Maces are handsome, of the time of Charles.

The Mayor's Chair, which was removed during the corporate disputes, was of oak carved. It is still in existence, and in a private person's possession.

The earliest documents connected with the Corporation, which we have been able to discover, are two very curious and highly interesting rolls of the accounts of the town. The first from Easter, 11th Rich. II, (1388) to Easter, 12th Rich. II, (1389;) and the second from Easter, 22nd Rich. II, (1399) to Easter, 1 Henry IV, (1400.) They are preserved among the Dering MSS., and are among the most valuable of the extracts, which we have been so kindly allowed to make, from that interesting collection of documents relating to the Cinque Ports. The items comprise payments for the wages and expenses of the members of parliament; of the mayor and jurats at the Court of Shepway; of journeys to the Brodhill; of 13s. 4d. for the mayor's expenses to London; of £3 10s. to the bailiff to Great Yarmouth; of salaries to the mayor, town clerk, and town sergeant; of thatching the town hall, and of 6s. 8d. for rent of the hall; of 12d. for labour in the time of affliction (general illness;) of presents of fish to Sir Edw. Dallyngerigge of Bodyam, and to the Prior of Canterbury; of 12d. each for messengers from Dover, and of 4d. each for messengers to Rye; of 55s. 4d. for the expenses of the men of the county coming to the succour of the town on Friday and Saturday, the 21st and 22nd August, 1388; of removing stones from the cliff; of wood for the beacon at Fairlight, and of wages for watching the same; of 14d. for a rope for the bell of St. Giles' church; and of 12d., in 1389, for sounding the curfew, which practice would seem to have been discontinued on the introduction of a striking clock into the town, for in 1399 the charge for the curfew has disappeared from the accounts, and instead of it an item of 5s. a quarter appears for the care of the clock; and foreigners are required not to be in the streets after a certain hour "of the clock." There are other items in the last account for the mayors of Hastings and Rye, with two clerks, copying the charter of the liberties of the ports, and many expenses incurred in the numerous arrests of ships in the Camber, which took place in the latter part of the year 1399.

ELEVENTH AND TWELFTH RICHARD II, (1388.)—Expense denariorum commitatis ville de Winchelse....per manus Roberti Harri, Majoris, a die Lune in Septimina Pasche anno regni Regis Ricardi secundi post conquestum undecimo usque eundem diem anno regni ejusdem Regis duodecimo.

A festo Pasche usque ad Nativitatem Sancti Johannis Baptiste.

Primo in expensis apud Schepweyam die Martis proxime post Septiminam Pasch. xljs. iiijd.; et pro xv equis ad hoc allocatis xvs.—It. in expensis ad unam Gestlyng, tentam hic die Veneris proxime sequente iiijs. viijd.—It. in expensis Majoris et Willielmi Skele, apud London pro Parliamento, per ix dies, xxxiiis. ivd.; et pro iii equis xs.—It. in expensis ad removendam navem Simonis Salerne extra solam, et aliis expensis, vs. ixd.—It. Idem Major cuidam nuncio Domini Regis die Sabbati in Septimina Pentecoste xijd.—It. pro pisse missa Domino Edwardo Dallyngerigge, una cum cariagio vis. vd.—It. in expensis Prioris et aliorum Monachorum de Bello, die Jovis proxime ante Festum Sancti Barnabe xd.—It. pro bruera empta ad becnam de Ffarlegh xvd.—It. Johanni Simoni pro warda facienda ibidem per unam Septiminam circa Festum St. Barnabe iiijd.—It. dedit uno gayto[1] Dovorr portanti breve pro compoto Benedicti Cely, in eadem Septimina xijd.—It. soluit pro cariagio petrarum circa clivam xvid.—It. soluit Edwardo Marthemme pro mora sua ad parliamentum per septem Septiminas liiijs. iiijd.—It. soluit Domino Johanni Devereux custodi Quinque Portuum xil. iis. iiijd.—It. soluit Joye, pro batello suo usque Ryam ad habendum colloquium cum custode die Sabbati proxime ante Festum Johannis Baptiste vid.—It. dedit uno gayti Dovorr portanti mandatum pro Majore, ballivo, et duobus hominibus essendis apud Dovorr die Lune proxime ante Festum Sancti Barnabe xijd.—It. in expensis Majoris, Ballivi, et duorum hominum ibidem die Lune proxime ante Festum Nativitatis Sancti Johannis Baptiste xis. iiijd.; et pro quatuor equis vis.—It. soluit Roberto Burghamme pro labore suo xijd.—It. soluit Roberto Burghamme portanti retornum nostrum apud Castrum Dovorr, de bonis seductorum foris xxd.—It. dedit uno gayto Dovorr portanti diversa brevia de compoto Majoris xijd., die Dominica proxime ante Festum Nativitatis Sancti Johannis Baptiste.—It. pro una corda ad campanam Sancti Egidii xiiijd.—It. pro pisse missa Priori de Cantuaria vis. iiijd.—It. soluit Majori pro feodo suo xxs.—It. Johanni Gotes, clerico, pro eodem xs.—It. Johanni Wynder, servienti viis. vjd.—It. Petro Flemyng, pro collectione petrarum juxta clyvam viijd.

Summa xxiijl. vs. id.

[1] Watchman.

A festo Nativitati Sancti Johannis usque Festum Sancti Michaelis.

It. soluit Johanni Simond pro warda de Farlegh, per iii Septiminas xii*d.*—It. dedit uno valetto de Ria, portanti patentes pro Brodhill, die Jovis proxime post Festum Sancti Margarete iiij*d.*—It. in expensis Henrici Ffynch et Johannis Gotes ad eandem die Lune proxime sequente apud Romene una cum allocatione batelli v*s.*—It. dedit uno gayti Dovorr portanti mandatum pro Parliamento die Jovis proxime post Festum Assumptionis Beate Marie xij*d.*—It. pro warda de Farlegh per alias iii Septiminas xij*d.*—It. dedit uno gayti Dovorr portanti diversa brevia die Dominica proxime ante Festum Sancti Egidii xij*d.*—It. in expensis Majoris, et Rogeri de Dovorr apud Bellum ad habendum colloquium cum Abbate eodem die xij*d.*—It. soluit Henrico de Worth, pro diversis laboribus tempore afflictionis xij*d.*—It. soluit Roberto Burghamme, eundo Dovorr, cum retorno nostro de Parliamento, et cum retorno de Hastings xij*d.*—It. Henrico Cely et Mattheo Goldyne pro Parliamento iiij*li.* xiii*s.* iiij*d.*; et eodem Henrico pro mora sua ibidem post dictum Mattheum viij*s.* iiij*d.*—It. Roberto Burghamme, pro servicio suo ibidem v*s.*; et pro iii equis xv*s.*; et pro cera empta vi*d.*—It. in expensis Majoris apud London, pro compoto suo de anno precedenti de diversis brevibus xiij*s.* iiij*d.*—It. soluit Thome Tayllor, Ballivo Magni Jernemuth iij*li.* x*s.*—It. Willielmo Wastel, pro curfew sonendo xij*d.*—It. in expensis factis super homines de patria venientes, pro salvationem ville die Veneris, et die Sabbati proxime post Festum Assumptionis Beate Marie (21st and 22nd August) lv*s.* iiij*d.*, ut patet per parcellas.—It. soluit Majori pro feodo suo xx*s.*—It. communi clerico x*s.*—It. communi servienti vij*s.* vj*d.*

Summa xv*li.* x*s.* viij*d.*

A festo Sancti Michaelis usque Nativitatem Domini.

Idem Major dedit uno gayti Dovorr, portanti mandatum pro Johanne Gotes essendo Dovorr die Veneris proxime ante Festum omnium Sanctorum xij*d.*—It. Roberto Burghamme portanti retornum nostrum, de Hastynges et Rie, Dovorr xij*d.*?—It. dedit uno gayti Dovorr portanti mandatum pro Majore, Ballivo, et iii hominibus essendis Dovorr die Mercurii proxime ante Festum Sancte Lucie xij*d.*—It. in expensis Mathei Goldyne, Johannis Herde, et Johannis Gotes, apud Dovorr et dictam Brodhill per quatuor dies, eundis, et rediundis xiiij*s.* iiij*d.*, una cum allocatione batelli eundis et redeund. xxij*d.*—It. pro allocatione equi Mathei Goldyne xvj*d.*—It. in expensis Majoris et Clerici apud Riam ad habendum colloquium cum Thoma Tayllor de redditibus Jernemuth x*d.*, et pro batallo allocato vj*d.*—It. soluit Roberto Burghamme, portanti retornum nostrum apud Dovorr de Inquisitione de diversis bonis inventis per mare xx*d.*—It. soluit Majori pro feodo suo xx*s.*—It. communi clerico x*s.*—It. communi servienti vij*s.* vj*d.*

Summa iij*li.* xvj*d.*

A festo Nativitatis Domini usque Festum Pasche.

It. dedit Roberto Essex die Lune proxime post Festum Circumcitionis Domini vi*s.* viij*d.*—It. Ricardo Sednor clerico castri Dovorr in Crastino iii*s.* iiij*d.*—It. uno gayti Dovorr venienti cum eodem portanti diversa brevia xij*d.*—It. dedit uno nuncio Regis die Sabbati proxime sequente iiij*d.* —It. uno famulo de Rya portanti patentes pro Brodhell tenenda die Lune, proxime post Festum Sancti Vincentii iiij*d.*—It. in expensis Johannis Jakeman et Rogeri de Dovorr ad eandem iv*s.* viij*d.*—It. pro batello eis allocato xvi*d.*—It. soluit Johanni atte Halle, pro una secta de tempore Roberti Londeneys, quondam Majoris v*s.*—It. eodem pro alia secta per ipsum facta de tempore Roberti Harri, Majoris vi*s.* viij*d.*—It. Johanni Sneppe eunti cum eisdem ad dictam Brodhull viij*d.*—It. soluit Roberto Arnold ad prosequendam allocationem xv*e* ad Festum, Purificationis Beate Marie xiij*s.* iiij*d.*; et pro allocatione equi sui iij*s.* iiij*d.*—It. pro papere, pergameno, et sera emptis ij*s.* vj*d.*—It. pro uno storio[1] ad domum communem iiij*d.*—It. dedit nuncio Comitis Cantie venienti ad inquirendum de quibusdam hominibus captis pro suspectis in dominio suo xij*d.*—It. dedit uno servienti Dovorr portanti diversa brevia die Dominica medie xl*e*[2] xviij*d.*—It. soluit Johanni Gerneys, pro curfew sonendo xvj*d.*—It. ad portandum vexillum nostrum et cartas libertatis iiij*d.*—It. dedit Johanni Wynder eundo apud Hastyngs, pro concilio eorum habendo sub quibus sigillis retornabimus apud Dovorr cum indiget vj*d.*—It. dedit Johanni Tyson pro labore suo tempore gwerre hoc anno vj*d.*—It. soluit Johanni Gotes pro equo suo usque Schipweyam et usque Dovorr ij*s.* vj*d.*—It. Rogero de Dovorr, pro expensis suis apud Bellum iiij*d.*—It. Johanni Wynder eundo quater apud Hastyngs, iii apud Ryam, semel apud Bellum iij*s.* iiij*d.* —It. Roberto Burghamme pro diversis laboribus tempore gwerre ij*s.*—It. soluit eidem Roberto ad portandum retornum nostrum usque Dovorr, de brevibus tangentibus Benedictum Cely viij*d.*—It. Thome Gannok pro equo suo usque Dovorr de anno precedente xviij*d.*—It. pro allocatione domus commune[3] de anno isto vi*s.* viij*d.*—It. pro compoto Majoris apud London, de hoc instante anno xiij*s.* iiij*d.*—It. Majori pro feodo suo xx*s.*—It. clerico pro eodem x*s.*—It. servienti pro eodem vij*s.* vi*d.*

Summa vj*li.* ij*s.* ij*d.*

Summa totalis xlvij*li.* xix*s.* iij*d.*, et sic excedunt receptus expense vi*li.* xiiij*s.* xi*d.*

It. Walterus Yonge, et Thomas Robynhod debent de vinis suis hoc anno xiij*s.*—It. idem Thomas debet pro carbonibus prout. . . . .—It. Margareta Londoneys iij*s.* iiij*d.*—It. Thomas Lang, Willielmus Lang, et Willielmus Smith xiij*s.* iiij*d.*

The next is a roll of the town accounts from Easter 1399, to Easter 1400, (22 Rich. II, and 1 Hen. IV.)

A membrane lost, the total of xiij*li.* ix*s.* v*d.* alone being preserved.

It. deliberatum Johanni Jakeman, constabulario dicte . . . . . . pro seipso . . . aliis marinariis ut in auro et in victualli. . . .—It. sol. uxori . . . . servise[4] ix*s.*—It. sol. Thome Thondyr[5] pro . . . . duobus barellis de flore, et pro pane, et pro pistura dicte panis xxi*s.* x*d.*—It. sol. pro octo barellis beer xxi*s.* viij*d.*—It. sol. Roberto Holdenne pro uno carkoys de carne bovine xi*s.* vj*d.*—It. sol. pro dimidio quaterii de sale xvj*d.*—It. deliberat. Johanni Jakeman, constabulario dicte navis ut in auro xviij*s.* viij*d.*

Summa iiij*li.* iiij*d.*

[1] Thatch [?] or shutter. Vide Du-Cange. [2] Midlent. [3] Sic in orig.
[4] Ale brewer. [5] Most probably for the fitting out of ships.

Mem. quod dictus Major et quinque constabularii dictarum quinque navium emerunt quatuor lestas de beer, pretium le lest xxxis.; et dictus Major et constabularii solverent pro le custumam et dicte quatuor lestas de beer fuerunt deliberat. dictis quinquis constabulariis in custumâ, in toto pretium le lest xxxiijs. iiijd.—It. sol. Johanni Gotes pro magno custumo vs. xjd.—It. sol. Roberto Arnold, pro le petit custumo viijs.

Summa sol. pro le custumo xiijs. xid.

It. sol. Willielmo Cowpare pro imposicione capitum in pypys, in bunnys,[1] et in barellis, et pro hopys, et pro ligacione eorum iijs. xd.—It. sol. Johanni de Essche, Andree ate Melle, Roberto Fflemyng, Willelmo Wareyner, portatoribus pro cariagio, et pro portagio iiijs. iijd.—It. sol. Willielmo ate Grove pro tribus cariagiis ixd.

Summa viijs. xd.

It. sol. Johanni Tounstalle pro octo bunnys iijs. iiijd.—It. sol. dicto Johanni pro quatuor barellis ijs. viijd.—It. sol. Johanni dicto pro tribus bunnys emptis de Johanne Vellard xviijd.—It. sol. dicto Johanni pro uno bunne empto Sewale Crudde vd.—It. sol. dicto Johanni pro uno bunne empto de Johanne Perhamme vjd.—It. sol. Johanni Perison pro quatuor bunnys xvjd.—It. sol. Thome Thondyr, pro uno barell viijd.—It. sol. dicto Majori, pro duobus bunnys xd.—It. sol. dicto Majori, pro duobus barellis xvjd.—It. sol. dicto Majori, pro uno pype xvd.—It. sol. Waltero Yong, pro duobus pypecokeris, et pro uno bunne ijs. xd.—It. sol. dicto Waltero, pro duobus barellis xiijd.—It. sol. Rogero de ——, pro uno bunne et pro uno barell xd.

Summa xviijs. ixd.—Summa totalis istius viagii $\overset{\text{xx}}{\text{iiij}}$vili. ijs. vid.

It. datum uni gaito Dovor portanti unum breve pro Majore, Ballivo, et pro sex aliis Juratis die Veneris proxime ante Pentecosten, anno ut supra xijd.—It. in expensis Majoris, Ballivi, et sex aliorum Juratorum versus Dovre, cum tribus servientibus et undecim equis .... In primum apud Apolder in domo Thome Lang, in diversis expensis iijs. vjd.—It. apud Romene in domo Johannis Gardener, ad cenam iijs. xjd. ob.—It. sol. in dicta domo pro prandio equorum iijs. vjd.—It. sol. apud Dovre pro prandio in domo Ricardi Arnold vjs. iiijd. ob.—It. sol. in dicta domo pro prandio equorum iiijs. xjd.—It. sol. apud Hethe, pro diversis expensis ijs. —It. apud Romene in domo Johannis Gardener, pro cena soluit iiijs. xd. —It. sol. in dicta domo pro prandio equorum iijs. vd. ob.—It. apud Apoldere in domo Thome Lang pro jantaculo[2] sol. ijs. iiijd.—It. sol. in dicta domo pro prandio equorum ijs.—It. sol. pro passagio octo hominum a Wynchelse usque Apoldere et retorno xxd.—It. sol. pro le Verye[3] apud Oxene undecim equorum xxijd.— It. sol. pro le Verye apud Wynchelse dictorum undecim equorum xxijd.—It. sol. pro labore trium servientium iijs.—It. sol. pro allocatione dictorum undecim equorum xviijs. iiijd. ob. —It. datum eodem tempore locum tenenti Castri Dovorr ...... li. inde pars Wynchelse xxs.

Summa iiijli. vs. vijd.

It. sol. Johanni Tounstalle, pro feodo suo xs. vjd.—It. Roberto Fflemyng, pro collectione malitot[4] xijd.—It. sol. Johanni Elys, pro collectione malitot carnificum xijd.—It. sol. Johanni Thetford pro custodio de orlogio[5] ville vs.—It. sol. Johanni Gotes communi clerico, pro feodo suo xs.

Summa xxvijs. vjd.

Summa totalis istius termini $\overset{\text{xx}}{\text{iiij}}$xvili. xviijs. viijd.

[1] Sort of cask. [2] Lunch, as we should call it. [3] The ferry.

[4] A tax on wool. [5] This is an early notice of a striking clock.

Expensis comitatis dicte ville, viz., a festo Nativitatis Sancti Johannis Baptiste usque ad festum Sancti Michaelis Archangeli, anno regis Ricardi, vicessimo tertio.

It. sol. Alano Brensete pro suo labore usque Neddyrfeld iiij*d.*—It. sol. pro expensis Johannis Tounstalle cum equitavit Domino Willielmo Ffynnes milit. pro suggestione facta de Thoma Bette pro allec[1] viij*d.*—It. sol. pro expensis dicti Johannis cum equitavit cum episcopo Cicestrensi ad sectandos rumores de Castro de Pevense viij*d.*—It. datum uni minstrello Regis xx*d.*—It. sol. pro diversis expensis cum Ballivus de Hasting, Major de Ria, et duo clerici cum eis, fuerunt hic apud Wynchelse ad copiandam cartam de libertatibus portuum ij*s.*—It. sol. pro expensis Johannis Tounstalle cum equitavit cum Roberto Yellyng, ad comitem pro ponte apud Panelle xx*d.*—It. sol. pro sex pellibus de percamino xviij*d.*

Summa viij*s.* vj*d.*

It. datum uni gaito portanti unum breve Brodhull . . . . ent die Lune proxime post festum Sancti Margarete xij*d.*—It. in expensis . . . . Johannis Tounstalle ad eundem Brodhell cum tribus servientibus versus Romene-In primum apud Lyde in domo Johannis Grange xviij*d.*—It. sol. pro . . . . . . duorum equorum, versus Lyde ij*d.*—It. sol. pro cena apud Romene in domo Johannis Gardener ij*s.* viij*d.*—It. sol. in eadem domo in mane pro prandio iiij*s.*—It. sol. pro . . . . . . equo Johannis Tounstalle in dicta domo xij*d.*—It. pro allocatione unius equi a Romene usque Snergate, et pro reductione dicti equi usque Romene sol. vj*d.*—It. sol. pro allocatione unius batelli a Winchelse usque ad Camere,[2] et a Camere usque ad Snergate iij*s.* iiij*d.*—It. sol. pro duobus servientibus xvj*d.*—It. sol. pro allocatione equi Johannis Tounstalle xij*d.*—It. sol. pro le Veryes et pro diversis expensis dicti equi vj*d.*

Summa xvij*s.*

It. datum uni gaito Dovorr portanti unum breve, pro uno concilio tento apud Dovre die Dominica proxime post festum Sancti Jacobi Apostoli xij*d.*—It. in expensis Majoris et Ballivi cum quatuor Juratis dicte ville et tribus servientibus, et ix equorum.—In primum apud Apoldore, in diversis expensis iij*s.*—It. sol. apud Romene in domo Johannis Gardener ad cenam vj*s.* iiij*d.*—It. sol. in dicta domo pro prandio equorum ij*s.* vj*d.*—It. apud Dovre in mane ad jantaculum vj*s.* ij*d.*—It. ibidem ad prandium v*s.* ix*d.*—It. ibidem pro prandio equorum iij*s.* vj*d.*—It. in redeundo apud Romene in domo Johannis Gardener sol. pro cena iiij*s.* iij*d.*—It. ibidem sol. pro prandio equorum in dicta domo iij*s.* iiij*d.*—It. sol. pro jantaculo et pro prandio equorum iij*s.*—It. pro le Veryes apud Oxene et apud Winchelse, equorum et novem hominum iij*s.*—It. sol. pro tribus servientibus iij*s.*—It. pro allocatione novem equorum xv*s.*

Summa iij*li.* . . . . vi*d.*

It. sol. Vincent Vynch pro sua moracione apud Romene ad cognoscendum utrum illi de portibus orientalibus vellent mandare London, pro navibus in servicio Domini Regis ij*s.* ij*d.*—It. sol. dicto Vincentio pro allocatione Domus Regis vj*s.* viij*d.*—It. tradit. Waltero Yong, Ballivo Jernemuthe iij*li.*, et dimidie.

Summa iij*li.* xviij*s.* iiij*d.*

[1] Pickled herrings. [2] The Camber.

It. sol. Johanni Tounstal pro feodo suo x*s*. vj*d*.—It. Roberto Flemyng pro collectione maletot xij*d*.—It. Johanni Elys pro collectione maletot carnificum xij*d*.—It. Alano [. . . . . .] pro custodio orlogii ville v*s*.—It. Johanni Gotes pro feodo suo x*s*.

Summa xxvij*s*. vj*d*.—Summa istius termini ix*li*. xi*s*. viii*d*.

In dorso. Expensis comitatis dicte ville a festo Sancti Michaelis, anno regis Ricardi secundi, xxiijo., usque ad festum Natalis Domini anno regis Henrici quarti, primo.[1]

It. datum cuidam gait. Dovorr portanti breve pro Parliamento tento . . . Sancti Michaelis, apud Westmonsterium xij*d*.—It. in expensis Willielmi Skele et Rogeri de Gate cum famulis . . . . ibidem commorantibus per quinque Septiminas vj*li*.—It. sol. dicto Willielmo pro sua moracione ibidem per tres Septiminas postea cum suo famulis, pro toto Westportu pro suis expensis xxxviij*s*. vj*d*.—It. sol. dicto Willielmo pro diversis, expensis circa campanillos et lanceas[2] xxiiij*s*. inde pars nostra vj*s*.—It. sol. . . . . . Barbour pro suo labore, et pro sua moracione ibidem ix Septiminas apud dictum Parliamentum v*s*.—It. sol. dicto Willielmo Skele pro allocatione . . . . equorum London et retro x*s*.—It. sol. . . . . uni equi Rogero . . . . London x*s*.

Summa ix*li*. x*s*. vj*d*.

It. . . . . cum duobus Juratis et duobus servientibus apud Riam pro . . . Gesteling, ibidem tent. die Mercurii post festum Omnium Sanctorum v*s*.—It. pro uno batello Apeldore et retro viij*d*.—It. in expensis Johannis Michell . . . . . cum veniebat ad recipiandum ballivam de Wynchelse, nomine Johannis Lodewyke in domo Thome Bente iiij*s*. ij*d*.—It. sol. pro diversis expensis die Dominica proxime post festum Sancti Martini, cum solucione Roberto Ffryshlake, Ballivo, pro ballivâ suâ pro primo termino iiij*s*. vj*d*.

Summa xiiij*s*. iiij*d*.

It. sol. Laurencio de parte boriali pro suo labore usque Hastyngs, portanti literam pro uno Brodhull, tento die Jovis in festo Sancti Edmundi Archiepiscopi Cantuarie apud Romene iiij*d*.—It. in expensis Walteri Yong, Johannis Jakeman, et servientium eorum ad eundem Brodhull vj*s*. vj*d*.—It. sol. pro le Verys apud Winchelse de tribus equis vj*d*.—It. sol. pro labore Roberti Burghamme . . . . equitante nocte ad contramandandam quondam Schypweyam xij*d*.—It. sol. pro allocatione . . . . ad eundem Brodhull iij*s*.

Summa xi*s*. iiij*d*.

It. dat. cuidam gait. Dovorr portanti breve de Schypweya xij*d*.—It. sol. ad eandem Schypweyam pro expensis Majoris cum tribus Juratis, et tribus servientibus apud Apolder, in domo Thome Lang vj*s*. iiij*d*.—It. ad Romene pro cena vj*s*. iij*d*.—It. in eodem loco pro prandio x equorum iiij*s*. vj*d*.—It. ad jantaculum in eodem loco ij*s*. vi*d*.—It. apud Romene pro diversis expensis iij*s*.—It. . . . . apud Romene et diversis expensis iiij*s*. x*d*.—It. . . . . pro ferrura duorum equorum iiij*d*.—It. apud Apoldre, in domo Thome Lang, pro cena v*s*. x*d*.—It. ibidem pro prandio equorum ij*s*. ij*d*.—It. sol. pro le Verys apud Oxene pro dictis x equis xx*d*.—It. sol. pro le Verys

[1] Richard II abdicated 30th Sept., 1399.

[2] Probably for bells and staves for the canopy at the Coronation.

apud Wynchelse pro dictis x equis xx*d.*—It. sol. pro quodam batello a Wynchelse ad Apolder et retro xx*d.*—It. pro labore trium servientium ij*s.* vj*d.*—It. pro allocatione x equorum ad Schypweyam vidlt, pro quolibet equo xvj*d.*, summa xiij*s.* iiij*d.*—It. dat. custodi nostro pro promissione sua centum marcas, et locum tenento x marcas, et aliis officiariis quinque marcas inde pars nostra xij*li.* xv*s.* vij*d.*—It. sol. pro batello viij*d.*

Summa xv*li.* xiiij*s.* x*d.*

It. sol. Johanni Tounstalle pro feodo suo de isto termino x*s.* vj*d.*—It. Roberto Flemynge pro collectione maletote xij*d.*—It. Johanni Elis pro collectione maletote carnificum xij*d.*—It. Johanni .... endenne pro custodio de orlogio ville v*s.*—It. Johanni .... clerico pro feodo suo x*s.*

Summa xxvij*s.* vj*d.*

Expensis comitatis dicte ville a festo Natalis Domini, anno regis Henrici quarti, primo, usque ad festum Pasche proxime futuro eodem anno.

In primum datum cuidam .... Dovorr portanto breve Domini Regis, pro collectoribus subsidii et duodecim denariorum die Veneris, in festo Sancti Stephani xij*d.*—It. sol. Roberto Burghamme portanti retornum dicti brevis ad Castrum Dovorr ij*s.*—It. dat. cuidam nuncio portanti breve pro uno Brodhull, tento apud Romene die Lune proxime post festum Epiphanie Domini iiij*d.*—It. in expensis ibidem Johannis Salerne, Willielmi Skele, jun., cum duobus servientibus vij*s.* x*d.*—It. dat. per manus Johannis Salerne cuidam gaito Dovorr portanti breve Domini Regis de passagio xij*d.*—It. sol. pro labore duorum servientium cum eis xvj*d.*—It. sol. pro uno batello pro eis, bina vice, ad Cameram xviij*d.*

Summa xv*s.*

It. sol. pro uno batello Roberti Warde ad Cameram, ad arrestand. naves, per virtute brevis Domini Regis, prima vice iiij*s.* vij*d.*—It. sol. eodem modo, secunda vice, pro batello cum x hominibus ad Cameram xliiij*d.* —It. sol. eodem modo, tertia vice, pro batello cum xij hominibus iiij*s.* iiij*d.*—It. sol. pro expensis dictorum ix,[1] hominum x*d.*—It. dat. cuidam nuncio portanti breve pro uno Brodhull, tento apud Romene die Jovis proxime ante festum Purificatione Beate Marie iiij*d.*—It. in expensis ibidem Majoris Vincencii Vynch, Walteri Yong, cum tribus servientibus xij*s.* x*d.*—It. ibidem dat. cuidam gaito Dovorr portanti breve Domini Regis ad arraiandum homines ad arma[2] xij*d.*—It. sol. pro tribus servientibus ij*s.*—It. pro allocatione trium equorum Vyncencii Vynch iij*s.*—It. sol. pro allocatione duorum equorum a Romene usque ad Snergate, et pro reduccione ad Romene et retro x*d.*—It. sol. pro uno batello cum iiij marinariis ad Romene, et ibidem expectantibus pro una nocte, et duos dies videlt pro quolibet marinario vj*d.*, et pro batello x*d.*, et pro Very equorum xix*d.*—Summa totalis iiij*s.* v*d.*

Summa xxxvij*s.* x*d.*

It. dat. duobus nunciis ad portandum duas literas, unam ad Riam, et alteram ad Hastings, pro uno Gestelyng tento apud Hastings, die Jovis proxime post festum Purificationis viij*d.*—It. in expensis ibidem Vincentii Vynch, Rogeri de Gate, et Johannis Tounstall, cum duobus servientibus iij*s.* ix*d.*—It. sol. pro duobus servientibus viij*d.*—It. sol. pro allocacione quinque equorum ibidem ij*s.* ij*d.*—It. sol. cuidam gaito Dovorr portanti,

[1] Sic in orig. [2] Sic.

breve Domini Regis ad traducendum naves versus Cales cum victualibus carcatas xij*d*.—It. sol. Roberto Mostardo pro portagio cujusdam brevis locum tenenti Castri Dovorr, pro licentio traducendi naves ij*s*.—It. sol. pro uno batello ad Cameram ad arrestandum unam Francigenam et Flanderensem cum xiij hominibus iiij*s*. viij*d*.—It. sol pro uno batello, alia vice, cum ix hominibus ad Cameram eodem modo iij*s*. iiij*d*.—It. sol. pro uno batello cum viij hominibus, tercia vice, ad Cameram ad arrestandum naves, et pro eorum expensis iij*s*. iij*d*.—It. sol. pro papiro et pro cero xij*d*. —It. sol. pro batello ad Cameram, quarto vice, cum xij, hominibus ad arrestandum naves, et pro eorum expensis vij*s*. viij*d*.

Summa xxx*s*. vi*d*.

It. sol. Ricardo Carp . . . . pro se et duobus famulis suis ad scindendum quendam arborem in cimiterio Sancti Egidii, ad faciendum pavys[1] de eo iiij*s*. ij*d*.—It. sol. Waltero Flemyng pro le sawnyng de dicto arbore videlt pro vc $\frac{xx}{vj}$; et xij*s*. pedes de bordys pro targis, pretium; le centum xv*d*. Summa viij*s*. ij*d*.—It. sol. Willielmo Prune pro emendacione duorum murorum qui ceciderunt cum dicto arbore xv*d*.—It. sol. pro duobus batellis cum xxvi hominibus ad Cameram ad arrestandum quatuor Castellanos, et ad portandum vela navium illorum ad terram viij*s*. xi*d*.—It. sol. pro portagio de velis illorum a mare ad ecclesiam Sancti Thome, et pro portagio de harnasio illorum ad terram xxx*d*.—It. sol. pro labore Edwardi Hopyare et Austini Dertemuthe, bina vice, ad Kenele xij*d*.—It. sol. pro batello Roberti Warde cum viij hominibus ad querendum duas naves extra le Podele ad villam, et iiij bonettas[2] de homine de Campan iij*s*. x*d*.—It. sol. dicto Roberto pro batello suo ad querendum tres bonettas de quedam homine de Rochelle extra le Podell ad terram xij*d*.—It. sol. pro batello Willielmi Ffolde cum xv hominibus ad querendum quendam Franciscum ad terram, qui fugiebat extra portum ad mare vij*s*. viij*d*.—It. sol. pro expensis dictorum xv hominum in dicto batello xij*d*.

Summa xxxix*s*. vi*d*.

It. tradit. per manus Majoris Vincentii Vynch ad prosequendum ad concilium Domini Regis, London, pro renovacione carte de libertate nostra cum aliis hominibus Eastportubus viij*li*. v*s*. viij*d*.—It. sol. pro labore Roberti Burghamme ad Neddyrfelde, ad portandum dictum aurum dicto Vincentio Vynch x*d*.—It. sol. pro allocatione unius equi dicto Roberto ad Neddyrfelde, ad idem tempus viij*d*.—It. sol. dicto Roberto pro peticione monete ad Riam pro dicta renovacione carte nostre iiij*d*.—It. dat cuidam gayto portanti breve pro Brodhull, tento die Lune proxime post festum Sancti Mathei Apostoli iiij*d*.—It. in expensis ibidem Roberti Arnold, Rogeri de Gate, cum famulo eorum vj*s*. x*d*.—It. pro labore Johannis Lyndregg famuli illorum ibidem viij*d*.—It. sol. pro allocatione trium equorum illic et retro iij*s*.—It. sol. Thome Bregiar pro quadam proclamacione facta quod extranei non spaciarent in villa post certam horam orlogii in nocte[3] ij*d*.—It. dat. cuidam gaito Dovorr portanti breve, pro Majori et Ballivo ad computandum London, coram Baronibus de Scaccario Domini Regis xij*d*.—It. sol. Vincent Vynch pro allocatione Domus Regis vi*s*. viij*d*.

Summa ix*li*. vi*s*. ij*d*.

We have not discovered any account of the receipts of the town; but from the foregoing accounts, we may infer that they arose principally from port dues.

[1] Shields. [2] Sails. [3] This is a very curious entry.

CORPORATION DISPUTES.—The abuses in the Corporation were rife in the days of James I, and the attempt to monopolise power was as strong as in the times of William IV; although, in the 17th century, there was a more summary mode of settling corporation disputes, as to the choice of their officers, than by applying to the Court of Queen's Bench for a mandamus or quo warranto, as is evident from a letter addressed to the mayor and jurats in 1609, communicated in 1816 to the Society of Antiquaries,[1] by Mr. William Bray, the treasurer.

A letter to the Mayor and Jurats of the Town of Winchelsea for the time being.

Whereas uppon complaint heretofore made both to this Boorde and unto o^r very good Lord, the Lo. Warden, in particular, of many defects and disorders crept into yor corporacon by a strong combinacon of a few factious persons that had ingrossed ye governmt thereof into their owne hands, who would admitt noe encrease in nomber, either of juratts or freemen, whereby the scope in the eleccon of the mayor might be more large, wch was then (amongst many other) a mayne greevaunce to the inhabitants, the place having att that tyme bene for many yeares together supplyed only by three; for reformacon whereof we addressed o^r lres for election to be made into y^t office for ye yeare following of Thomas Pelham, the only juratt y^t had bene held out of that place, while ye mayrolty was contynued in three. But in ye last yeares election, whether out of ignourance or perswacon wee know not, wee are informed ye freemen swarved from our scope and intencon, and contrary to the Lord Warden's exp'sse comaundmt made choyce of one into that office y^t was neither antientest juratt, nor yet capable of any governmt, being before suspended by his Lopp., and the mayor inhibited to call him to ye Bench, who, under p'tence of seigniority, as being sometymes a juratt, (wch place he had many yeares before waved and given ov^r) challenged to himself a right by relacon. to ye time of his first admittance, wch was long before lost. Forasmuch as it is thought fitt, that in ye successive election of the mayor, the juratts should from henceforth be chosen to succeede in that office by seigniority and place of eldershipp, as they are in order of auntientnesse recorded in ye towne booke kept for that purpose, and have held and exercised y^t place w'thout discontinuance according to ye example of

[1] Arch. vol. 18, pp. 291-3.

Romney and Sandwch, as ye best meanes to establishe peace, and to cutt of ye cause of envye and partiallity (ye seedes of yt dissencon) wch hath bene soe long and soe unhappily nourished amongst yow. These are, therefore, to require yow to observe ye said orders for ye better governemt of ye towne and reformacon of former abuses, unlesse it shall happen yt just cause of excepcon may be taken to ye partie, wch by yt course is to be elected. And whereas we are informed yt Paul Wymond, an auntient juratt, is a very honest discrete man, and fitt to be chosen for this yeare following: we have thought good, for avoyding of variannce at this tyme, to recomend unto yow ye said Wymond to be chosen mayor att yor next election, not doubting but both in respect of or recomendacon and to shew yorselves conformable to these or directcons, yow will not only make choice of the said Paul Wymonde[1] to be mayor this yeare, but alsoe have care that hereafter ye juratts successively from him downewards, according to every man's seigniority as they have bene elected and recorded in ye towne booke, and exercised their place wthout discontinuance (not admitting of any antiquity by relacon to any former admittance waved before, and lost in all true construccon of law) be elected to ye office of mayor, except some sufficient cause be first alleadged to the contrary unto or very good Lord, the Lo. Warden, before ye election. And soe, &c.

Dat. 19o Aprill, 1609.

Concordat cum Registro, Jo. Corbett.

Signed by six of the Lods. Councell, viz.: Lo. Threr., Lo. Pri. Seale, Lo. Admirall, Lo. Chamberlayne, Earl of Worcester, Lo. Wotton.

Additional light is thrown upon this dispute with the Council, the mode of conducting the corporate affairs, and the value of the corporation property at this period, from the diary of Mr. Thomas Godfrey,[2] who came to reside here at this time. He says,

On Sunday, the 30th of Aprill, 1609, I was made a freeman of Winchellsea, no one man giveing his voice against me, and on Tuesday after I was, together with Mr. Thos. Greene, employed by the Corporacon, who allowed us 5s. apeece per diem to goe to London to our Lord Warden to deliver a pettision from them, and to make intersession for them in theire

[1] Who afterwards acted so partially in his office that he was committed by the House of Commons.

[2] Lands. MSS., 235, p. 2.

disobeying of the Lords of the Councell, lately concerning the elleccon of theire mayor, at wch time we brought down from my Lord the orders of succession in that office; and at the next assembly, being the ninth of May, 1609, according to those orders, I was sworne a jurat, Wm. Bishop being mayor; in which orders it was comanded that, notwithstanding, though Mr. Farmer and Mr. Cooper had been long on the Bench, yett Mr. Greene and myselfe were to take the place of them, and to be mayors in succession before them, and then likewise was it decided that thoe Mr. Eglistone had been a jurat formerly, yett he was to come after Mr. Boteler, who was elected together with him, the second time that he was called and sworne before him, for it was decreed by ye Lords of the Councell, that Eglistone cou'd have no relation to his being a jurat formerly, in respect that he waived the Bench voluntary.

The 16th of June, 1609, being one of the auditors, who for that purpose were chosen at an assembly before we took ye accompts of the old, the chamberlains who were in the yeare that Mr. White was mayor, viz., Wm. Rayman and Abednigo Standen, at the house of Thos. Cobb, at ye sign of the Square, whose receipts for that yeare upon true accot came to £303 18s. 8d. q., and theire paymts £184 6s. 2d. ob., besides £20 8s. 3d. that they reced in allowances for, the rest was £99 4s. 2d. ob. q.

At the Brotherhood, held this yeare at Romney, Mr. White was fined £10 for returning of Mr. Cooper a jurat into the King's . . . . . . when he was mayor, and for other speeches wch he had used against the Brotherhood.

There was returned to the Brotherhood and Guestling holden at New Rumney, ye 24th July, 1610, from Winchelsea, Mr. Robt. Boteler, gent., mayor of the town, Mr. John Egliston, gent., myself, and Mr. Francis Whitton, gent., jurats of ye same town; Tho. Isted, gent., com. clerk; Wm. Wimond, chamberlain; Abednigo Standen, freemen.

Memdm that the ——— of Aprill, 1610, I being the Mayor's Deputy, Geo. Brooks was disfranchised by a generall consent, for many matters alledged openly against him in court.

I was chosen to be one of the auditors for ye chamberlains' accompts, in anno, 1610, which was deferred till the 3rd of Augst, by reason of some differences, wch till then were not decided: we kept it at Mrs. Standing at ye King's Arms: wee found the totall receipts of that yeare to be £257 13s. 1d. q., the payments £92 2s. 2d., and £16 4s. 10d. ob. q., which they reced in allowances, the which added to the former maketh the totall payments to be £108 7s. ob. q., the which taken out of ye receipts of £257 13s. 1d. q., the rest wherewith the new chamberlains stand charged is £149 6s. ob.

The promise of amendment, like many other promises, was made to be broken. Ten years only elapsed before the Corporation asserted their right to remove from the list of freemen, all such as (having been admitted) should remove from the town and cease to be liable to the local taxes: and they were obliged to justify their conduct to the Lord Warden, which they did in the following letter.[1]

RT. HONBLE. OUR VERY GOOD LORDE.—It pleased your Honor to direct unto us your lres of the 24th of May, (wch came the 20th of this present) concerning Mr Robt. Butler,[2] Lieut. of Camber Castle, wherein (as in all things) we desire to shew ourselves most ready to be commanded by your Lp., humbly desiring your Ldp. to understand the truth of our cause, wch is, that we never disinfranchised the said Mr. Butler. But there is an ancient usage and custome of our towne, that if any freeman do remove his dwelling out of our towne, and the liberties thereof, by the space of a year and a daie, he loseth his freedom, and is as if he never had been free. Mr. Butler, by the space of two years together, did remove his dwelling out of our towne to the Camber Castle, (which is within our liberties but not of them) and was no advocate of our towne, neither paid any lot, scot, or taxe there; whereupon at an assembly there was an order made, the said Mr. Butler not to have pasturage in our commons, that yeare nor thereafter, without a new graunte; never (since) which time (till nowe of late) hath he desired to be of the corporation againe, but hath published to many that he was glad that he was out of our company, and that he wd not for £40, be of it againe: also he hath dissuaded others from being, or bearing office in this corporation, and hath joined himself to those, who seek our hurte: especially we do humbly desire your Honble. Ldp. to consider, that if Mr. Butler be made a freeman here, he is capable of the office of the receipt of the revenues of our poor towne, and having another place so fitly to resort unto, may go away with all, without any accompt: or may tarry here to take the benefit of the commons from divers poor men, (which have comfort thereby) and when any charge cometh may withdraw himself, and thus committing our cause to your Ho.: consideration, praying to the Lord to preserve your

[1] Addl. MS., 5705, p. 157, stated to be transcribed from the MSS. of Sir Charles Hedges, Judge of the ——— in the possession of Wm. Macham, L.L.D., a member of the Coll. of Advocates, Drs. Coms., 1771, No. 358.

[2] The name should be Boteler.

Honor, in helth, to his good pleasure, to the happiness of this kingdom, we rest your Honor's much bounden.

Wynch., 22 June, 1620.

The Mayor, Jurates, and Comminaltye of Winchelsea.

Addressed,

To the right honle Edw. Ld. Zouch St. Maure Cantelupe, Ld. Warden, Chancellor, and Admiral of the Cinque Ports, and 2 Ancient Townes, with their members, and one of the Lords of his Maj.'s honble. Privy Councel; give these.

For a time matters in the Corporation were peaceably conducted; but about 1760, Mr. Arnold Nesbit[1] purchased property in and near the town, and the fiercest contests were carried on.

In 1766, came on before Lord Mansfield, the celebrated Winchelsea Causes,[2] in which the Court of the King's Bench, was, for the first time, clearly of opinion that twenty years was the *ne plus ultra*, beyond which the court would not disturb a peaccable possession of a franchise; but that in every case within twenty years their interference would depend upon the particular circumstances of the case before them. There had been a great many rules nisi for quo warrantos; but after this opinion of the court, four only remained. One was against Edwin Wardroper, who had been in possession for nineteen years and eight months after re-election, (made for greater caution) and for twenty-seven years from his original election: the relators had voted at his election of mayor: and this rule was discharged with costs: another rule was against Nathaniel Dawes, who had been nineteen and half years in quiet possession: the third, and strongest case, was that of Richard Wardroper, who was elected a freeman on 13th May, 1760, against whom the affidavit was sworn on 4th Nov., 1766; this rule was also discharged: and the fourth rule was against Thomas Marten. Mr. Dawes had been elected a freeman on

[1] An entry is made in 1769, of his being admitted a freeman, and every earlier hundred book has disappeared!

[2] Burrow's Reports, vol. 4, pp. 1962, 2022, and 2120.

22nd September, 1747; he did not then reside, but soon after his election he hired a house in the town, and had dwelt there ever since, with his wife and family: had served all the parish offices: two of the three informers were present at his election and voted for it: he had generally voted at all the assemblies at the same time with all the three informers, none of whom had objected till within the preceding nine months: he had served the office of jurat from the year 1756: and had been twice mayor, to which office he was, in 1762, elected unanimously. Marten had been elected a freeman on 1st October, 1753: he had ever afterwards attended and voted without any objection, even from the informers, though they knew he was not rated at the time of his election. The court discharged the rules on the grounds; Firstly: That the objections did not lie in the relators' mouths, as they all knew the constitution of the borough, and had voted with the defendants, and had acted with them, and had assented to many persons deriving rights under Dawes:

"They come now," said Lord Mansfield, "to complain of their own iniquity: they come to set aside effects of which they themselves have been the cause: they come to desire that they may represent the King to prosecute guilt of which they themselves are partakers: they have laid a snare for the Corporation: drawn it into error: and, after having been temptors, desire to put on the character of accusers. *Non tali auxilio, nec defensoribus istis.* The cause of the king and the public, for the usurpation of a franchise, ought not to be trusted in such hands." Secondly; because they shewed no right or interest of their own or of any other person which depended upon invalidating the title of Dawes; but the objection was such, that so far as the borough or the crown was concerned, it had been substantially cured ever since his election, and no new constitution had been usurped upon the crown: it would be acting with the utmost rigour of the *summum jus*, if the *King himself* were to pry with eagle eyes into such defect; and certainly ought not to be indulged by the court[1] to private informers, accomplices in the usurpation. And

[1] This has now grown to be the admitted practice of the court. Rex *v.* Parry, 6 Ad. and Ellis, 821.

thirdly; the consequences of granting the application might be fatal to the borough, and the example thereby set, that men might lie in wait and lay a scheme for many years to draw a corporation into acts which they may afterwards, for occasional and corrupt views, turn to their destruction. The parliament had entrusted the court with the authority to give a *private* informer leave to prosecute the usurpation of a franchise in the King's name; but the court were all clearly and unanimously of opinion that these informers ought not to have that leave, and that "it never ought to be granted to *any* informers, who shall appear under all the same circumstances in the same *unfavourable* light."

Mr. Nesbit, who was the real cause of these disputes, had been returned as member, on the government interest, in 1754, and was content enough with the state of the Corporation at that time: but by purchases of land, he established an interest independent of the Treasury; and it was after an attack, in 1762, upon his interest, by the treasury, under the auspices of the Earl of Egremont, who, in that year, had purchased Mr. Carryll's property, that the assumed defects in the title of the different members of the corporation to their offices were brought forward. During these contests, and to raise money for the defence of the Corporation, the town clerk, Mr. Wardroper, pledged the original Customal[1] to Mr. Wilson, (the charters had been surrendered temp. Chas. I, to Sir E. Dering, for the then Lord Warden of the Cinque Ports.) It is said to have been redeemed from him; but it has never re-appeared; and when the last attempt was made, in 1830, to obtain the freedom of the town for all the inhabitants paying scot and lot, and residing for a year and a day, the non-production was not inconvenient for the ruling body.

We print this Customal from a copy preserved and printed in Lyons' History of Dover Castle, &c.[2] He does not state, however, where the original was.

[1] At a Guestling held at Dover, 17th Eliz., (1574) in reference to disputes with the city of London, among the customals there was read "an ancyent roulle in parchment for Winchelsey." Boys' Sandwich, p. 776.

[2] Lyons' Dover, vol. 2, p. 370.

THE CUSTOMAL OF THE TOWN AND PORT OF WINCHELSEA.

1. *Chusing of Mayor.*—Every year, the Monday after Easter, all the inhabitants assemble in a certain place called the hundred, and there, by common consent shall chuse a mayor. In case the mayor that is chosen be not present, to accept his charge, the mayor that was before shall not be discharged, until the other be charged by his predecessor.

2. *Punishment of the Mayor for not accepting the office, and his oath.*—If the mayor that is chose absent himself, and will not accept and receive his charge, all the whole commons shall go and shut in his chief tenement. But if the mayor that is chosen be present, and will his charge accept, he shall be charged, and swear thus:—

I, A. B. shall bear faith to our Sovereign Lord the King of England, and to the commonalty of Winchelsea, and the franchises and usages of the same rightfully shall maintain, and the common profit shall keep; and to rich and poor shall do right, as near as can be. So help me.

And in case the mayor die before the yearly election, the twelve sworn men here, in course, to the same shall do their turns, until the time be in the year, for the assembly to chuse another mayor; then he so chose shall do his office, until the day of election. And in this case, the mayor charged shall be one of the best of the twelve sworn men.

3. *Appointing Jurats.*—Also the mayor shall chuse the same day, twelve sworn men, the most wise within the town, the which shall swear to the King, and the commons; and shall chuse a common clerk, which shall swear to the commonalty, and shall bear faith to all the said commons, and truly their councils shall keep to his power.

Also, the same day the mayor shall chuse a sergeant, the which shall do his charge in manner as follows. That he shall bear faith to the mayor, and the commonalty, and duly shall do execution, as appertaineth to his office, after the usage used in the town in times passed. So help me God, and All Saints.

4. *Of receiving a Bailiff.*—In the right of the bailiff, the king may remove at his will; and in case the bailiff die, or the king remove him from his office, then the king shall send his commission, with a writ of attendage, to the mayor and jurats, under the seal of the Chancery; the which bailiff shall shew his commission to the mayor and jurats, and after that, shall be accepted, and charged by the mayor, and his charge shall be this:—

By the allegiance you owe to the Sovereign Lord the King, that you do due execution and right, without blemish of the franchise, after the usage used in old time in the town, as is aforesaid.

And after that, the bailiff shall chuse a sergeant, for which he shall answer, who shall be charged.

5. *Of the Coroner, and his office.*—Item, in case a man be found dead within the franchise, by misadventure, or by deed of any man, by land or water, the mayor shall have sight of the body, as coroner, and the bailiff do come a countie; at which countie the mayor shall make an inquest of the death of the body present. Anon, the mayor, as coroner, shall charge the bailiff for to attach the indicted, and if he may be found, he shall be brought into the ward of the bailiff within the franchise; but if that the indicted may find, after his imprisonment, sufficient mainprise for to be at the law, the bailiff shall let go to the same, until a hundred be ordained by the mayor and bailiff, at which hundred the indicted shall come, and

shall be arraigned of the felony, and there shall be proclamation made by the mayor and bailiff; and there if any will come to pursue in due form against the indicted of felony of above said, that he come; and if none do come for to pursue, then be it returned, till proclamation be made, in the same form, by two hundreds after; and if none do come at the third hundred, that will pursue the indicted, he shall go quit of his indictment. And be it for to wit, that no hundred shall be holden after the other less than fifteen days. And if any come to pursue against the indicted, by appeal, and the indicted be arraigned of the felony, and if he say nay in the felony, then he be charged by the mayor to have his acquittance, in manner as follows: that is to wit; thirty-six men of his own province, of good fame in the liegance of England, that they be ready at the next hundred that to him shall be assigned; the which thirty-six men the apellor shall take their names written, into the hands of the bailiff, and the common clerk shall read their names, as shall do every appealed; and if any of the thirty-six men be in default, or answer not for him who is appealed of the felony, be he adjudged to death, to be hanged at the gallows.

6. *Acquittance of a Felon.*—It is ordained, in the usages of Winchelsea, that when a man ought to be acquitted by thirty-six men, that first the names of the thirty-six men shall be delivered to the bailiff by the man who is appealed, in writing; and those thirty-six men ought to be called by their names; and if any of them, when called, be absent and answer not, then the man that is appealed shall be put to death. And if they all appear, and answer by name, the which being called, then of the King's grace that shall be the best twelve of the said thirty-six men, and the grace of the mayor; and of the sworn men, twelve, so that the mayor and bailiff of them all chuse twelve, the which left them, to swear what the man who is appealed shall swear on a book, that he is not guilty of that which he is appealed of, as God him help, and the Holy Church, and so kiss the book.

After that, the twelve men that have been chosen to swear, shall confirm the same oath, that the man appealed made, and so the man appealed to quit.

If any of the twelve men withdraw their hands, and will not swear, then shall he who is appealed be put to death; and if he be acquit, then shall the apellor be attached, by his body, and all his goods, to the will of the king. All men condemned in this manner, shall be hanged in the Salt Marsh, on the north side of the town of Winchelsea, in the salt water of the same town.

7. *Holding of Pleas, Treason excepted.*—Also, all manner of the pleas of the coroner, of life and member, may be determined and ended before the mayor, bailiff, and jurats, within the said liberties of the said town of Winchelsea, out-take the plea of counterfeitors of the King's coin, and of the King's seal; and also except the plea of those who imagine the King or the Queen's death; the which pleas appertain and belong to the Court of Shepway. But such manner of pleas of the coroner, of life and member, ought to be taken in the whole hundred.

8. *Sanctuary.*—Also, if any man flee to Holy Church, the mayor, as coroner, shall go to him, and of him know the cause of his flying; and if he will the felony acknowledge, by the recognizance registered, or enrolled, anon he shall leave all his goods and chattels as forfeited, of which the bailiff shall answer to the king; and he shall dwell in the church, if he will, forty days, and he shall chuse the port or passage where he will pass; and if he will make abjuration before the forty days ended, he shall

be accepted. And anon, after his abjuration he shall take his cross, and the mayor shall make proclamation on the king's behalf, that no man, upon forfeiture of life and member, do him any evil, or grievance, inasmuch as he him holdeth in the highway towards the said port.

9. *Of admitting Freemen.*—Also, may the mayor and jurats make men free in such manner; that if any stranger come to Winchelsea, to dwell there, having lawful craft, and being of good conversation, for a year and a day, and desirous to be of the franchise, come before the mayor and jurats, in open assembly, beseeching to be of the franchise; upon which award, he shall pay to the comen of the franchise, having which award only, and his name shall be written in the common register, and after he shall take his oath :—

I shall faith and true bear, and true man be, unto the King of England, and to the commonalty of the town of Winchelsea, from this day forward; and the estate of the common franchise to my power shall maintain; and scott and lott of my goods and chattels shall pay. So God me help, and All Saints. And so kiss the book; and so he is accepted to the franchises.

10. *Recognizance by a Femme Covert.*—And the mayor and jurats may have recognizance in this manner. That if any husband, his wife having any tenement, or rent, within the said franchise, to any givver or seller, and of which the said wife, by way of heritage, or of purchase, or in any other manner, was feoffed or seized, or by reversion of any tenement, rent, or possession, after the death of any man, to her appertaining, the same wife shall come before the mayor and the bailiff and every of the jurors, and she shall be examined by every of the jurats; and she shall be examined by the same mayor and jurats, in the absence of her husband, whether she be contented of the said gift, or selling, or not; and the charter shall be read there, in English words, before the same wife, and if she say that she be well pleased, and not to that constrained by her husband, but of good will, and in her good memory, and acknowledge the same deed, the recognizance shall be enrolled into the comen rolls, as it appeareth after the manner. And after recognizance so done, the said wife, nor her husband, may not, in the said tenement, rent, or possession, after claim, but they be excluded all time to come, and for ever.

11. *A Fine, confessed by a sick woman, available.*—Also, they be wont to take such recognizance before the mayor and any of the jurats, in the court, in case the wife be in good mind, and in full health, and there personally come. But if the wife of the man be sick or feeble, that for feebleness she may not come to the court, and she would such acknowledge by recognizance, she shall send for the mayor and some of the jurats, and they shall come for to hear her will. When they be come, the same there they shall examine in manner aforesaid; if she consent firm and stable, be the recognizance for all to come, and for ever.

Also, if the wife of any man make knowledge, that in a case the conditions be, that she and her husband should be again feoffed of the aforesaid tenement or possession, jointly to their heirs, or to the husband's term of his natural life, and to the wife, and to her heirs, or in other manner, the mayor and jurats shall behold, and ratify these conditions, for the right and equity to be had and used in the said franchises at all times.

12. *Mortmain for Masses.*—Also, the mayor and jurats and commonalty may grant and confirm the ratification of lands and tenements, rents, and other possessions, within the franchises, being as much to a chauntry of masses, the sustenation of hospitals, and to Holy Church, viz., to Saint

Thomas and Saint Giles, Winchelsea, without licence of the king, or any other lord, any rent of the aforesaid lands and tenements, rents, and other possessions having.

13. *Receiving Pleas.*—Also, the bailiff or his sergeant shall receive all manner of plaints, as well of stranger as of in-dweller, after their nature, and they shall make attachment or summons; and if the plaintiff or defendant be strangers, their plea shall be holden from day to day, if it be not of land, or of the crown; and if it be of the two, or of the one, they shall be holden from fifteen days to fifteen days, viz., on Tuesday; every manner of plea shall be holden in the court-house of our Sovereign Lord the King; the same to be tried for member or for life, the which shall be holden in the hundred. In case of trespass, bloodshed, hamsoken, or mayhem, the defendant shall be attached by his body, to come unto the prison, if he cannot find sufficient pledges to be at the next court; at which court, if he come not, be he and his pledges in mercy; and for to be set at liberty, pledges against the next court; and so until he be justified for to answer to the party for why. In such cases be there no delay in court.

14. *Plea of Debt and Covenant.*—In every plea of debt, and covenant broken, and chattels withholden, be it between freemen or strangers, or between two strangers or two freemen, the bailiff shall take pledge to pursue; and if he may not find pledge, be his faith on the yard, and his day shall be limited unto him if he be a stranger, the morning afterwards; and if they be both abiding, both the one and the other, they shall have their day from fifteen days to fifteen days, as is above said, in the said court-house. And the bailiff shall summons against the stranger with the premises at the first court, and if he come not, be he attached; and if he come not at the second court, be he distrained from court to court, till he will justify. And when the parties be come into court, in their proper persons, or by their attornies, the plaintiff shall come to the defendant to ask leave for to account, which ought to be given; and the defendant in the same manner if he come to the mayor, he shall have leave. But in no manner of plea, where the sergeant is at the bar, no leave then shall be given to plead again. And in case the demand lay before them specially, by two men and himself, the third being at the making of the said deed; and in case that he may not pursue specially, the party defendant shall go without day; and the plaintiff be in mercy. And in case that the demandant may prove his deed, the defendant shall be in mercy, and make agree with the parties and have damage.

15. *Proceedings with Heirs and Executors.*—Also, in case that heirs and executors be impleaded, and the demandant have no speciality, the demandant ought to prove the debt by certain folk, two or three of the sight and hearing, and he shall be heard.

16. *Arresting of Goods of a Foreign Debtor within the Franchise.*—Also, if a man of the franchise see his foreign debtor within the franchise, well may the said freeman arrest the chattels of his debtor in the franchise, and going freshly to the bailiff, to him commit the said arrest, so that none deliverance be made in the absence of the said bailiff to deliver and the two parties, and neither of the two shall be amerced to each other. And in whatsoever manner of plea, in the which a man is adjudged, be he foreign or denizen, before the mayor and the bailiff in the court, he shall do hold in person, until he make agreement with the party in right of damage returned in the court; and shall be taxed by the mayor and jurats of the party, if the party condemned of him will ask.

17. *A Freeman to have Summons against a Freeman.*—In case any freeman complaineth against another freeman, he must come into the court

by summons, or by attachment, and the party defendant will account against him; he that is impleaded may delay the same day by these words:—

Sir Mayor, please you to wit, that I am a freeman, and I am not bound anon to answer to the party, by the reason I have no summons, nor as a freeman, before this day, for to be against him in this court; for which Sir, I ask my fee summons by law, as freeman ought to have in this court.

18. *A Woman covert de Baron.*—Item, if a woman covert de baron, viz., having an husband, be impleaded of a plea of debt, covenant broken, or chattels with-holden, and she be bound for merchandise, she shall answer without the presence of her husband.

19. *Plea of Land.*—Every plea of land shall be in a place called the court-house, appertaining to our Sovereign Lord the King, which plea may not be holden without the presence of the mayor, and be that holden from fifteen days to fifteen days, viz., the Tuesday, whether it be between stranger or freeman, or between two strangers or two freemen, of all lands, rents, and tenements within the franchise. And all manner of pleas of lands, rents, and tenements within the franchise, may be tried there by simple plaint, without the writ of our Sovereign Lord the King, save the writ of right, called Du Droit Patent, in the which he shall say, that if a man do not, the Sheriff of Sussex shall say to the Warden of the Cinque Ports, that all manner of writs ought to be pleaded in that manner, as it is in the King's court, save in some writs many delays, as in assize and mort d'ancestor, and in others less.

There as their pleas being common pleadings, the pleas by themselves, or their counsels, the mayor shall record the process of the trespasser, and the other; and as the nature of the process, the said mayor and jurats shall go to judgment, the which judgment shall be given by the mouth in playn court. And if any difficulty be in such judgment, be it lawful for the mayor and the jurats to have together the speaking of their combrethren of the Cinque Ports, how and in what manner they shall do right, and the parties after the plea before them pleaded; which judgment shall be delayed until the next court ensuing.

20. *Proceedings in Plea of Life and Member.*—Also the bailiff, when appellor doth appeal any man of life or member, shall attach the defendant by his body, &c., that the bailiff take pledges against the appellor, for to pursue his appeal; and if the appeal be such that the defendant be like to die, then the bailiff shall attach and sequester (by the advice of the mayor and the sworn men, or any of the sworn men) all the moveable goods of the defendant; but the said bailiff may not alienate the goods in no wise. If the defendant be convicted, all his goods shall be forfeited to the King; and all his house and rents, within the King's liberties, shall be forfeited to the King for a year and a day; and after that, they turn to the right heirs of the said defendant; and if he have none, to the Lord of the fee.

21. *A Freeman appealled.*—Also, when the appellor and the appealled shall come before the mayor and the bailiff's sergeant, he shall hold the defendant's hand; but when that he shall answer, he shall be unbound, and the bailiff shall rehearse, to the men that shall be there, the cause of the man that is appealled, and then the appellor shall appeal the defendant; and if the defendant contrary to the appellor, then he ought to say he is not guilty of the appeal that is put upon him, and that he will acquit himself thereof, after the liberty of the said town; and at a certain day assigned the defendant, have thirty-six men, good and true, the which shall swear with him that he is not guilty; and that day ought to be

assigned unto such time, and that the defendant may send into the place of his dwelling after such men, so that he shall be a stranger; and none of the thirty-six men shall be refused their oath, so that they be known for good men and true, whether they be stranger or denizen.

22. *Cutting a Purse.*—Also, when any man is found cutting a purse, or with the money stolen out of purses in any other place; then, at the suit of the appellor, one of the ears shall be abscided; and then shall he be led to the limits of the town, and forswear the town, never to be seen there afterwards, under pain of losing the other ear; and if he be found the second time cutting of purses, and may be proved that he loses his ear for the like cause, and if he bear any sign whereby a thief may be known, then he shall lose the other ear, and abjure the town, under pain of losing his life. And if he be found a third time in manner abovesaid, then he shall die, whether that he be signed in that town, or in any other place.

23. *Proceedings in Theft and Trespass.*—Also, if any theft, or any trespass be done in the port, or the town, as well by land as by water; also, if any person come to dwell in any of the said towns or ports, to bear open slander against the said port or town; then the mayor shall attach him, and deliver him to the bailiff into prison; for the bailiff shall receive all manner of such attachments, done by the mayor's hand, and deliver them, after that the trespass be there considered. And the man attached for that false slander shall abide in prison, and no man pursue for him; and afterwards he shall be delivered by pledges, but so shall govern himself well and truly afterwards; that if he may not find us pledges, then he shall forswear until he can.

24. *The Bailiff not to attach upon suspicion, without consent of the Mayor.*—Also, though the bailiff have any man suspected, he may not attach him in any case, without assent of the mayor and jurats, neither may he detain without their assent.

25. *Felony in Foreign.*—Also, if any man, free or stranger, for any felony or trespass in foreign country, come to the said town for the cause of help, he shall not be attached within the said town, as long as he governeth himself within the said town well and truly; without that the Warden of the Cinque Ports command that the said man be attached by assigning his cause; and if he may not find six men to undertake his body, within the said liberty, when it shall be asked; and if they come to serve him, he shall be had out of prison.

26. *Escape of Felony.*—Also, when any man of the said liberty, or a stranger, do any felony within the liberty, and flee from the said liberty for dread of the same felony, the mayor may send for him again, within that lordship or freedom wheresoever he be, within the realm of England, except the liberty of Holy Church, and have him delivered by the freedom of the same town, and there to be punished for his trespass; and so it hath been used of old time, unto this day.

27. *Bloodshed.*—Also, the bailiff may attach any man without any assent, where the man draweth blood of another in violence; he may put him in prison, if he that is hurt will pursue; and he may also put him to pledge, for the peace to be kept. And if any man will make any rescue against the bailiff for drawing of blood, the mayor and the sworn men shall help him, if they be required, on the King's behalf; and that may the mayor and every jurat do, when they see any man striking, or disturbing the King's peace.

28. *Of true Men's Goods seized.*—Also, if the goods of any true man be arrested among the goods of a felon, which goods the felon haply had by borrowing, and the owner might prove the goods his, and the felon

with-say it not, the goods shall be delivered unto the owner; for a thief may not for-say another man's goods to be his own, and will not appeal him, and he shall then lose the goods. And when a man is appealed and the suit of the appellor be judged to death, then the appellor shall have the goods that he challenged in the appeal.

29. *Distress for Rent.*—Also, if any man hold any tenement, by the which he ought to pay free rent to any man, and suffer the said tenement to be ruinous, or to fall, so that he who ought to have the free rent have none thereof, neither may find there none distress to the value; then let him, after seven months and one day, come unto the playne hundred, before the mayor and jurats, complaining thereof his right with-held. Then the mayor and the sworn men shall give him full power to set distress, if the owner the arrearage will not pay; and if the owner cannot, then let him come to the next hundred, and complain to the mayor as he did before; and when it shall be adjudged, that he go to the said tenement or land, and solemnly, by the sight of worthy men, he shall open the door of the tenement, and lift it out of the hooks; and if no man come within twelve months and one day, then it shall be judged, that he shall stick a stake in the earth, and that there shall be made proclamation; and if any man or woman ask any right in the said lands and tenement, let them come within six months and one day, from the time of this proclamation, and satisfy the asker of his arrearage; and if he acknowledge, after the liberty of the said town, the cause why he would not do it, before any pain of losing the said tenement and lands within the twelve months and one day, and no man come to make any, or to do in the manner aforesaid, then, in the next hundred following, it shall be judged, that the seizin of the lands and tenement shall turn to the asker of the said rent thereof due. But if any man or woman, within the said year and a day, before the payment made, acknowledge him to pay all that is due of the said tenement or lands, then he may save his lands and tenement; and if he will avow and say he holdeth not the lands and tenement of the asker, then they may plead; for in that case, the asker may not receive his asking, but by plea.

30. *Of Strepe and Waste.*—Also, if any man or woman hold anywise demise of land within the town for their lives, and if the reversion thereof belong to another man, if he waste the demise, or suffer it to be wasted in any wise, then the mayor and the sworn men, at the pursuing of him that owneth the reversion, shall constrain him to repair and support the said tenement, while that be insufficient; and if he be not sufficient, then the mayor and the sworn men shall take his goods, and sell them, to the reparation of the said demise; and if he will not, then he shall lose the said demise.

31. *Withernam.*—Also, the mayor and jurats may take withernam of citizens of London, and in any other place where they repair unto, for any manner of thing done against the liberties; and the withernam may be taken for many cases.

If a freeman come unto the mayor and jurats, praying to have letters under the mayor's seal, or the common seal of the town, to pray for him to citizens of London, or to burgesses of Calais, or any other place thither side the sea, or beyond the sea, to recover debt against another man dwelling there, in which debt he is bound to the said combaron and freeman of Winchelsea aforesaid, as he saith; and, if at the first letter, the citizens, or the burgesses aforesaid, do not execute their letters to recover the debt; or they write not again, permitting to do well execution, then send them letters a second time; and if they do not answer in manner abovesaid then send them letters a third time, on the part of the commonalty of the said town, under the common seal; and if at the letters the third time so sent, they do not in the manner abovesaid, and the pursuer come before the mayor and the sworn men, swearing on the gospel, that he into such a city, or burgh, such manner of letters, after his freedom and right, had sent, and the said citizens and burgesses had failed in his right, and will not execute his letters; then it shall be judged, that all that commonalty shall be condemned in the said debt, for default of righteousness, and that all that commonalty be distrained for the whole debt aforesaid; so that it may be proved to be very right, before the mayor and sworn men, that the said debt be true, and right to be paid.

And in case the said men of the aforesaid towns and burghs, for the same cause leave, and flee from the aforesaid town and haven of Winchelsea, and do go to other of the Cinque Ports, then the mayor and the sworn men shall send, by their letters, to the said ports, the record and proofs of the aforesaid debt, and judgment; and then they, after their custom and usage, shall make distraining and final execution, by the record and process aforesaid, the which the aforesaid mayor and sworn men of Winchelsea made, and sent to them.

32. *Buying and selling in Foreign.*—Also, if any freeman of the said town of Winchelsea dare not buy, nor sell, in any place of England, in London, Scotland, or France, or in any other place, by land or by water, or if they be distrained unrightfully, or pay any custom, or toll against the liberties, through any means of any commonalty, of their knowledge, or without knowledge, so that they may write their name, and so by their letters thus sent to the city or burgh, wheresoever they may be, once, or twice, or thrice, as it is aforesaid, by any of the freemen of the said town; but, and if they cannot offer any reasonable cause for themselves, in writing, or by any otherwise, then it shall be adjudged, that withernam shall be taken of all the commonalty; and so always that it be taken and held, untill the said commonalty direct the said trespass, in due form, what harms and expences for their rightful damage had and sustained.

33. *Of the Lord of a Franchise distraining a Portman.*—Also, if any lord distrain any merchant of Winchelsea, for pickage or standing on the ground, and if he be prayed by the mayor, by his letters, without delivering his distress, then may they take a withernam on him and all his tenants.

Also, the freemen of Winchelsea may be purchasers of all merchandize, where that they may be at the buying, or selling, so that the buyer and seller either be free or stranger; but if it be so, that the buyer or seller may put on him any lawfull cause, where through that he shall claim no part thereof, and if he be convicted of for-swearing, or to have no part of merchandize, for because, if he went from the town abovesaid, from the King's service, or from war, and come not in again by a certain day assigned, or if he do any forfeit against the said liberties, so that it be adjudged that he lose the said liberties; but there may be no stranger partner with a freeman as abovesaid, whatsoever he be, without his goodwill.

34.—*Barons of the Ports may sell in Foreign.*—And as the men of the Cinque Ports were wont to be let of their liberties most on the coast of Ireland, Edward the King, uncle to Edward the Third, confirmed the said liberties, under his charter, which see.

35. *Brewers may make and sell Ale in Foreign.*—Also, if there be any brewer of the said town, a freeman, who makes ale, and sells in foreign in harvest time, and the lord of the fee or the borough distrain for that

selling, against the liberty, then the mayor, through that complaint, shall send his letter and his seal to the said lord, to deliver that distress; for barons of Winchelsea are free to buy and sell throughout England. And if he do not, after these letters, then there shall be taken a withernam on all the tenants of the abovesaid lord.

36. *Holding Pleas.*—Also, all manner of pleas, real and personal, of which no mention hath been made, the mayor hath competence of his fellows, sworn to natural laws; on the which, and of the which, all manner of customs according to law, which being founded, and proceeding forth from Shepway; and the coronation of the king and the queen, the said town of Winchelsea hath as the other barons of the Cinque Ports.

37. *Alienation of Lands.*—Also, in case that a stranger, or a freeman, hath lands, rents, or tenements, within the same franchise, and he bind the same lands, rents, or tenements, to any stranger or freeman; or be he bound by recognizance made in the common rolls; or else the said lands, rents, and tenements, be alienated; he shall have execution to levy the debt of the said lands, tenements, and rents, without plea of it to be found by recognizance.

38. *Complaints to be heard either in the town or at Shepway.*—Also, in case that any man of the said town, do complain of any man of the said town, in any other place but the same town, he shall be punished for the despite to the comen, or else that it be in defence of the right of the comen, as aforesaid; and then it shall be tried before the warden, at Shepway, and no where else.

39. *Freeman may claim a share of Merchandize sold.*—If any merchant, denizen, or stranger, any merchandize at Winchelsea do put to sale, and they at the same town which be at the beginning of the said merchandize together, and also they of the said franchise being absent, and their part ought to be claimed by them that be then present. Be it also, that the said merchandize be equally divided, every man his part.

40. *Division of Merchandize.*—Also, if any stranger buy any merchandize in the franchise, being in absence of the folks of the franchise, they shall have half of the aforesaid merchandize, against the stranger, if they will ask it.

41. *Wardship.*—Also, if a man or woman die, and their heir be within age, the mayor shall have the sight of the child, and also of the goods and chattels, rents, and lands; and, by the said mayor and sworn men, the child shall be put to ward, to the most next of his blood, and to whom no heritage may in any wise extend. And also all the said goods and chattels to his said keeper, by indenture made between the mayor and keeper, till the full age of the child; and that the same part of this indenture shall be delivered in the comen treasury. And, if so be that he have none of blood living, then the mayor shall take the aforesaid goods to a sufficient man of the said commonalty, for to restore to the child at his full age, in the same manner as it is above said.

42. *The Mayor Visitor of the Hospitals.*—Also, the mayor shall have the visitation of the hospitals of Saint John and Saint Bartholomew, of Winchelsea, every year once; and there be in the said hospital brethren and sisters, sometimes more, and sometimes less; and there shall be no brother nor sister taken into the hospitals, but by assent of the mayor and commons aforesaid. And the rules of the hospitals aforesaid shall be read before the mayor, or in time of his visitation, which he shall ask and enquire for, if they be well holden, or not; also if any brother or sister do bear them in such manner, by which they be culpable, or an annoyance to the house. The mayor shall enquire of all the brethren and

sisters being there; and if he or she be then thereof annoyant, the mayor shall do him remove, if he will. And the mayor may, by the assent of the sworn men, if he may find in the same comen men or women that be covenatable, who have been in good love and fame all their time, and have neither goods nor chattels whereof to live, the said man or woman shall be sent into the said hospital, to take the sustenance of the said brethren and sisters, without paying anything to the said hospital.

43. *Chusing Brokers.*—Also, the mayor and the comen shall chuse common brokers, certain men to keep the weights and measures, as well of the corn as of the cloth, both linen and woollen, the which shall be sent to do right, as well to strangers as freemen.

These writings were compiled by Thomas Hokernam, town-clerk of Winchelsea, A.D., 1557.

KING'S AND TOWN'S RENTS.

The following are the rents as entered in the book formerly belonging to Mr. Wm. Lucas Shadwell, under date of 1716.

	s.	d.
The heirs of Edward Martin.		
For a house and ground in 13th quarter, called the *Firebrand*	1	7½
Ground there, where once stood a house	0	2
Ditto in 1st quarter, late Cheston's	0	10
A house and ground in the Strand	0	11
A barn, &c., in ditto	0	11½
The Pendants of the Hill there	2	1
A house and ground in 13th quarter	1	0½
Total 7s. 7½d.		
The heirs of Robert Bristow, Esq.		
For the *Wallnut Tree marsh*	8	0
A barn in the Strand	0	3
A house and ground in ditto	0	8
Another house and ground in ditto	1	4
Ground in 7th quarter, late Clerk's	1	0½
Another piece, 7th quarter, late ditto, formerly Farnham's	0	3
House in 7th quarter, tenant Parnell	2	0
Other ground there	1	0½
House and ground, 9th quarter, tenant Wm. Gyles	0	10½
Piece of ground in the Strand, late Longley's	0	10
Total 16s. 3½d.		
Thos. Jenkins, tanner.		
For a house in 13th quarter, late Head's	2	4½
A piece of ground where once stood a barn, ditto	0	4
A house and ground in 6th quarter, late Fowle's	0	8½
Ground in 8th quarter, late Ince's	5	2
Ditto in 2nd ditto ditto	0	2½
Ditto in 8th ditto ditto	1	8½
Other ditto in ditto, formerly *Three Kings' Taverne*	0	5
A dwelling house in the Strand	1	2½
Total 12s. 2½d.		

	s.	d.
Mr. Samuel Newman.		
For an orchard in the 9th quarter	4	9½
Ground in 35th quarter	1	3¾
Other ditto in ditto	1	11
Ground in 14th quarter, where stood a house and barn	1	4
Ditto in 9th ditto where once stood a house	0	7½
A piece of ditto in 10th quarter, late Mr. Seymore's	0	9
Morley's marsh, in the Strand	1	6
The *Stone Rock House* and ground there	1	2
A stable and ground in 13th quarter	0	4
An orchard in 18th ditto	1	9½
The *Ferry marsh*	3	4
Squire field, in 28th quarter	4	9
A house and ground in 7th quarter	1	7½
Ditto and ditto there, late Cheston's	1	8¾
A garden belonging to the same	0	3¼
A house and ground in the *Strand*	5	3¾
Ditto and ditto in 3rd quarter	0	8½
For a piece of ground at *Monday's Market*	0	2
An orchard in 10th quarter	3	5½
Land in 23rd ditto	0	8½
A field in 27th ditto	2	1
A barn and land in 28th ditto	6	4¼
A field in 33rd ditto	1	10
Land in 36th ditto	0	7
King's Green, in 34th ditto	5	0
A house and ground in 28th ditto	1	1
Ground in 3rd ditto, late Westbrooke's	2	6
A house and ground in 2nd quarter	2	3
An orchard in 20th quarter	3	3
A piece of ground in 19th, where once stood a barn	3	3
A field in 21st quarter	4	3
For ground in 15th quarter	3	2½
More ditto there	4	8¼
Saffron Garden, in 22nd quarter	0	7¾
A house and ground in the Strand	1	8
An orchard in 1st quarter	3	0
Butchery Orchard, 19th quarter	4	1
Total £4 7s. 3¾d.		
The heirs of John Hayes, Esq.		
For a house and ground in the 10th quarter	6	4
Ground in 26th quarter	5	3½
Relfe House, in 12th quarter	1	1½
Tinker's Garden, 17th ditto	3	1
The Pendants of the Hill there	0	10
Friar's Orchard, in 4th quarter	5	8¼
For *Ballad Singer's Platt*, in the 14th quarter	2	7½
A field in 27th quarter	5	2
The *Thorne*, in 24th quarter	3	4½
The Summerlands, in 20th ditto	3	2½
The *Salutation*, in 2nd ditto	1	7
A house and ground, 8th ditto, Fissenden's	1	3
The whole 16th quarter	7	0½
The Pendants of the Hill	0	6

	s.	d.
A field in 11th quarter	3	3
More ground in ditto	3	0¾
Bartholomew's field, in 39th quarter	6	0
Furze Bank ditto, 22nd ditto	7	4
St. John's field, in 34th quarter	13	9
A field in 30th quarter	4	9
More for land, late Tookey's	1	4
A field in 29th quarter	3	7
Total £4 10s. 2½d.		
John Swaine.		
For a house and ground in the 8th quarter	0	6
Ground in 2nd quarter	1	4½
Trojan's Hall, 19th quarter	0	11½
Land in 20th ditto	2	9
A field in ditto	5	4½
Total 10s. 11½d.		
The *Parsonage* of *St. Thomas the Apostle*	1	4
Ditto *St. Gyles*	1	3
Total 13s. 6½d.		
Cadwell.		
A house and ground in 18th quarter	2	5¾
His house in 5th quarter	3	0
A house, &c., 13th ditto	0	2
Total 5s. 7¾d.		
William Tidgwell.		
A house and ground in 14th quarter	0	5½
Ground in ditto	2	2½
More ditto in ditto	0	4
Total 3s.		
Mr. Young.		
For a house, &c., in the 13th quarter	0	7½
Thomas Cooper.[1]		
For the *Horse-head-House*, 9th quarter	1	0½
Ground in 6th quarter	0	4½
Total 1s. 5d.		
Zacheus Dicheson.		
A house and ground in 6th quarter	0	6½
A lane thereto adjoining	0	2
Total 8½d.		
Widow Stately.		
For her house in 12th quarter	2	0½
Mr. Short.		
For a house in 2nd quarter	2	11
John Samson.		
For a house in 6th quarter	1	0
John Benden.		
For part of the *Castle* field	0	6½

[1] In the Church Register, under date 1717-8, is the following entry, which establishes the correctness of the date of Mr. Shadwell's rental. Jan. 14, buried Thomas Cooper, juratt.

	s.	d.
John Richardson.		
For a house and ground in the 8th quarter	1	5
The house adjoining	0	2
Total 1s. 7d.		
Mr. Pares.		
For a house and ground in 8th quarter	1	9
John Carryll, Esq.		
Part of *Holy Rood*, in 38th quarter	9	11½
More in 39th quarter	3	0
Total 12s. 11½d.		
The heirs of Edward Marten.		
Ground in the Strand	4	4
The Pendants of the Hill, by the tan house	0	2
Cooke's Green, in 1st quarter	0	2
The Pendants of the Hill, in the Strand	0	2
The other ditto at the Mount	0	2
Two pieces of lanes in 1st quarter	0	2
The Pendants of the Hill, in the Strand, part of a lane there, and a barn	6	1
Ground at *Monday's Market*	3	0
Total 14s. 3d.		
Robert Bristow, Esq.		
For part of the *Wallnut Tree marsh*	1	0
A piece of ground near the tan yard	0	10
A house in the Strand, &c., tenant Tamsett	1	6
A lane near that house, tenant Ashenden	1	0
Several other lanes and slipps of ground	0	4
For the standing of a fence against a barne	0	4
Mr. Parnell's house in 7th quarter	2	8
Total 7s. 8d.		
Mr. Walsh.		
For a chimney platt in 13th quarter	0	4
His stable in ditto	0	4
Total 8d.		
Mr. Samuel Newman.		
An inclosure before his house, 10th quarter	0	4
The porch belonging to his barn there	0	4
The *Ferry marsh*	10	4
For the *Squire field*, 28th quarter	6	8
Coney field	2	0
The Pendants of the Hill, near *Pipe Well*	0	4
Land in 19th quarter	1	6
The *Brewhouse* marsh	0	2
House, ground, and lane in the Strand, tenant Jarret	1	0
The Furze Land field	1	0
A lane between the *Mill Banks*	0	0½
Part of the Town ditch and two lanes there	0	6
A spot of ground in 2nd quarter for a stable	0	4
Butchery Orchard, 19th quarter	7	0
Crooked Acre and part of a lane	3	0
Part of a lane adjoining thereto	0	1
Total £1 14s. 7½d.		

	s.	d.
Thomas Jenkins, tanner.		
For *Black Well*, in his tan yard	2	6
A piece of a lane, 8th quarter, lately belonging to the Inces	1	0
Land in 3rd quarter, ditto	3	0
A house and ground, late Head's	8	0
Total 14s. 6d.		
John Swaine of Hasting.		
For land in 2nd quarter, called Riches	0	4
Part of *Pooke lane*	0	1
Total 5d.		
John Carryll, Esq.		
For *Holy Rood*	3	0
Mr. Pares.		
For land behind the Court Hall	2	0
Mr. John Short.		
For a house and ground in 1st quarter, tenant Mr. Cruttenden	0	8
The heirs of John Hayes, Esq.		
For the Pendants of the Hill, near the Thorne	0	1
The Town ditch, a green, and a lane near *Pell Morrice*	0	6
A barn and ground in 12th quarter	3	4
The Pendants of the Hill there	2	0
Part of two lanes there	1	0
More for other ground there	0	2
The house called the *Salutation*	0	4
The standing of the sign post	0	6
The *Ferry Salts*	5	0
The *Thorne*, in 24th quarter	3	0
Two lanes adjoining	0	8
The *Ferry House*	1	0
A spot of ground called Fissenden's barn	0	4
Bartholomew field, 39th quarter	0	2½
Pooke lane, near Crooked Acre	0	6
The Pendants of the Hill, late Fissenden's	1	0
St. Leonard's Green, and a piece of a lane near *Gallows Hill*	6	0
Total £1 0s. 1½d.		
Widow Stately.		
For a house and ground, 12th quarter	0	10
Mr. Young.		
A house and ground, 13th quarter	3	0
Benjamin Jackson's widow.		
A house and ground, 5th quarter	2	6
John Sampson.		
Ground adjoining to his house	0	2
Part of a lane, 6th quarter	0	1
Total 3d.		
William Tidgwell.		
The Pendants of the Hill, 6th quarter, adjoining to Sampson's house	0	1
More for the Pendants of the Hill adjoining	0	2
Total 3d.		
Making together, £18 6s. 0½d.		

In the oldest account book belonging to the Chamberlain of the Corporation, (1753) which is signed by Edwin Wardroper, mayor, and by W. Marten, Nathl. Dawes, Thos. Orby Hunter, Arnold Nesbitt, Thos. Marten, Alex. Nesbitt, John Crawfurd, John Knight, and John Peters, is the following entry among the receipts :—

	£	s.	d.
To a year's King's rents and Town's rents due at Midsummer, 1753	19	1	10
Less unpaid	1	8	3½
	£17	13	6½

The difference, probably, being for waste land let subsequently to the compilation of the former rental.

The latest Rental, by which the Chamberlain now collects, is as follows: no new rental having been made for several years, the old names of former owners frequently occur instead of the present proprietors.

THE KING'S AND TOWN'S RENTAL.

	s.	d.
FIRST QUARTER.		
King's Rents.		
Edward Jeakins	0	10
Ditto	2	11
Total 3s. 9d.		
Town's Rents.		
Ditto for *Cook's Green*	0	2
Ditto	0	2
Ditto	0	8
Total 1s.		
SECOND QUARTER.		
King's Rents.		
Thomas Lloyd, Esq.	2	3
Edward Jeakins	0	2½
Thomas Lloyd, Esq., *Salutation Tavern* and ground	1	7
Ditto	1	4½
Total 5s. 5d.		
Town's Rents.		
Ditto	0	4
Ditto, part of *Pook lane*	0	1
Ditto, *Salutation Tavern*	0	4
Ditto, for the standing of a sign post	0	6
George Tilden, a spot of ground to set a stable on	0	4
Total 1s. 7d.		
THIRD QUARTER.		
King's Rents.		
Josiah Boots	0	8½
Thomas Lloyd, West brook	2	6
Edward Jeakins	1	8½
Total 4s. 11d.		
Town's Rents.		
Ditto	3	0
Thomas Lloyd, Esq., for the standing of the blacksmith's shop	2	6
Total 5s. 6d.		
FOURTH QUARTER.		
King's Rents.		
Thomas Lloyd, Esq., for *Fryer's Orchard*	5	8½

FIFTH QUARTER.

King's Rents.

	s.	d.
George Bray	3	0

Town's Rents.

	s.	d.
Ditto	2	6

SIXTH QUARTER.

King's Rents.

	s.	d.
Joseph Hoad	0	8
Robert Alce	0	4
George Stace	0	6½
Charles Terry	0	4½
Ditto, for a lane adjoining his property . . .	0	2
George Tilden . . .	0	8½
Charles Terry, for the Pendents of the Hill (sold May 20th, 1680) . .	0	1
Ditto, ditto, ditto .	0	2
Ditto, part of a lane .	0	1
Ditto, for standing of pallisades before his house . .	0	6
. . . . Hoad	0	2

Total 3s. 9½d.

SEVENTH QUARTER.

King's Rents.

	s.	d.
Thomas Lloyd, Esq. .	1	0½
Ditto	0	3
Ditto	2	0
Ditto	1	0½
Ditto, a piece of ground whereon the Stone Rock House formerly stood .	1	2
Ditto, for a house and ground, whereon a brewhouse formerly stood -	1	8¾
Ditto	0	3¼
Ditto	1	7½
Ditto	2	8
Ditto	0	2
Edward Jeakins . . .	5	2
Ditto, for a piece of ground whereon stood heretofore the *Three Kings' Tavern*	0	5
Thomas Lloyd, Esq., for barn and ground .	1	3
Ditto	0	6
Ditto	1	9
Ditto	1	5

Total £1 2s. 5¾d.

Town's Rents.

	s.	d.
Ditto, a piece of ground behind the Court Hall .	2	0
Edward Jeakins, for piece of a lane	1	0
Thomas Lloyd, Esq., for ground taken from the Court Hall plat . .	0	6

Total 3s. 6d.

NINTH QUARTER.

King's Rents.

	s.	d.
Edwin Dawes, Esq., for an orchard, late Sir William Ashburnham's, Bart., the the only son and heir-at-law of the late Lord Bishop of Chichester .	4	9½
Ditto	0	7½
Ditto	1	0½

Total 6s. 5½d.

Town's Rents.

	s.	d.
Ditto, for a porch, where stood a barn . .	0	4

TENTH QUARTER.

King's Rents.

	s.	d.
Thomas Lloyd, Esq. .	0	9
Ditto, for an orchard where stood a house . .	3	5½
Ditto, for ground where stood a house . .	6	4

Total 10s. 6½d.

Town's Rents.

	s.	d.
James Bray, for an inclosure before the house .	0	4

ELEVENTH QUARTER.

King's Rents.

	s.	d.
Thomas Lloyd, Esq., for a piece of ground, almost the whole quarter .	3	3
Ditto	3	0¾

Total 6s. 3¾d.

TWELFTH QUARTER.

King's Rents.

	s.	d.
Ditto, for a barn and ground called the *Cherry Garden*	1	1½
Richard Stileman, Esqr's., heirs, piece of garden ground	2	0½

Total 3s. 2d.

Town's Rents.

	s.	d.
Ditto	0	6
Thomas Lloyd, Esq., Cherry Garden, barn, and ground	3	4
Thomas Easton . .	0	4

	s.	d.
R. Stileman's heirs	0	6

Total 4s. 2d.

THIRTEENTH QUARTER.

King's Rents.

	s.	d.
Richard Lamb, for a house called the *Firebrand*	1	7½
Ditto	0	2
Thomas Lloyd, Esq.	1	0½
Richard Stileman, Esqr's., heirs	0	2
Ditto	0	2
Edward Jeakins	2	4½
John Elliott	0	2
George Harrod	0	7½

Total 6s. 4d.

Town's Rents.

	s.	d.
William Sargent, for a chimney plat	0	4
Ditto, for the standing of a stable (sold Aug. 2nd, 1681)	0	4
Edward Jeakins, for a house	8	0
George Harrod	3	0
Ditto for the standing of a sign post	0	6

Total 12s. 2d.

FOURTEENTH QUARTER.

King's Rents.

	s.	d.
Edwin Dawes, Esq.	1	4
Edward Jeakins, a piece of ground whereon stood a barn	0	4
Thomas Lloyd, Esq., a piece of ground called the *Ballad Singer's Plat*	2	7½
George Harrod, two houses	0	5½
Richard Maplesden	1	2
Thomas Easton	0	8
Ditto	0	7
Ditto	0	7
George Harrod	2	2½
Ditto	0	4

Total 10s. 3½d.

FIFTEENTH QUARTER.

King's Rents.

	s.	d.
Thomas Lloyd, Esq.	3	2½
Ditto	4	8¼

Total 7s. 10¾d.

SIXTEENTH QUARTER.

King's Rents.

	s.	d.
Ditto, for a field, being the whole quarter	7	0½

SEVENTEENTH QUARTER.

King's Rents.

	s.	d.
Thomas Lloyd, Esq., for a field called *Tinker's Garden*	3	1

EIGHTEENTH QUARTER.

King's Rents.

	s.	d.
Ditto, for an orchard	1	9½
Walter Fuller	2	5¾

Total 4s. 3¼d.

NINETEENTH QUARTER.

King's Rents.

	s.	d.
Thomas Lloyd, Esq., for a piece of ground called *Little Monday's Market*	0	2
Ditto, for *Trojan's Hall* alias *Jew's Hall*	0	11½
William Leere	0	10½
Thomas Lloyd, Esq.	3	3
Ditto, *Butcher's Orchard*	4	1

Total 9s. 4d.

Town's Rents.

	s.	d.
Ditto, *Little Monday's Market*	3	0
Ditto	1	6
Ditto, *Butchery Orchard*	7	0

Total 11s. 6d.

TWENTIETH QUARTER.

King's Rents.

	s.	d.
Ditto, for a field called *Summer Land*, part of the Thorn	3	2½
Ditto	2	9
Ditto, an orchard	3	3
Ditto, Burnt House Orchard	3	4

Total 12s. 6½d.

Town's Rents.

	s.	d.
Ditto, *Summer Lands*	5	0
Ditto	0	4

Total 5s. 4d.

TWENTY-FIRST QUARTER.

King's Rents.

	s.	d.
Ditto, *Cheston's field*	4	3

TWENTY-SECOND QUARTER.

King's Rents.

	s.	d.
Ditto, the *Furze Banks*	7	4
Ditto, *Saffron Garden*, adjoining Cheston's field	0	7¾

Total 7s. 11¾d.

TWENTY-THIRD QUARTER.

King's Rents.	s.	d.
Thomas Lloyd, Esq., a lane, part of *Fryers* . .	8	2

TWENTY-FOURTH QUARTER.

King's Rents.		
Ditto, a house and ground called *The Thorn* .	3	4¼
Town's Rents.		
Ditto, for *The Thorn* .	3	0
Ditto, two lanes near ditto, and Gallows Hill . .	0	8
Total 3s. 8d.		

TWENTY-FIFTH QUARTER.

King's Rents.		
Ditto	5	3½

TWENTY-SIXTH QUARTER.

King's Rents.		
Ditto, a field, being a whole quarter . . .	5	4¼

TWENTY-SEVENTH QUARTER.

King's Rents.		
Ditto, part of Fryer's called *Little King's Green* .	2	1
Ditto, *Chapel field*, or St. John's field . .	5	2
Total 7s. 3d.		

TWENTY-EIGHTH QUARTER.

King's Rents.		
Ditto Squire's field .	4	9
Ditto, a piece adjoining ditto, where stood a barn	6	4½
Ditto, part of the Fryers, where stood a house -	1	1
Total 12s. 2½d.		
Town's Rents.		
Ditto, Squire's field . .	6	8

TWENTY-NINTH QUARTER.

King's Rents.		
Ditto, Peckham field .	3	7

THIRTIETH QUARTER.

King's Rents.		
Ditto, part of Great Gallows Hill	4	9

THIRTY-FIRST QUARTER.

None.

THIRTY-SECOND QUARTER.

None.

THIRTY-THIRD QUARTER.

King's Rents.	s.	d.
Thomas Lloyd, Esq., a field, part of *Fryers* . .	1	10

THIRTY-FOURTH QUARTER.

King's Rents.		
Ditto, land called *King's Green* . . .	5	0
Ditto, *St. John's field* .	13	9
Total 18s. 9d.		

THIRTY-FIFTH QUARTER.

King's Rents.		
Ditto, a piece of ground near the Pewes . .	1	3¾
Ditto	1	11
Total 3s. 2¾d.		

THIRTY-SIXTH QUARTER.

King's Rents.		
Ditto, land, part of Fryers	0	7

THIRTY-SEVENTH QUARTER.

None.

THIRTY-EIGHTH QUARTER.

King's Rents.		
Sir William Ashburnham, part of *Holy Rood* (the late Lord Bishop of Chichester's - - -	9	11½

THIRTY-NINTH QUARTER.

King's Rents.		
Thomas Lloyd, Esq., for *Newgate* alias *Bartholomew field* . . .	6	0
Sir William Ashburnham, other part of *Holy Rood*	3	0
Total 9s.		
Town's Rents.		
Ditto, Holy Rood . . .	3	0
Thomas Lloyd, Esq., Newgate or Bartholomew field	0	2½
Total 3s. 2½d.		

KING'S AND TOWN'S RENTS, PAYABLE OUT OF THE QUARTERS.

	s.	d.
Edward Jeakins, for malthouse and brewhouse	0	11
Ditto	0	11½
Ditto, for Well field	2	1
Ditto, Wallnut Tree marsh	8	0
Thomas Mays, for ground at the Strand	0	3
James Drury, ditto, and house at ditto	0	8
Thamas Mays, ground at Strand	1	4
Edward Jeakins, Longley's marsh, at ditto	0	10
Thomas Lloyd, Esq., Pear Tree marsh	1	6
Ditto, Morley's ditto	3	4
Ditto, for ground at the Strand	5	3¾
Rev. Drake Hollingbery, Parsonage of St. Thomas the Apostle	1	4
Ditto ditto of St. Giles	1	3
Thomas Lloyd, Esq., Pendents of the Hill, near Tinker's Garden	0	10
Ditto	1	4
Edward Jeakins, Pendents of the Hill	0	6
Sir William Ashburnham, part of Castle field	0	6½
Thomas Lloyd, Esq., house and ground, Strand	1	8
Edward Jeakins, ditto, ditto, ditto	1	2½
Henry Martin, Floatage ground ditto	4	4
Edward Jeakins, Pendents of Cliff and Well field	0	2
Ditto, Pendents of the Hill, where the ashes formerly stood	0	2
Ditto, Pendents at Strand, and part of a lane there	6	1
Ditto, Wallnut Tree marsh	1	0
Ditto, piece of Ground near the tan yard	0	10
James Drury, house and ground at Strand	1	6
Ditto a lane near ditto	1	0
Thomas Mays, several lanes and slips of ground (sold to Richard Breene, May 18th, 1680)	0	4
Ditto, for standing of fence where once stood a barn	0	4
Thomas Lloyd, Esq., for Morley marsh	10	4
Edward Jeakins, for Blackwell, in his tan yard	2	6
Thomas Lloyd, Esq., for Brewhouse marsh	0	2
Ditto, grounds and part of lane, Strand	1	0
Ditto, Furze Banks	1	0
Ditto, for a lane between the Mill Banks	0	0½
Ditto, part of Town's Ditch and two lanes adjoining	0	6
Ditto, Pendents of the Hill, near the Thorn (purchased Aug. 2nd, 1680)	0	1
Ditto, Town's Ditch and green leading to Pet Morris (sold May 30th, 1682)	0	6
Ditto, Pendents under *Tinker's Garden*	2	0
Ditto, part of two lanes	1	0
Ditto	0	2
Ditto, Ferry Salts	5	0
Ditto, Ferry House	1	0
Ditto, *Pook lane*, near Crooked Acre	0	6
Ditto, Pendents	1	0
Ditto, St. Leonard's Green, and piece of land near Gallows Hill	0	6
Ditto, Crooked Acre, and a lane there	3	0
Ditto, a lane joining Crooked Acre	0	1

	s.	d.
Thomas Lloyd, Esq., Coney field	2	0
Edward Jeakins, Pendents, near Pipe Well gate	0	4
Sir William Ashburnham, Water Bailiff's prison	6	8

Total £4 8s. 11¾d.

MAYORS,

SO FAR AS THEY HAVE BEEN DISCOVERED.

1306.	34 Edward I.	Henry Paulin. MSS. in Chapt. Ho. West., Press z., No. 11.
1308-9.	2 and 3 Edward II.	Gervase Alard, jun. Dering MSS.
1313-4.	7 "	Robert Paulyn. Ib.
1333.	7 Edward III.	Henry Vynghe. Addl. Charters, Brit. Museum, No. 970.
1354.	28 "	Robert Arnald.[1] Rot. Parl., vol. 2, p. 263 a.
	"	Valentine de Dovor. Dering MSS.
1358.	32 "	Robert Arnold. Ib.
1376-7.	50 "	Robert Baddyng. Ib.
Before	11 Richard II.	Robert Londeneys. Ib.
1388-9.	11 and 12	Robert Harri. Ib.
1389.	12 and 13	William Skele. Bat. Abb. Rec.
1400.	1 Henry IV.	Vincent Finch. Dering MSS.
1405.	January 26th.	John Helde. Bat. Abb. Rec.
1407.	May 1st.	John Thundyr, jun. Ib.
1412.	September 20th.	John Tonstall.[2] Ib.
1415.	November 6th.	Roger Atte Gate. Ib.
1420.	May 1st.	Thomas Thunder, jun. Ib.
1425.	April 5th.	The same
1426.	April 5th.	William Worth. Ib.
1430.		Roger Atte Gate. Ib.
1433.	May 21st.	John Godfrey. Ib.
1434.	October 22nd.	William Fynch. Ib.
1443.	June 20th.	Thomas Sylton. Ib.
1446.	July 2nd.	Godard Pulham. Ib.

[1] There was a complaint against him by John de Bures, who, coming to Winchelsea on his voyage to Brittany, had his ship seized on a plaint and judgment obtained in the Winchelsea Court by John de Menil, and the whole of her freight of large value sold by Sir Ralph Caus, Knt., Vyncent Finch, John his brother, and John Menil. Rot. Parl., vol. 2, p. 263 a.

[2] On 25th July, 1412, the Mayor of Winchelsea (for the time being) was appointed one of the Conservators of Truces with Flanders, to repair the ports, &c. Rym. Fœd., vol. 8, p. 765.

1474.	February 20th.	Richard Davy. Bat. Abb. Rec.
1483-4.	January 31st.	John Fysshe. Rot. Pat.
1522-3.	14 Henry VIII.	Thomas Ashborneham. Dering MSS.
1544.	36 "	John Watts. Carlt. Ride MS. Benevolence
1571-2.	4th Elizabeth.	Thomas Wildforth. Dering MSS.
1601-2.	January 21st.	Richard Martham, when the Charter to the Cinque Ports was granted. Jeake's Charters.
1606.	4 James I.	Thomas Pelham. Arch. vol. 18, p. 291.
1608.	6 "	Mr. White. Godfrey's Diary, Lans. MS., 235.
1609.	7 "	William Bishop. Ib.
1610.	8 "	Robert Boteler. Ib.
1623.	21 "	Paul Wymond. Journ. Ho. of Com.
1641.	17 Charles I.	No name.[1]
1700.	12 William and Mary.	Edward Marten. Journ. Ho. of Com.
1701.	13 "	John Hopper. Ib.
1707.	6 Anne	Robert Ashdowne. Ib.
1709.	8 "	John Parnell. Ib.
1713.	12 "	The same.[2] Ib.
1747.	21 George II.	Edwin Wardroper. Hastings Corp. Boundaries.

1754.	Edw. Wardroper[3]	1766.	Walter Gybbon, deputy
55.	No name preserved	67.	Richard Wardroper
56.	Edw. Wardroper	68.	No name preserved
57.	William Marten	69.	William Marten[5]
58. 59.	No names preserved	70.	Joash Adcroft
		71.	Nathaniel Dawes
60.	Edw. Wardroper	72.	Thomas Marten
61.	Richard Wardroper	73.	William Marten
62.	Nathaniel Dawes[4]	74.	Thomas Marten
63. 64.	No names preserved	75.	William Marten
		76.	Thomas Marten
65.	Edw. Wardroper, deputy	77.	William Marten

[1] By the Act, 17 Chas. II, c. 33, the Mayor (for the time being) and Daniel White, a jurat, were appointed Commissioners to call together the inhabitants and collect a loan towards the relief of Ireland. Scobell's Acts and Ordinances, p. 24.

[2] In the Register of Burials, is the following entry: "1713, Nov. 23. Buried, John Parnell, Esq., then mayor. He dyed of the small pox."

[3] The names, from 1754 to 1768, (except 1762) are from the audits of the Chamberlain's accounts; but as the accounts were only audited at intervals, the names are not regularly given each year.

[4] Burrow's Reports.

[5] From the Hundred and Assembly Books after 1768.

1778. Thomas Marten
79. William Marten
80. Thomas Marten
81. William Marten
82. John Peters
83. Thomas Marten
84. Joash Adcroft
85. Thomas Marten
86. Joash Adcroft
87. Thomas Marten
88. Joash Adcroft
89. Thomas Marten
90. Richard Lamb
91. Thomas Marten
92. Richard Lamb
93. Thomas Marten
94. George Stace
95. Thomas Marten
96. Barwell Brown
97. Godfrey Scholey
98. Barwell Brown
99. John Shakespear
1800. Barwell Brown
1. The Rev. Thomas Raddish, clerk
2. Barwell Browne
3. The Rev. Thomas Raddish
4. Thomas Lloyd
5. Barwell Browne
6. Thomas Lloyd
7. Barwell Browne
8. The Rev. Thomas Raddish
9. Barwell Browne
10. The Rev. Thomas Raddish
11. Barwell Browne
12. The Rev. Thomas Raddish
13. Barwell Browne
14. The Rev. Thomas Raddish
15. Barwell Browne
1816. The Rev. Thomas Raddish
17. Barwell Browne
18. Alexander Tullock[1]
19. Barwell Brown
20. Alexander Tullock
21. Barwell Browne
22. Alexander Tullock
23. Barwell Browne
24. Alexander Tullock
25. Barwell Browne
26. Alexander Tullock
27. The Rev. Samuel Philip Sheppard
28. Alexander Tullock
29. The Rev. Samuel Philip Sheppard
30. Alexander Tullock
31. The Rev. Samuel Philip Sheppard
32. William Lipscomb
The same afterwards
33. George Morant
34. Thomas Dawes
35. John Tilden
36. Joseph Hennah
37. John Beaumont
38. Richard Stileman
39. Richard Stileman
40. Thomas Dawes
41. Richard Stileman
42. Thomas Dawes
43. Richard Stileman
44. Joseph Hennah
45. Ditto
46. Ditto
47. Ditto
48. Ditto
49. Ditto
50. William Sergeant

BARONS AT CORONATIONS.

The Barons of the Cinque Ports, to the number of thirty-two, had the privilege of bearing the canopy, with four silver staves, over the King and Queen at Coronations. Of this number four were sent from Winchelsea. The costume varied from time to time. At the coronation of James II the barons wore doublets of crimson satin, scarlet hose, and

[1] Tullock and Sheppard were merely the Duke of Cleveland's managers: they were non-resident and nick-named "Grass-mayors."

scarlet gowns faced with crimson, black velvet shoes, with caps of the same, fastened to their sleeves.[1] At the coronation of George III and his Queen, on 22nd Sept., 1761, the barons from Winchelsea, who supported the canopies, were[2]

Thos. O. Hunter .	King's canopy.	Richd. Wardroper	Queen's canopy.
Geo. Gray . .	King's canopy.	John Nicholl . .	Queen's canopy.

They wore robes of scarlet cloth, like an Oxford Master of Arts' gown, faced with scarlet satin, with long slit sleeves, and a large cape of scarlet satin, lace ruffles at wrist, scarlet satin breeches with white satin knots at the knees, scarlet satin waistcoats lined with white, and a small square open cuff of white satin, white silk hose, black velvet shoes with scarlet thongs and heels, and white satin rosettes, black velvet round Spanish cap, sword with cross-carved gilded handle in white satin scabbard, and a white satin belt.[3] At the coronation of George IV, in 1820, the barons from Winchelsea wore as the dress, a vest of scarlet satin trimmed with tissue lace, and buttons worked of the same, the sleeves slashed and trimmed with lace, trunk hose of blue satin slashed with scarlet satin, trimmed as above, red silk stockings, white kid shoes with rosettes of scarlet riband, and trimmed as above, a surtout of dark blue satin, quite plain, black Spanish hat and feather, upstanding frill for neck.[4]

[1] Holloway's Rye, p. 72.

[2] Mantell's Coronations, p. 20.

[3] Ex. inf., Mr. Geo. Slade Butler. The canopy was of gold brocaded tissue, with bullion fringe seven inches deep, lined with silver tissue and silver fringe. The bell was silver gilt, of the ordinary hand-bell size. Mantell says the stockings were scarlet.

[4] Holloway's Rye, p. 73.

PARLIAMENTARY HISTORY.

The right of returning Members to Parliament was first exercised by Winchelsea, at the same time as by the Cinque Ports, 42 Edw. III. The persons then, and for the next two centuries, elected, were the principal inhabitants of the town; but by degrees, as the representation became an honor and not a burden, strangers, who were admitted to their freedom for this purpose only, were, by degrees, introduced. The Lord Warden claimed the right of nominating one member; subsequently the representation fell completely into the hands of the Treasury, and ultimately into those of a Patron. The right of election was in the mayor, jurats, and freemen; but for the patron's purposes, the number of freemen was reduced so low, that in 1792, the number of legal voters was only three, and in 1832, it was only nine.

The History of the Corporation will have given our readers a clear insight into the mode by which the object of the patron was effected, and we must refer those who wish for a detailed history of the parliamentary contests, to Horsfield's History of Sussex.[1] We may, however, state here, that for his illegal conduct, especially in excluding the Tildens from voting, the mayor, Paul Wymond, was, in 1623, committed by the Commons to prison: and that, in 1700, Mr. Edward Marten, the mayor, was also committed for "threats and indirect practices."

The last instance, which we have discovered, of anything like an approach to independence on the part of the electors, was in March, 1680-1, when the following address was agreed upon.[2]

To their Barons, Sir Steven Lenon and Creswel Draper, Esquire, elected in their absence, March 4, 1680-1, and ordered by the mayor and jurates to be presented to them; the said Mr. Draper serving for them in the last parliament.

Mr. Draper,

You may assure your self that we are very highly satisfied with your

[1] Parl. History, by W. D. Cooper, vol. 2, app. p. 72. [2] State Tracts, 1692.

unwearied pains, as also of your honest discharge of the great trust we reposed in you in the last parliament, by our hearty thanks we now return you, and by our unanimous electing you again to serve for us in the next parliament to be holden at Oxford.

And gentlemen, as for you both, we know you are so sensible of our condition, that we need not tender you our thoughts in many particulars; only the preservation of His Sacred Majesty's person, our religion, and properties, which are of the greatest concern and most dear unto us, and especially in order thereunto we commend unto you, and desire you to use your utmost endeavours.

1.—That there may be a full and perfect discovery of that most hellish and damnable Popish plot in England and Ireland, and all other sham plots, which have been wickedly contriving and acting for many years past.

2.—That effectual means be used for uniting all his Majesty's protestant subjects against the common enemy, both at home and abroad.

3.—That all effectual means and ways may be provided to secure us against a Popish successor, and particularly against James Duke of York.

4.—That you will endeavour as far as in you lies, that a law may be made for putting our free-lands and houses under a voluntary register, that thereby this kingdom may be a just and honorable fund, whereby moneys may be taken up upon all urgent occasions, and so prevent the great ruines we now lie under for want thereof.

5.—That you will use your utmost endeavours to put a brand upon those abominable monsters which were the pensioners in the late long parliament, that thereby the generations to come may be deterred from attempting the like unheard of villiany.

6.—That you will vigorously and carefully represent to the rest of your fellow members the present condition of the royal navy, as also of the stores, castles, and forts, which are under God the bulwarks of England; and that such effectual ways and means may be found out and prosecuted for the better securing and improving the navy; as also that none may be employed therein but such persons as are of known integrity and loyalty, both to the King and nation; and that all debauch'd and unskilful persons now employed may be removed, and men fearing God, loving truth, and hating covetousness, may be put in their places: that so our present fears may be abated, and thereby the dreadful growing power of France may be timely checked.

Gentlemen,—In the pursuance of these good ends, and such other as you shall think conducing to the happiness of the King and kingdom, we shall stand by you with our lives and fortunes.

In 1700 the Treasury were the patrons: but they did not escape contests; for, in 1710, their candidates, Robt. Bristow, Esq., and Sir Francis Dashwood, polled ten each, and their opponents, William Penn and Richard Jones, polled twelve each, of whom, however, the mayor rejected all but two. In 1741, their candidates were opposed by E. H. Beaghan, and Samuel Jeake, Esqrs. In 1747, their candidates were the Hon. J. Mordaunt, who polled fifteen, and Thomas Orby Hunter, Esq., who polled twelve, against three votes given for Visct. Donerayle. In 1754, Mr. Arnold Nesbit was returned by the Treasury, and afterwards succeeded so far in establishing his own private interest, that, in 1768, his candidates wholly defeated the Government: Thos. Orby Hunter, polling twenty-three, and the Earl of Thomond, twenty; whilst Sir Thomas Sewell and Richd. Burton Philipson, Esq., polled only eight each. In 1790, the patronage became the property of Richard Barwell, Esq., and the Earl of Darlington: the latter afterwards purchased Mr. Barwell's interest, and was the patron when the Reform Act of 1832, disfranchised this town.

The parishes of St. Thomas and St. Giles have been placed within the Electoral District of Rye town, and the right of vôting for the members for that town is exercised by the inhabitants of £10 houses in Winchelsea, of whom, forty-one are on the present register.

The Boundary Act of 1832, did not alter the right of the £10 householders within the Liberty of St. Leonard to vote for Hastings, and there is one registered voter for the borough eight miles distant.

The list of the members returned to parliament between 1473 and 1553 has been lost; but the Dering MSS. contain valuable entries of members from the Cinque Ports during this period. It will be seen from the following list that so late as the time of Elizabeth, the mayor was not unfrequently returned as a member to parliament.

MEMBERS OF PARLIAMENT.

EDWARD III.

1369.	Robert Bettercock	Robert Londeneys
72.	Robert Baddyng	
73.	Robert Londoneys	Thomas Sibb
74.	Robert Harrys	Gervase Loveron
77.	Robert Baddyng, mayor	Robert Arnold

RICHARD II.

78.	Robert Loudon	William Wells
79.	William Skele	Roger Danere
83.	The same	John Pulham
84.	The same	Thomas Bett
84.	John Pulham	The same
86.	The same	William Martyn
87.	William Skele	John Pulham
88.	The same	Robert Harri, mayor
89.	Henry Cely	Math. Goldyne
90.	William Skele	Roger Dover
92.	The same	Vincent Ewele
93.	Robert Arnold	Thomas Bett
95.	Vincent Fynch	William Skele
97.	The same	John de Helde

HENRY IV.

1400.	Robert Gate	William Skele
2.	Vincent Fynch	John Salerne
7.	John Sugern	Robert Fishlake
10.	Roger Bates	John Tounstell

HENRY V.

13.	Roger atte Gate	Thomas Young
14.	The same	William Cotton
19.	Vincent Finch	John Warton
20.	Roger atte Gate	Edw. Hopyere
21.	The same	Alexander Beuley

HENRY VI.

22.	The same	John Tamworth
24.	Thomas Young	Alexander Beuley
25.	Thomas Thondyr	The same
26.	John Frenshe	William Cotton

1427.	Roger atte Gate	John Tamworth
28.	William Alard	William Moorfot
29.	The same	The same
30.	Thomas Thondyr	Godard Pulham
32.	William Finch	William Pope
35.	Thomas Thondyr	The same
36.	William Alard	Richard Hendnes
41.	John Godfrey	Thomas Sylton
44.	William Alard	The same
48.	John Godfrey	Geoffry Pulham
49.	John Clive	John Westbourne
50.	John Cobbey	Alan Honywood
52.	Thomas Silton	John Convers

EDWARD IV.

73.	Robert Bossele	Richard Davy

HENRY VII.[1]

1st.	John Convers	John Godard
12th.	Richard Marcham	Richard Barkeley, valectus corone Domini Regis

HENRY VIII.

1st.	Thomas Ashborneham	Robert Sparowe
14th.	The same, mayor	The same
25th.	Thomas Ensyng	George Lowes
33rd.	John . . . . . ., mayor	Philip Chewte

EDWARD VI.

	Ciriac Petytt	Joseph Beverley
7th.	William Eglestone	Michael Blount
1553.	William Roper	

MARY.

54.	The same	Henry Crispe, Knt.

PHILIP AND MARY.

54.	William Eglestone	John Cheney
55.	Thomas Smyth	John Poyton
57.	George Howard, Knt.	John Fowler

[1] The list, from 1473 to 1553, is taken from the Dering MSS.

ELIZABETH.

1558.	Goddard White	Henry Vane
63.	Richard Chambrey	The same
71.	Thomas Wildford	Robert Eyre
72.	Thomas Wildford, mayor	Richard Barry
83.	Giles Fletcher, L.L.D.	Herbert Pelham
86.	Adam Moyle	Thomas Eglestone
88.	Herbert Morley	Adam Moyle
92.	Adam Ashbornham	Ashburnham Pecke
97.	Ralph Evans	Thomas Culpepper
1601.	Moyle Finch, Knt.	Hugh Beeston

JAMES I.

3.	Adam White	Thomas Unton
14.	Edward Barcit, Knt.	
20.	Thomas Finch, Knt. and Bart.	Edward Nicholson
23.	John Finch	Edward Nicholas

CHARLES I.

25.	Ralph Freeman, Knt.	Roger Twisden, Knt.
	Nicholas Sanders, Knt.	The same
28.	William Twisden, Bart.	Ralph Freeman, Knt.
40.	Nic. Crispe[1] (excluded)	John Finch: ob. 1642
	Henry Oxenden (vice Crispe, secluded)	Samuel Gott[2] (vice Finch)

COMMONWEALTH.

58-9.	John Busbridge	Robert Fowle
60.	William Howard, second son of E. Lord Howard, of Eserick	Samuel Gott
61.	The same	Sir Nicholas Crispe
78.	Creswel Draper	Thomas Austine
81.	The same	Sir Stephen Lenon

[1] 2 Feb. 1640-1. Upon Mr. Perd's report from the Committee of Monopolists, it was resolved upon the question that Sir Nicholas Cripps is a monopolist, in joint execution of the patent for coperas stores, and so within the Order of the House made against monopolists, and ought not to sit as a member in the house, and that a warrant issue for a new writ. Journ. of Ho. of Commons, vol. 2, p. 77.

[2] William Smith of the Middle Temple, elected a burgess for Winchelsea, 1604. Hayley.

JAMES II.

1685.	Creswel Draper	Lord Middleton[1]
		Arthur St. Leger Viscount Doneraile (vice Middleton)

WILLIAM AND MARY.

88.	Richard Austine	Samuel Western
90.	The same	The same
95.	The same	The same
98.	John Hayes	Robert Bristow
1701.	The same	Robert Austine

ANNE.

2.	The same	George Clerk
7.	The same	George Dodington
8.	Robert Bristow	The same[2]
		Sir Francis Dashwood, Knt. and Bart. (vice Dodington)
10.	The same	The same
13.	The same	George Dodington

GEORGE I.

14.	The same	George Bubb Dodington
22.	The same	The same[3]
		Thomas Townsend (vice Dodington)
27.	The same	John Scrope[4]
27.	The same	Sir Arthur Croft, Bart.[5]
		Peter Walter (vice Croft)

GEORGE II.

34.	The same	Edward Hungate Beaghan
41.	Arthur Visc. Doneraile	Thomas Orby Hunter
47.	John Mordaunt	The same
54.	Thomas Orby Hunter	Arnold Nesbit

[1] In 2 Jac. II, Lord Middleton was returned in pursuance of a pretended claim in the Crown, that the Lord Warden of the Cinque Ports has a power to recommend and nominate one baron for each port to any parliament.

[2] Made his election for Bridgewater.

[3] Made his election for Bridgewater.

[4] Made his election for Bristol.

[5] Made his election for Beeralston.

1754.	George Gray[1]	
60.	Thomas Orby Hunter	Arnold Nesbit

GEORGE III.

61.	The same	Percy, Earl of Thomond[2]
		Thomas Sewell
68.	The same[3]	Percy, Earl of Thomond[4]
	Arnold Nesbit (vice Hunter)	William Nedham (vice Earl of Thomond)
74.	The same[5]	Charles W. Cornwall
	William Nedham (vice Nesbit)	
80.	John Nesbit	The same
84.	The same	William Nedham
90.	William Viscount Barnard[6]	Richard Barwell
92.	Sir Frederick F. Vane, Bart.[7]	
	John H. Addington (vice Vane)	
96.	William Currie	The same[8]
		William Devaynes (vice Barwell)
1801.	The same	The same
2.	Robert Ladbroke	William Moffatt
6.	Sir F. Vane, Bart.	Calverley Bewicke
7.	Sir Fred. F. F. Vane, Bart.	The same
	Sir Oswald Mosley, Bart. (vice Vane)	
12.	Hon. W. J. F. Vane. He changed his name to Powlett[9]	The same

[1] Made Steward of the manor of Old Shoreham, county of Sussex. A new writ ordered March 31, 1760.

[2] Made Cofferer of His Majesty's Household. A new writ ordered November 28, 1761. He was elected for Minehead.

[3] Died. A new writ ordered January 10, 1770.

[4] Died. New writ issued in 1774.

[5] Made his election for Cricklade. A new writ ordered February 21, 1775.

[6] Succeeded to the Peerage as Earl of Darlington. A new writ issued October 9, 1792.

[7] He was chosen for the city of Durham.

[8] Made Steward of the manor of East Hendred, county of Berks. A new writ ordered November, 1796.

[9] Made Steward of the manor and hundred of East Hendred, in the county of Berks; and a new writ ordered July, 1815.

1815.	Henry Brougham (vice Powlett)[1]	
16.		Right Hon. Henry Vane Visc. Barnard (vice Calverley Bewicke, deceased)[2]
18.	The same	George Mills
	GEORGE IV.	
20.	The same	Lucius Concannon
23.		William Leader (vice Concannon)
26.	The same	Right Hon. Henry Viscount Howick (now Earl Grey)
	WILLIAM IV.	
30.	John Williams	Hon. Henry Dundas[3]
31.		Stephen Lushington (vice Dundas)
31.	The same. He was afterwards made a Justice of the Queen's Bench	James Brougham

These were the last two members. They supported the Reform Bill, and the disfranchisement of this petty borough.

---

[1] The election took place 21st July, 1815, when "Henry Brougham, of Brougham, in the county of Westmoreland," was unanimously elected, &c., "and being present at his election, took the oath of freeman, and the oath of a baron, and also the oaths of allegiance, supremacy, and adjuration." Corporation Records. This attendance was not usual: the members were ordinarily nominated in their absence on the receipt of a letter from the patron. The oath of a freeman was taken in pursuance of a resolution come to at a Guestling held on 22nd July, 14th Elizabeth, when it was ordered that none should "be chosen member of parliament for any of the ports, unless he were a freeman and an inhabitant of some one of the ports." Harris' Kent, p. 481. If a new member did not attend at the election, the oaths were respited.

[2] Election 12th February.

[3] Made Steward of East Hendred. New election 4th April, 1831.

INDEX.

INDEX.

The following Index does not include the Names of the Householders at the building of the New Town, in 1285 (see p. 44); of the Masters and Constables of Vessels (see pp. 55, 59, 68); of the Freemen exempted in the Non. Inq. (see p. 87); of the Bailiffs of the Town (see p. 114); of the Bailiffs to Yarmouth (see p. 119); of the Rectors (see pp. 141, 144, 191); of the Mayors (see p. 237); or of the Members of Parliament (see p. 244.)

HENRY OSBORNE, Printer, 55, George Street, Hastings.

CPSIA information can be obtained
at www.ICGtesting.com
Printed in the USA
LVHW012101261122
734032LV00005B/284

9 780342 411